THE WARS OF THE IROQUOIS

The Wars of the
I R O Q U O I S

A Study in Intertribal
Trade Relations

GEORGE T. HUNT

THE UNIVERSITY OF WISCONSIN PRESS

Published 1940
The University of Wisconsin Press
Box 1379, Madison, Wisconsin 53701

The University of Wisconsin Press, Ltd.
70 Great Russell Street, London

Printings 1940, 1960, 1967, 1972, 1978

Printed in the United States of America
ISBN 0-299-00164-4; LC 40-3755

ACKNOWLEDGMENTS

WHATEVER contribution to scholarship this book may contain is in large measure the result of the labors and talents of persons other than the author. Particularly he wishes to express his thanks to Professor John D. Hicks of the University of Wisconsin for his unfailing encouragement, without which it is doubtful whether the work would ever have been attempted; to Dr. Louise Phelps Kellogg of the State Historical Society of Wisconsin, for her constant help and advice; to Professor Chester V. Easum of the University of Wisconsin, for reading the manuscript and making many valuable suggestions; to the staff of the Historical Society Library, especially Miss Genevieve Winchester, for their unfailing courtesy and cooperation; and to Mr. Robert C. West of the University of California for his collaboration in preparing the map of the Huron trading empire.

G. T. H.

Western Reserve University
August, 1939

CONTENTS

THE WARS OF THE IROQUOIS

I. THE PROBLEM OF THE IROQUOIS

IN MOST RESPECTS the circumstances of the contact between white man and native in North America are unique in the history of such relationships. In other centuries and in other regions, where the frontiers of superior civilizations had long been in contact with the periphera of inferior civilizations, the conditions of these frontier-peripheral areas were well established and relatively familiar, and the process of infiltration and conquest was comparatively gradual. The Russian advance into Siberia, the French and English movement into and beyond India, the penetration of the Orient by the peddling shipmasters of the West, all these were conditioned by the fact that each civilization had already considerable knowledge of the other. In Africa the Nile Valley and the Mediterranean shore had constituted a frontier area before historic times, and even in the southern part of the African continent contacts had been more or less continuous for nearly four hundred years before actual colonization and exploitation were begun.

In North America, on the other hand, a well advanced civilization, in which the mechanism of exploitation was already highly developed, met the Stone Age face to face, in an invasion almost simultaneously continental in extent. There had been a few premonitory invasions along the St. Lawrence River, Coronado's horsemen had retreated from the far Southwest, a few mailed footmen had floundered through southern swamps to the Great River, a few Englishmen had died at Croatan, but these tentative ventures of the sixteenth century had come to nothing. The Wars of Religion cut short the beginning made by Cartier; Texas remained virtually uninhabited; and one hundred and thirty years passed before another white man glimpsed the Mississippi.

3

In the thirty years following 1603 the whole Atlantic seaboard swarmed with settlement. Champlain established New France at Quebec and Three Rivers; Holland built forts far up the Hudson; England was at Plymouth, in Massachusetts Bay, Virginia, and Maryland, and struggling for a foothold in Maine. The entire coast was explored and mapped. The Stone Age faced the insistent seventeenth century on a fifteen-hundred-mile front which moved swiftly and relentlessly forward. This advance was no matter of slave raids, ivory, or gold. What these white men wanted was what every native had or could get, furs or land, and the trade that was opened was a trade in which every native could take part. As a matter of fact, he was usually frantically eager to take part in it.

The abundance of furs and the inexhaustible market for them made North America a unique theater of interracial contacts. On other continents the desire of traders had been for materials or products considerably less plentiful and less easily obtained by individuals, but here the ease of acquisition, the apparently limitless supply, the ready market, and the permanence of the white settlements permitted the constant participation of every native, expanded the business of trade to unprecedented proportions, and changed, almost overnight, the fundamental conditions of aboriginal economy.

If it is true that "the relations into which the Europeans entered with the aborigines were decided almost wholly by the relations which they found to exist among the tribes on their arrival,"[1] it is certainly equally true that the intertribal relations of the aborigines were in the future to be decided almost wholly by the relations existing between them and the Europeans, especially in those areas in which the fur trade was the chief factor in those relations. On the question of land, the tribes could, and often did, cooperate, and yield or resist together, but the fur trade divided them immediately into groups—those who had fur and those who had none. The great desirability of the trade goods to the Indian who had once known them became shortly a necessity, a very urgent necessity that permitted no renunciation of the trade. As new desires

[1] George E. Ellis, "Indians of North America," in Justin Winsor, ed., *Narrative and Critical History of America* (8 vols., Boston and New York, 1884–89), 1:283.

wakened and old skills vanished, the Indian who had fur, or could get it, survived; he who could not get it died or moved away. But whatever he did, life for him could never again be what it had been: old institutions and economies had profoundly altered or disappeared completely at the electrifying touch of the white man's trade, which swept along the inland trails and rivers with bewildering speed and wrought social revolution a thousand miles beyond the white man's habitations, and years before he himself appeared on the scene. English powder burned on the Mississippi a half century before the English cabins reached Lake Ontario,[2] and the Ottawa tribe had fought a commercial war with the Winnebago of Wisconsin, forcing French trade goods upon them, ten years before the hesitant French settlement had reached Montreal.[3] In truth, the Indian world had in many respects already vanished before the white man saw it, and it is not strange that in his great hurry he formed opinions of it that were somewhat wide of the truth. Those who wonder at the foolishness of the Indians who fought each other to extinction instead of combining to stay the white man's advance are usually the same who attribute their intertribal wars to "insensate fury" and "homicidal frenzy."[4] Tribal motives must necessarily be mysterious to the historian who ignores the social and economic metamorphosis brought about by the trade.

The area in which the fur trade was most significant was the northeastern quarter of the continent, where two great waterways led through inhospitable mountains and highlands into a region which in the seventeenth century and long thereafter teemed with

[2] The powder was burned by the Iroquois in their assault upon the Illinois in 1680. Oswego, the first English settlement on Lake Ontario, was founded in 1726.

[3] Nicolas Perrot, *Memoir on the Manners, Customs, and Religion of the Savages of North America*, translated from the French by Emma H. Blair, in her *Indian Tribes of the Upper Mississippi Valley and Region of the Great Lakes*, 1:293 (Cleveland, 1911). The date is not exact.

[4] Francis Parkman, *The Jesuits in North America in the Seventeenth Century* (*France and England in North America*, pt. 2, Boston, 1867), 434, 444, 447; John A. Doyle, *Virginia, Maryland, and the Carolinas* (*English Colonies in America*, vol. 1, New York, 1882), 13–14. Doyle merely remarks upon the suicidal feuds and what the Indians could have done if they had united; he does not comment on the reason for the disunity. Parkman, in his *La Salle and the Discovery of the Great West* (12th ed., Boston, 1892), 204, again ascribes their actions to "homicidal fury," though he admits that once, in 1680, "strange as it may seem," there appeared to be another motive.

furbearers. The St. Lawrence-Ottawa and the Hudson-Mohawk routes led to the Great Lakes and the Mississippi-Ohio country. with their innumerable tributary streams where were to be found more beaver than in any similar area in the world. Commanding both these routes lay the Huron Iroquois, composed of a half dozen consanguine tribes which with the Algonquins of the upper St. Lawrence must have represented a population of nearly one hundred thousand. Yet after only thirty years of intermittent warfare the Iroquois proper, probably the least numerous of the tribes, never numbering more than twelve thousand, were in sole possession of the region east of Lake Michigan, having dispersed, incorporated, or exterminated all their neighbors; they were even credited, though somewhat mistakenly, with a shadowy empire extending west to the Mississippi, and from Carolina to Hudson Bay. As to the importance of the Iroquois, it has been said that their steady alliance with the Dutch and English of the Hudson River colony was "the pivotal fact of early American history."[5]

With intertribal relations and activities centering as they did about the tribe most active in intertribal affairs, the Iroquois, the question, why did the Iroquois do the things that they did, becomes not only pertinent but vital to an understanding of colonial history. The answers thus far given by historians are three, none of which is in the least convincing.[6] The first of these is the theory that they were possessed of an "insensate fury" and "homicidal frenzy," a theory advanced by Parkman. The second is that a superior political organization, the League of the Iroquois, produced by a superior Iroquois intellect, rendered the Five Nations invincible. This thesis was propounded by Lewis H. Morgan, who even ascribed to the Iroquois the paradoxical motive of exterminating

---

[5] John Fiske, *The Dutch and Quaker Colonies in America* (2 vols., Boston, 1899), 2:172. For representative opinions see Frederic L. Paxson, *History of the American Frontier* (New York, 1924), 52; Herbert L. Osgood, *The American Colonies in the Seventeenth Century* (3 vols., New York, 1907), 1:420–421; Lewis H. Morgan, *League of the Ho-dé-no-sau-nee, or Iroquois* (new edition, edited by Herbert M. Lloyd, New York, 1904), 11; Parkman, *Jesuits in North America*, 447; "Governor Dongan's Report on the State of the Province," in Edmund B. O'Callaghan, ed., *Documents Relative to the Colonial History of the State of New York* (15 vols., Albany, 1853–87), 3:393; "M. Du Chesneau's Memoir on the Western Indians," *ibid.*, 9:165; Andrew M. Davis, "Canada and Louisiana," in Winsor, *Narrative and Critical History*, 5:2.

[6] For a critical estimate of the literature on the subject see page 185.

their enemies in order to establish universal intertribal peace.[7] To these may be added a third theory, that a great supply of firearms, furnished by the greedy Dutch West India Company and unavailable to their enemies, gave rein to a natural passion for conquest and butchery, which they indulged at random but with almost unimaginable enthusiasm.

Even a cursory contemplation of the generally known facts, however, will raise further questions. If a natural superiority or an innate fury was responsible, it is curious that neither of these traits was manifest in the very closely consanguine tribes, such as the Hurons, the Erie, the Neutrals, and others which the Iroquois conquered. Neither does this thesis explain why the naturally superior and ferocious Iroquois had fled from the Algonquins of the St. Lawrence in the years preceding the coming of Champlain, and were on the defensive, stockaded in invaded territory until after 1620. Even if there had been some virtues inherent in the Iroquois blood stream, that stream had changed very early and very completely, for as early as 1656 a priest found that there were more foreigners than natives in Iroquoia, eleven different nations being represented in the country of the Seneca.[8] In 1660 it would have been hard to find twelve hundred Iroquois of pure blood, according to Lalemant, who anticipated Parkman by remarking, "It may be said that, if the Iroquois have any power, it is only because they are knavish and cruel."[9] Even the casual reader feels, after reviewing the achievements of the Iroquois, that knavery and cruelty could hardly have been the mainspring of their mighty and significant labors.

With respect to the great efficiency claimed for the League, a re-examination of only a few sources leads to the conclusion that in the period of Iroquois conquest the League was little if any more effectual in achieving unanimity of action than were the loose Powhatanic and Cherokee leagues, or even the Algonquin confederacy or the Choctaw republic. Despite the bluster of Mohawk orators, there is not a single recorded instance of unanimous

[7] *League of the Iroquois*, 72.

[8] Reuben G. Thwaites, ed., *The Jesuit Relations and Allied Documents* (73 vols., Cleveland, 1896–1901), 43:265.

[9] *Ibid.*, 45:207, 211.

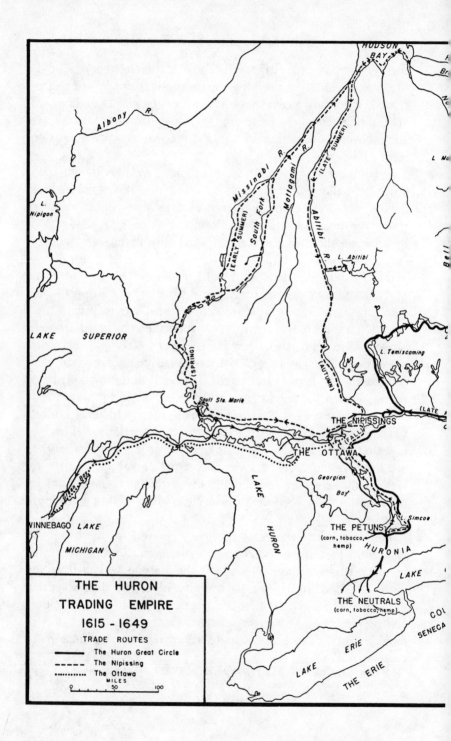

THE HURON
TRADING EMPIRE
1615-1649

TRADE ROUTES
——— The Huron Great Circle
----- The Nipissing
········· The Ottawa

MILES
0   50   100

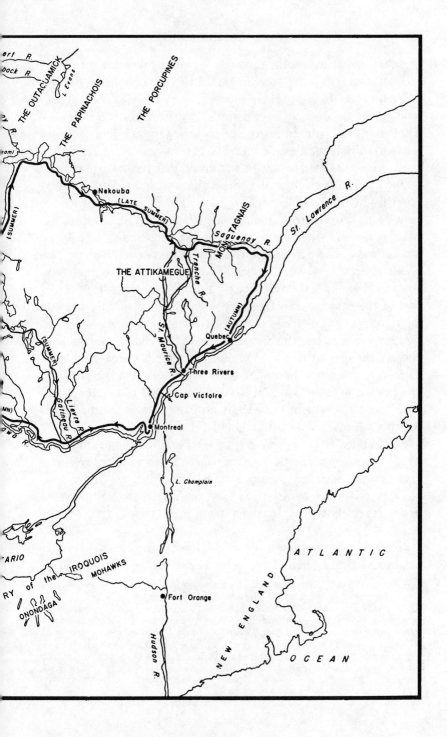

THE OUTACOUAMICK

THE PAPINACHOIS

THE PORCUPINES

ert R.

bock R.

L Evans

ami

(SUMMER)

●Nekouba

(LATE SUMMER)

Saguenay R.

MONTAGNAIS

St. Lawrence R.

THE ATTIKAMEGUE

Trenche R.

St. Maurice R.

(SUMMER)

(SUMMER)

Gatineau R.

(MN)

Lièvre R.

R.

●Quebec

(AUTUMN)

●Three Rivers

Cap Victoire

●Montreal

L. Champlain

ARIO

RY of the IROQUOIS MOHAWKS

ONONDAGA

●Fort Orange

ATLANTIC

NEW ENGLAND

Hudson R.

OCEAN

or anywhere near unanimous action by the League prior to 1653, and none save in peace treaties thereafter. The Mohawk orators had a way, confusing to their enemies, as they well knew, of pretending, when on their own business, to speak for the League.[10] The habit has confused historians no less. Osgood, however, has recognized that the League could at best only prevent fratricidal strife among its members.[11] In any event, that result was achieved by the other, less celebrated, confederacies with more marked success than by the League of the Iroquois. The Hurons, for instance, kept peace with their Algonquin neighbors with no organization whatever, no ties of consanguinity, no common tongue or social institutions[12]—in fact, with nothing more in common than an economic interest—while throughout a series of five wars there was no such thing as unanimity among the Five Nations. Rarely did two of the cantons combine in an attack, and then only because their commercial interests were for the time identical. Never did two cantons combine for defense. Mohawks and Onondaga both cheered the French attack upon the Seneca, and Seneca and Onondaga were steadily antipathetic to the Mohawks, who, as the eastern canton, held the Hudson River country and the Dutch trade. The Mohawks sought ceaselessly to exploit their brothers, and were at swords' points with them half the time. All that prevented a vicious intra-Iroquois war was the fact that the common interest of all three in opposing the French and the French Indians was ever greater than their conflicting interests. At that, much Iroquois blood was spilled by Iroquois, and perhaps more embassies of peace traveled within Iroquoia than from Iroquoia to foreign tribes.

If all this is true, one may ask, why has the League been so celebrated by historians, and why has it for seventy-five years

---

[10] See, for example, Kiotsaeton to the Governor, in *Jesuit Relations*, 17:253: "Onontio, lend me ear. I am the mouth for the whole of my country; thou listeneth to all the Iroquois in hearing my words"; this when he had to return to his own country to get ratification for a peace concerning only his own people. See also Grangula to La Barre, in Louis A. Lahontan, *New Voyages to North-America*, edited by Reuben G. Thwaites (2 vols., Chicago, 1905), 1:82–83, 85. There are many more examples.

[11] Osgood, *American Colonies*, 2:420–422; Parkman, *Jesuits in North America*, 344; John A. Doyle, *The Middle Colonies (English Colonies in America*, vol. 4, New York, 1907), 119.

[12] See below, Chapters 3 and 4.

been given credit for accomplishing things it did not accomplish? The most important single reason is probably Lewis H. Morgan's book *The League of the Iroquois*. Morgan was a true scholar in spirit, a conscientious observer, and a tireless worker, but he was not a historian, and he had access to few or none of the sources which could have informed him on the history of the League he so carefully observed.[13] It is perhaps not strange that when he viewed the perfected League of 1850, knowing little of Iroquois history except tradition,[14] he should have assumed that the perfection of political organization he saw then was more than two centuries old. The League as he saw it in the nineteenth century offered a plausible explanation for a hitherto unexplained phenomenon of the seventeenth century, and without critical investigation it was temptingly easy to interchange result and cause. The very excellence of his general work unfortunately perpetuated this specific error, which was widely adopted by historians.[15] To those who read the sources, however, it becomes quite clear that the League as Morgan saw it did not wage the wars of the Iroquois nor make them possible, but that in a very real sense it was the wars that made the League which he and others were privileged to examine two hundred years later. The League, then, cannot be an answer to the Iroquois problem.

In the matter of armament also, the assets of the Iroquois have been overstated. The two thousand muskets which they are cred-

[13] When Morgan wrote his *League of the Iroquois*, the *New York Colonial Documents* were only in the process of publication, and the *Jesuit Relations* were also as yet unpublished, so he took his background from Cadwallader Colden, who probably knew less about the subject than Morgan himself. For a discussion of Colden's work see below, page 185.

[14] A great deal of nonsense has been written about the reliability of Indian tradition in factual matters. Charles Eastman was a full-blood Sioux, and his *Indian Heroes and Great Chieftains* is written mainly from information obtained directly from the older people of his tribe, but George E. Hyde, after checking it with known facts, says that "it presents a spectacle of poor and distorted memory that is appalling, as nearly every date and statement of fact is incorrect." *Red Cloud's Folk* (Norman, Oklahoma, 1937), 54. See also pages viii, ix, and 60 for other cases in point. Mr. Hyde is one of the regrettably few writers in the field of Indian history who has his feet on the ground, and who deals with source material in a scientific manner.

[15] It was adopted by both Parkman and Fiske, and it influenced Channing, Doyle, and Turner. The youthful Turner writes, in his doctoral dissertation, that "thus by priority in securing firearms, as well as by their remarkable civil organization," did the Iroquois rise to power, citing Morgan directly. *The Early Writings of Frederick Jackson Turner* (University of Wisconsin Press, 1938), 97.

ited with having possessed in 1640[16] shrink upon investigation to a possible four hundred, and even this is probably too generous an estimate. In that year a French prisoner testified that a "heavily armed" war band of five hundred Iroquois had exactly thirty-six arquebuses.[17] The supposed greed of the Dutch West India Company is called into serious question when it is discovered that they tried desperately to stop what trade in guns there was, and that both the Company and the settlement at Beverwyck passed and attempted to enforce ordinances against it, even going so far as to ordain the penalty of death. Among the Dutch on the Hudson and Connecticut the French were as bitterly accused of trading arms to Indians as were the Dutch in the French settlements on the St. Lawrence, and the justification was as ample in the one case as in the other. Moreover, the Susquehannah, whom the Iroquois conquered, were far better provided with arms than the Iroquois, possessing even artillery in their forts.[18]

There is no denying that these conditions, to which is attributed the Iroquois phenomenon, existed in some measure and undoubtedly had an aggregate importance, but the fact still remains that although they were paralleled elsewhere, in fact were paralleled again and again all over the continent, the phenomenon itself was unparalleled. No other tribe ever did what the Iroquois did, and yet the three theories of inherent qualities, superior organization, and superior armament fail to explain their achievements or to suggest a motive which could have driven them so far and down so hard a road.

The explanation must lie in some fundamental condition which thus far has not received the attention of the relatively few students of Iroquois history. The search should be not for the ineluctable ultimate origin, but for a general condition of Indian life, readily ascertained and recognized, from which the motivation of the Iroquois should appear to proceed inevitably. Since this general condition was peculiar in its effect upon the Iroquois, it follows

[16] Louise P. Kellogg, *The French Régime in Wisconsin and the Northwest* (Madison, 1925), 85.

[17] Testimony of Marguerie, transcribed by Le Jeune, in the *Jesuit Relations*, 21:37.

[18] For a full discussion of the Dutch trade with the Iroquois in firearms, see below, Appendix A.

that unless the Iroquois were themselves peculiar, it must have some connection with geography or climate; and when it is recalled that the rise of the Iroquois to power coincided with the spread of the white trade throughout their region and the regions beyond them, a second inference follows, namely that some peculiarity of the Iroquois position and the spread of the white trade may well have combined to produce a motivation sufficiently powerful to drive the Iroquois through a half century of bloody intertribal conflict with their brother tribesmen, the closely related peoples that almost surrounded them. The inference gains in strength when it is recalled that throughout the wars there runs ceaselessly the theme of trade and commercial arrangement, and that even the merciless Indian oratory, punctuated by gifts made in frank expectation of counter-gifts, is wound tightly about a core of commercial negotiation—of proposal and counter-proposal.

Such wars as those of the Iroquois must have had not only an insistent motivation, but also a disastrous alternative, or at least an alternative that was regarded as disastrous by those who waged them. It is quite likely that if the white trade had become a social and economic necessity to them, their position had life and death as alternatives. That position would have permitted neither compromise nor inactivity, and would explain why their wars were the first truly national intertribal wars on the continent, there being now for the first time a truly national motive. It is possible that William C. Macleod may have struck the lost chord in intertribal relations when he wrote that "the same principles of economic science apply alike to the economy of modern Germany and of the Shoshone Digger Indians, or any like economic group."[19] If the Iroquois were either facing disaster or thought that they were, they may well have turned, as do "enlightened" nations, to war. What is true is never so important, historically, as what people think is true, and while it may be convincingly reasoned, with that keen hindsight which historians often call insight, that the Iroquois would have been better off economically had they done anything other than what they did, this reasoning need not mean

[19] *The Origin of the State Reconsidered in the Light of the Data of Aboriginal North America* (Philadelphia, 1924), 41-42.

that the ultimate facts were clear to the Iroquois or that their motive was not (perhaps mistakenly) economic.

The thesis that when the Iroquois made war on a national scale they did so with somewhat the same ends in view as have their Christian brothers, is admittedly attractive. Such a thesis, however, requires abundant and indisputable documentary evidence, if it aspires to solve the Iroquois problem.

II. BEFORE THE CONQUEST

When the first white man, Jacques Cartier of St. Malo, ventured up the great waterway of the St. Lawrence, he unwittingly intersected a phase of that slow flux of native population, that advance and recession of tribes and cultures, which is always found in and is perhaps an inevitable characteristic of aboriginal life on a large and thinly populated continent. Apparently he cut across the final recession of the Huron Iroquois from the St. Lawrence uplands into the position they assumed in the seventeenth century.

Cartier's first voyage, in 1534, did not carry him beyond the mouth of the St. Lawrence. On his second, in 1535, he reached the native settlements of Stadacona and Hochelaga, at the present sites of Quebec and Montreal. Appended to his *Brief recit* is a vocabulary which, supplemented by archeological investigation and tradition, establishes the fact that the towns were Huron Iroquois. The loss of most of the manuscript of the third voyage, made in 1541, prevents certainty of anything more than the fact that the towns were still there at that time. When Champlain came up the river in 1603 they were gone, and Algonquin tribes were in possession and still advancing, having built forts up the River Richelieu.[1]

Concerning the reasons for the Iroquois retreat, there have been many considered opinions. The subject offers a wide scope to the imagination, the early records being almost silent save for vague and often contradictory traditions. Perrot preserved one such ac-

[1] Henry S. Burrage, ed., *Early English and French Voyages* (*Original Narratives of Early American History*, edited by J. Franklin Jameson, New York, 1906), 3–102; Richard Hakluyt, ed., *The Principal Navigations, Voyages, Traffiques, & Discoveries of the English Nation* (12 vols., Glasgow, 1903–05), 8 :183–209, 263–272; Jacques Cartier, *Brief recit & succincte narration de la nauigation faicte es ysles de Canada, Hochelage, & Saguenay & autres* (Paris, 1545), a photostatic copy of which is the in the library of the

count, but little can be made of it except to confirm the opinion that here a nomadic hunting economy had come into contact with a purely agricultural way of life. The traditions related to and by the Jesuits tell only of Algonquin triumphs and Iroquois recession.[2]

In 1848 a Tuscarora Indian published a traditional history of the Iroquois, which in lieu of anything more scholarly was widely accepted despite the early declaration by Garakontie, the great Onondaga, that it was nothing more than a long fable, a formula for state occasions. It was adopted with few reservations by Horatio Hale, a philologist, and used as the basis of his own theory of Iroquois origins. This was that the earliest home of the Huron Iroquois had been in the region of James Bay and the lower St. Lawrence, that "numbers increased, dissensions arose, the hive swarmed, and bands moved off to the west and south," followed by the advancing and presumably also swarming Algonquins. Concerning the fact that the region is a most inhospitable one for "swarming," Hale had nothing to say. In this theory he was immediately supported by others, and Schoolcraft's theory that Iroquoian culture was of southern origin was ignored.[3]

With the beginning in America of archeological science, scientific excavation and comparison of results, it was discovered that

State Historical Society of Wisconsin; three articles by William D. Lighthall: "Hochelagans and Mohawks: A Link in Iroquois History," in the *Proceedings and Transactions of the Royal Society of Canada*, 1899 (2d series, vol. 5), sec. 2, pp. 199–211; "Signposts of Prehistoric Time," *ibid.*, 1916 (3d series, vol. 10), sec. 2, pp. 475–480; and "The False Plan of Hochelaga," *ibid.*, 1932 (3d series, vol. 26), sec. 2, pp. 181–192; *The Works of Samuel de Champlain*, edited under the direction of H. P. Biggar (6 vols. Toronto, 1922–36), 1:141.

[2] Perrot, *Memoir*, in Blair, *Indian Tribes*, 1: 42–47; Sara Stites, *Economics of the Iroquois* (Lancaster, Pennsylvania, 1905); Adriaen van der Donck, "Description of the New Netherlands," translated from the Dutch by Jeremiah Johnson, in *New York Historical Collections*, 2d series, 1:192–194 (New York, 1841); Frank G. Speck, "Algonkian Influence upon Iroquois Social Organization," in the *American Anthropologist*, new series, 25:224 (1923). Speck says: "Agriculture has always been their mainstay of life, in fact, their economic basis." See also the *Jesuit Relations*, 45:205. A Huron account of the conflict is in *The Voyages of Peter Esprit Radisson*, edited by Gideon D. Scull (Publications of the Prince Society, vol. 16, Boston, 1885), 92.

[3] *David Cusick's Sketches of Ancient History of the Six Nations* (Lockport, New York, 1848); Peter D. Clarke, *Origin and Traditional History of the Wyandotts and Sketches of Other Indian Tribes of North America* (Toronto, 1870); Garakontie, quoted by Milet in the *Jesuit Relations*, 57:211; Horatio Hale, *Indian Migrations, as Evidenced by Language* (Chicago, 1883), reprinted from the *American Antiquarian*, vol. 5 (January and April, 1883); Horatio Hale, ed., *Iroquois Book of Rites* (Philadelphia, 1883); David Boyle, *Notes on Primitive Man in Ontario* (Toronto, 1895), and "The Iroquois," in

the Iroquoian culture overlay a more ancient one, which was Algonquin, and that the whole of Iroquoian culture, not alone the use of the Zea maize, seemed predominantly southern. Lewis Morgan had already been puzzled by the maize culture, and had suggested the Puget Sound–Columbia River region as a likely point of origin, thinking that the corn culture might have been picked up on the southeastward swing to the Ohio, although there existed neither a trace nor a tradition of such a journey, despite the formidable barrier of the Rockies and the intermediate plains. It is difficult to understand why scientific men were for so long passionately partisan to the doctrine of a northern origin of the Iroquois.[4]

The present view is that the Iroquois had a southern origin and pushed into the Lakes region from the southwest, following the line of the Ohio and splitting on Lakes Erie and Ontario. Those who later became Hurons passed north of the Lakes and established themselves in the Georgian Bay–Lake Simcoe region; the southern group followed the southern shore, the Susquehannah dropping off to the south. By 1535 they had advanced across the

Provincial Museum of Ontario, *Archaeological Report*, 1905, pp. 146–158; Daniel Wilson, "The Huron-Iroquois of Canada, a Typical Race of American Aborigines," in Royal Society of Canada, *Proceedings and Transactions*, 1884 (1st series, vol. 2), sec. 2, pp. 55–106; Henry R. Schoolcraft, *Historical and Statistical Information Respecting the History, Condition, and Prospects of the Indian Tribes of the United States* (6 vols., Philadelphia, 1851–57), 1:61–64.

[4] William J. Wintemberg, "Indian Village Sites in Oxford and Waterloo Counties," in Provincial Museum of Ontario, *Archaeological Report*, 1900, pp. 37–40; William M. Beauchamp, "Origins of the Iroquois," in the *American Antiquarian*, vol. 16 (1894); Clark Wissler, *The American Indian: An Introduction to the Anthropology of the New World* (New York, 1922); Morgan, *League of the Iroquois*, 2:187–188; "Iroquois Migrations," in William W. Beach, ed., *The Indian Miscellany* (Albany, 1877), 229; Francis S. Drake, ed., *The Indian Tribes of the United States* (6 vols., Philadelphia, 1884), 1:85. With Brinton's study of the traditions of the Delawares (Leni-Lenâpé) and his edition of their pictographic record, the Walum Olum, the connection between Iroquois and Delawares, argued almost sixty years before by Heckewelder, seemed almost certainly valid, and the curious myths supported by Cusick, Clarke, and Hale were dismissed. Livingston Farrand, however, writing in 1904, clung to the old theory, placing the Iroquois on the lower St. Lawrence, with the Algonquin center on the north Atlantic coast. See Daniel G. Brinton, *The Lenâpé and Their Legends* (Philadelphia, 1885); C. Staniland Wake, "Migrations of the Algonquins," in the *American Antiquarian*, 16:127–140 (1894); John G. Heckewelder, *History, Manners, and Customs of the Indian Nations Who Once Inhabited Pennsylvania and the Neighbouring States* (revised ed., Philadelphia, 1876); William Rawle's "Vindication" of this history in Pennsylvania Historical Society, *Memoirs*, 1:258–275; and Livingston Farrand, *Basis of American History, 1500–1900* (*The American Nation*, vol. 2, New York, 1904), 98.

St. Lawrence, and by 1603 had recoiled before the stiffened Algonquin resistance.

There is much in the genuine Iroquoian tradition to support this view; for example, the frequent reference to the "Tree of the Great Long Leaves," for which one whole section of the constitution of the Five Nations was named. Most of their contacts of both trade and war were in the south, and archeological evidence is most convincing. David I. Bushnell's *Tribal Migrations* is the most ambitious attempt yet made to substantiate this opinion, and although archeological evidence does not yet wholly support his series of maps, none of it directly contradicts them. On these maps the Iroquois are shown as originating in the general region of what is now southern Missouri and moving northeast, the Tuscarora and Cherokee breaking off in northeastern Kentucky and the remaining tribes displacing the Algonquin peoples of the eastern Lakes. They were there, an island in a veritable sea of Algonquin peoples, a disturbing cultural anomaly in the region, when Cartier came to their towns and when, three-quarters of a century later, Champlain slew their chiefs at Lake George.[5]

Throughout the sixteenth century the coasting traders and fishermen of the intruding whites apparently did a considerable business with the natives,[6] and the first Europeans to enter the continent found indications of widespread intertribal trade connections along well-established routes, which, with the impetus of Euro-

[5] Arthur C. Parker, *The Constitution of the Five Nations, or the Iroquois Book of the Great Law* (New York State Museum Bulletin no. 184, Albany, 1916), 8–11, and "The Origin of the Iroquois as Suggested by Their Archaeology," in the *American Anthropologist*, new series, 18:479–507 (October-December, 1916); David I. Bushnell, Jr., *Tribal Migrations East of the Mississippi River* (Smithsonian Miscellaneous Collections, vol. 89, no. 12, Washington, 1934); Wissler, *American Indian*, 221.

[6] In Peter Wraxall, *An Abridgment of the Indian Affairs . . . Transacted in the Colony of New York from the Year 1678 to the Year 1751*, edited by Charles H. McIlwain (Cambridge, Massachusetts, 1915), xii–xiii, the editor has a list of references on the coasting trade. Because most of the trade was in heavy skins, it is likely that these traders had tapped channels of intertribal exchange. Before the white man's arrival the native had considered the beaver of little value, and the heavy skins were much more valuable in Indian economics and manufacture. The early French records seldom mention their shipment; they were too heavy for the canoes and much less valuable per pound. That fact gave the Hudson's Bay Company an advantage in later years, for they had not the trouble of transportation on inland streams. Menendez, if he may be believed, got six thousand buffalo skins on one expedition. Parkman, *Pioneers of France in the New World* (*France and England in North America*, pt. 1, Boston, 1890), 230n.

pean trade goods, would carry them swiftly throughout the region. Furthermore, they found that the supposedly simple natives were far from ingenuous in the technique of trade, understanding well the desirability of excluding trade rivals from a profitable connection. Donnaconna, chief of the town of Stadacona, tried to keep Cartier from visiting Hochelaga by magnifying the dangers and difficulties of the route, hoping to keep the trade and the middleman's profit for himself, a tactic that was to be repeated thereafter as often as trader and Indian met. The *Brief recit* is the first written evidence of that motive which was, for more than two centuries, to determine the history of the Lakes region, perhaps eventually that of the continent.[7]

The trade between the Lakes region and the south can be traced by the wide use that was made of Lake Superior copper. Fontaneda found copper, probably from Lake Superior, in Florida. Cabeza de Vaca, in 1536, got a copper bell from Indians who told him that it had come from the north, where there were plates of it, and fixed habitations. Tonty found copper in the Illinois country, Smith found a huge trade in it in Virginia, and De Laet and Juet were impressed by the quantity of it that had been found in New Netherland. Artifacts and products of the far south were exchanged for it, and Sulte insists that Cartier became ill at Hochelaga on a pipe of Virginia tobacco.[8] "So many evidences of pre-historic intercourse

[7] Cartier, *Brief recit*, 15–18; Pierre F. X. Charlevoix, *History and General Description of New France*, translated from the French by John G. Shea (6 vols., New York, 1866–72), 1:117.

[8] Buckingham Smith, trans. and ed., *Letter of Hernando de Soto and Memoir of Hernando de Escalante Fontaneda* (Washington, 1854), 17; George P. Winship, "The Coronado Expedition, 1540–1542," in Bureau of American Ethnology, *Annual Report*, 1892–93, pt. 1, p. 350. Champlain thought that the copper was melted and smoothed out into sheets with stones. See *Works*, 2:123. Boyle claims that it was used only as a malleable metal. See his *Notes on Primitive Man in Ontario*, 85–88. Stories of the tempering of copper by the aborigines are without foundation. See the debate on this subject in the *American Anthropologist*, new series, 5:25–57 (1903). See also Henri de Tonty, "Memoir," in *Illinois Historical Collections*, 1:145 (Springfield, 1903); John Smith, *The Generall History of Virginia, New England, and the Summer Isles* (2 vols., Glasgow, 1907), 1:63, 71–73, 78, 126; Johan de Laet, "Extracts from the New World, or a Description of the West Indies," translated from the Dutch by George Folsom, in *New York Historical Collections*, 2d series, 1:299–300 (New York, 1841); Robert Juet, "Extract from The Third Voyage of Master Henry Hudson," in J. Franklin Jameson, ed., *Narratives of New Netherland, 1609–1664* (*Original Narratives of Early American History*, New York, 1909), 18–20; T. W. E. Sowter, "Indian Trade, Travel, and Transportation," in Ontario Provincial Museum, *Archaeological Report*, 1916, p. 26; Benjamin Sulte,

with the regions to the south have been found," writes an authority on this trade, "that it is safe to assume that the Lake Superior region furnished the greater part of the copper in use by the southern Indians, which . . . was traded for . . . the raw material obtainable only on the seaboard or the Gulf Coast."[9]

With the West there was a heavy trade in stone, both as artifacts and as raw material. Brown pipestone from the Chippewa River and red pipestone from the Minnesota came by way of the Lakes into Ohio and New York as far east as Onondaga and Oswego, and thence north into Canada. Flint from Ontario went west in the shape of "blanks"; and the finished points, traveling into Saskatchewan and Alberta, and north of Ontario, tipped the weapons of the Algonquin hunters. Obsidian from the Rocky Mountains, which was widely used in Ohio, was imported both as raw material and as artifacts; deposits of several hundred pounds have been found in the Hopewell mounds. There were evidently tribes who did nothing but manufacture even in that early day, for Tonty found that the Natchitoches and the Nasoui of the Red River "did no work except making very fine bows, which they make a traffic with distant nations."[10] The trade of the Huron and Ottawa nations was so extensive, and with the impetus of European goods became so dominant a factor in intertribal relations, that it will be considered separately in succeeding chapters.

Intertribal Relations: War

Aside from commerce, the most important relation between nations, primitive or modern, is probably war, and the tendency of the general historian, when dealing with primitive peoples, to mini-

"The Valley of the Grand River, 1600–1650," in Royal Society of Canada, *Proceedings and Transactions*, 1898 (2d series, vol. 4), sec. 2, p. 118. Sulte is obviously in error, for according to Cartier's own account the experiment took place at Stadacona, no one became ill, and the tobacco was home-grown. *Brief recit*, 31.

[9] Clarence B. Moore, "Mound Investigations on the East Coast of Florida," in *Additional Mounds of Duval and of Clay Counties, Florida*, etc. (Museum of the American Indian, Heye Foundation, Indian Notes and Monographs, Miscellaneous Series, no. 26, New York, 1922), 258. See also George A. West, *Copper: Its Mining and Use by the Aborigines of the Lake Superior Region* (Milwaukee Public Museum Bulletin, vol. 10, no. 1, Milwaukee, 1929), 64.

[10] Sowter, "Indian Trade," in Ontario Provincial Museum, *Archaeological Report*, 1916, pp. 30, 33; Henry C. Shetrone, *The Mound-Builders* (New York, 1930), 206–208; Tonty, "Memoir," in *Illinois Historical Collections*, 1:157.

mize the one and overemphasize the other is not difficult to understand, particularly in North America. Here, as has been said, the
European trade instantly divided the tribes into highly competitive
groups, and the competition for trade was, or soon became, a
struggle for survival. The native who had known and used the
keen steel tools of the white man was unlikely to renounce them
and was shortly unable to do so, so swiftly did the skills of the
Stone Age vanish. "The coveted tools or implements represented
a value not measurable by any reach of wild territory. A metal
kettle, a spear, a knife, a hatchet, transformed the whole life of a
savage."[11] A tribe whose enemies had the weapons which it lacked
had few alternatives, and all of them were unpleasant. It inevitably
made war upon the competitor.

So quickly did such hostilities arise after the entry of the European, and so fiercely did they continue, that observers were prone
to consider war as the usual intertribal relationship, not knowing
how they themselves had transformed these relations when they
appeared with the precious tools and weapons. The progress of
this transformation was very swift, and virtually as extensive as
the intertribal trade, because the one accompanied the other. So
swift was it, in fact, that it is doubtful whether first-hand observers
ever saw intertribal relations exactly as they had been before, even
on the coast. Most of those who could have observed them intelli-
gently were uninterested in such matters, and they were very few.
Most of those who were interested and capable of understanding
them arrived too late. Only a few capable and considered opinions
remain, but by piecing them together it is possible to arrive at a
few valid conclusions.

In all five books of the Walum Olum there are only a dozen
symbols connoting war, and most of these relate to a single invasion, yet the Walum Olum is the complete pictographic history of
the Delaware tribe. Champlain, marching to "war" with the

[11] Ellis, "Indians of North America," in Winsor, *Narrative and Critical History*, 1:
287. In evidence given before the British House of Commons concerning the monopoly
of the Hudson's Bay Company, it was said that the tribes rapidly lost their old skills
through disuse, and died of starvation when they were deprived of European supplies.
In this connection see the appeal of Onanguisset, a Potawatomi chief, against cessation
of trade and withdrawal of the posts, in *New York Colonial Documents*, 9:673.

Montagnais and the Hurons in 1609, was under the impression that it was in some sense a national war, and was amused and disappointed to discover that what he considered a mere skirmish was truly intertribal war as it was understood by the people of the region. "He saw what native warfare meant, and that to his allies this successful skirmish was victory enough." It was a fair average specimen, doubtless, of Stone Age warfare, "a random fight, a few deaths on the field and a few more at the stake, and nothing definite accomplished." While an Indian nation might be technically at "war" with all nations not in actual alliance, the military enterprises were no more than private ventures, in which the chiefs tried to restrain rather than encourage the martial ardor of their warriors. "It kept," says Sulte, "the form of a kind of noble sport." Viewed as war at all, the expeditions were few, the operations always feeble, and much the greater number abandoned without an effective stroke.[12]

It was remarked by the Jesuits that a stray killing or insult was enough to set two tribes at each other's throats, but they record no illustrative instance, and many instances illustrative of the contrary. Morgan, who remarked that warfare was most persistent between tribes speaking different stock languages, was unable to prove his point by reference to North America, where the great Indian wars were fought between closely kindred tribes.[13] The Dakota-Algonquin groups, in general, lived at peace, and the Hurons and Algonquins never fought each other. A difference in stock languages, in this region at least, did not determine intertribal relations.

Nicolas Perrot, who was, with the exception of Duluth, the greatest woods-rover of the French regime, and without question

[12] Brinton, *The Lenâpé*, 169–217; George M. Wrong, *The Rise and Fall of New France* (2 vols., New York, 1928), 1:180; Champlain, *Works*, 2:95–100, 125–134; 3:67–75; John Fiske, *New France and New England* (Boston and New York, 1902), 70; Morgan, *League of the Iroquois*, 68; Benjamin Sulte, "The Valley of the Ottawa in 1613," in Ontario Historical Society, *Papers and Records*, 13:31 (Toronto, 1915); William H. Harrison, "A Discourse on the Aborigines of the Ohio Valley," in *Fergus Historical Series*, vol. 5, no. 26 (Chicago, 1883), 33.

[13] As one example from the Jesuit records, see the *Jesuit Relations*, 43:101, 103, 135–137. Morgan's statement is found in his *Ancient Society* (New York, 1877), 172. The other great intertribal war, the Sioux-Chippewa, was between people of different stock languages, but with an admittedly economic motive.

the best authority of his century on Indian life, not excepting the Jesuits, wrote that "although ambition and vengeance are two passions which imperiously possess the minds of the savages, self-interest carries them still further, and has more ascendancy over them. There is no disgrace or injury which they do not overlook if those who have insulted them or injured them indemnify them with goods of sufficient value . . . self-interest corrupts them. . . . they make it their chief ideal as being that one in which they place all their confidence."[14]

This self-interest, which most writers underrate and others discover far too late in Indian history, was operative from the moment of the arrival of the European ships, and it may be said, in anticipation of a development traced in later pages, that thereafter tribes fought only their direct competitors. Trader fought trader and hunter fought hunter, but trader and hunter never fought each other. The trader, moreover, was always anxious to mediate between warring tribes to further the cause of peace, and thereby the interests of commerce.[15] The munitions industry did not then complicate the business of negotiation. William Bradford remarked upon the intertribal dissension created by the use of wampum, even among the small and weak New England tribes, and Hubbard came very near to the heart of the matter when he wrote: "Whatever honey in the mouth of that beast of trade, there was a deadly sting in the tail . . . which proved a fatal business to those that were concerned in it."[16]

In summary, it may be concluded that in prehistoric North America intertribal trade, particularly in the region of the Great Lakes, was extensive and was sufficiently well developed to ab-

[14] Perrot, *Memoir*, in Blair, *Indian Tribes*, 1:144. The Jesuits were careful observers and truthful and conscientious reporters of fact. Their weakness as sources lies in their interpretation of events and motives, which is narrowed, perhaps inevitably, by the religious perspective. Charlevoix and Faillon are not exceptions. Professor Wrong and Charlevoix ascribe the commercial motive, where they admit it at all, solely to the loot obtainable from the trading brigades. The matter goes much deeper than this.

[15] The Cree, who were not traders, were implacably hostile to the Sioux, who were also hunters. The Chippewa, on the other hand, were most anxious for peace between the Cree and the Sioux, and joyful at the prospect of its conclusion, since the Chippewa were traders. Dablon, in the *Jesuit Relations*, 58:17, 257.

[16] *Bradford's History "Of Plimouth Plantation," from the Original Manuscript* (Boston, 1899), 282–283; William Hubbard, quoted in Joel Munsell, *Annals of Albany* (10 vols., Albany, 1850–59), 2:8.

sorb immediately all the trade goods that could be sent from Europe. In the beginning intertribal rivalries were not keen, and intertribal war was a purely private and social enterprise. But before long the European trade was to create new rivalries, and whet old ones to the point where the issue became one of survival. When that occurred, intertribal relations assumed an entirely different aspect, and in 1626 the long and bloody wars of the Iroquois began somewhere west of Fort Orange.

III. THE IROQUOIS, 1609–1640

By MOST OF THE earlier writers the Iroquois were thought to have achieved, by the time the Europeans arrived, an aggressively dominant position among the tribes of the region they inhabited, and through them that view was unfortunately transmitted to the general historian. Albert Gallatin characterized them as conquerors, and stated that the few "Massawomecks" encountered by Smith in Virginia were probably Iroquois fulfilling their career of conquest. He thought, moreover, that the incident proved that these people had great power and wide domination. Garrick Mallery held the same opinion; and Fiske, by a direct misquotation, credited the Iroquois quite undeservedly with a hegemony over the New England tribes in 1609. Fiske writes: "They exterminated their old enemies the Adirondacks, and pushed the Mohegan over the mountains from the Hudson River to the Connecticut. When they first encountered white men in 1609, their name had become a terror in New England, insomuch that as soon as a single Mohawk was caught sight of by the Indians in that country they would raise the cry from hill to hill 'A Mohawk! A Mohawk!' and forthwith would flee like sheep before wolves, never dreaming of resistance." Fiske not only cited Colden as an authority on this matter, on which Colden was quite uninformed, but misquotes him. Colden says: "I have been told by old men in New England, who remember [sic] the time when the Mohawks made war on their Indians, that as soon as a single Mohawk was discovered . . . ," etc., which is quite different from citing the year 1609. It is true that the Mohawks became a terror to the Indians of New England, but not until many years after 1609, which was 118 years before Colden wrote. It is possible not only to limit considerably the supposed Iroquois hegemony of that year, but to prove that it did not exist at all, and that the Iroquois of the year 1609 were a beaten people, on the defensive and raided with impunity by their enemies.[1]

The "Massawomecks" met by Smith were a very small party of marauders, and were identified as Massawomecks by a Potomac Indian named Mosco, who accompanied Smith. There is no conclusive reason for supposing them to have been Iroquois. Though the testimony that "they inhabit upon a great water beyond the mountaines" and that they were "mortall enemies" of the "Sasquesahannocks" and Tockwoghs seems to suggest it, the statement that they "have their hatchets and commodities of trade from the French" weakens the identification, since none of the Iroquois had at that time any connection with the French. The statement concerning trade may also be discounted on the ground that among their effects captured by Smith there were none of European manufacture. As Smith's Indians knew nothing of the French, the statement is probably his own interpretation.[2]

The supposed dominance of these Massawomecks, whoever they were, may be fairly demolished. First, the small number indicates that at most it was a small raiding party such as Champlain had accompanied, and Smith himself, speaking of the Susquehannah as a "mightie people," distinctly gives the impression that at the worst they were holding their own. Second, Radisson's Huron account shows that the Iroquois were recoiling from them upon the Susquehannah through necessity and not in any attempt at conquest, and according to the account for those years in the Jesuit Relations they were "overthrown . . . and their nation humiliated" by the Susquehannah.[3]

[1] Albert Gallatin, "A Synopsis of the Indian Tribes of North America," in American Antiquarian Society, *Transactions and Collections*, 2:22, 75 (Cambridge, 1836); Garrick Mallery, "The Former and Present Number of Our Indians," in American Association for the Advancement of Science, *Proceedings*, 26:355 (1877); John Fiske, *The Discovery of America* (2 vols., Boston and New York, 1892), 1:46; Cadwallader Colden, *The History of the Five Nations of Canada* (2 vols., New York, 1904), xviii.

[2] Smith, *Historie of Virginia, New England, and the Summer Isles*, 1:126, 127, 131. These references may also be found in Lyon G. Tyler, ed., *Narratives of Early Virginia, 1606–1625* (*Original Narratives of Early American History*, New York, 1907). Further references are given by Nathaniell Poell and Anas Todkell, in *The Proceedings of the English Colony in America* (1612), reprinted *ibid.*, 143–144, 150.

[3] Radisson, *Voyages*, 92; *Jesuit Relations*, 14:205.

The Iroquois upon the Hudson River, 1609–1626

We turn now to the area in which the Iroquois were supposed to have been mighty. There are three bases for the claim that the Dutch recognized their power by treaty before the French made a treaty with them in 1624. The first is the statement made by four of the Iroquois tribes to Governor Slaughter in 1691. In the council of that year Slaughter urged the Iroquois to attack Canada, though the tribesmen were solely interested in obtaining better prices in trade. During the debate an Iroquois spokesman said: "We have been informed by our Forefathers that in former times a Ship arrived here in this Country which was matter of great admiration to us, especially our desire was to know what was within her Belly. In that Ship were Christians, amongst the rest one Jaques with whom we made a Covenant of friendship."[4] The attempt to make this statement fit the circumstance of any ship on the Hudson in the early part of the seventeenth century has only one argument to support it, the phrase "here in this country," and that is of doubtful validity. There are three arguments against it, the word "forefathers," the name "Jaques," and the fact that the Mohawks, the easternmost of the tribes and the one which of all the Iroquois always lived nearest the Hudson, were not even represented at the council. Had the Mohawks made the statement or lent it the authority of their consent it would have some, though little more, value.

The phrase "here in this country" is susceptible of two interpretations. It does not necessarily mean "in this *immediate* territory" but may well have a broader connotation, including even the St. Lawrence region, which was in truth the country of the "forefathers" and the country into which there had once come "one Jaques" Cartier with a ship.

The word "forefathers" offers a similar opportunity for two interpretations, the correct one, however, being considerably more evident. In view of the fact that only eighty-two years had elapsed since the coming of the first European ship, it would be strange if there had not been at the council of 1691 mature Iroquois whose immediate fathers would have told them of such an event had

⁴ *New York Colonial Documents*, 3:775.

they known of it, or who might themselves have met the ship in question. While it is not impossible that the reference was to the seventeenth century, the usual connotation of "forefathers" even in those times was greater antiquity than eighty-two years. The document, if it has any value at all, almost certainly refers to the voyages of Cartier, a century and a half before. Proponents of the other view, it would seem, face an insurmountable difficulty in the name "Jaques"; and the absence of the Mohawks from the council weakens the case fatally, for the Mohawks, the eastern canton of the Iroquois, were always the Iroquois nearest the Hudson River. It is more than doubtful whether Hudson's Indians were Iroquois at all; William M. Beauchamp, an archeologist of considerable standing, has decided that they could not have been. It is his view that the enemies of the Mohawks held the river for twenty-five leagues on each side. Further evidence will be offered in support of his contention.[5]

The second basis for the claim that the Iroquois were in power on the Hudson is a supposed treaty of 1618 in "the vale of Tawasentha" or Norman's Kill, a small stream flowing into the Hudson a few miles below the mouth of the Mohawk. In the *Albany Records* this supposed treaty is run to earth in an anonymous traditional account which resembles in every respect the traditional Delaware story, presented by Heckewelder, of a Dutch mediation between Iroquois and Delaware, and which, although undated, is presumably to be dated later than 1630. If considered as of 1618, it contains at least one positive anachronism in the separate identification of the Iroquois cantons, which was not possible to the Dutch until 1659 at the earliest, and probably not until 1662.[6]

[5] William M. Beauchamp, *A History of the New York Iroquois* (New York State Museum Bulletin no. 78, New York, 1905), 168; Nicolaes van Wassenaer, *Historisch Verhael*, in Jameson, *Narratives of New Netherland*, 67. There is but one possible solution of the "Jaques" difficulty. Granting an Anglicized pronunciation of the name, some think it might refer to a Captain Jacobs, who is known to have come to Albany in 1623. The later the date, however, the more valid become the arguments against the original claim.

[6] Professor John A. Doyle accepts the fact of the treaty, quoting John R. Brodhead, though criticizing him for his failure to cite authority. Fiske also accepts it, characterizing it as a solemn treaty concerning the exchange of firearms for peltries "in the groves of singing pinetrees, in the green and silent valley." Brodhead, Doyle's authority, quotes Joseph W. Moulton, who gives no authority. O'Callaghan quotes Colden, whose testimony is of no value whatever, and the *Albany Records*. See Doyle, *Middle*

The Dutch had never heard of this treaty they are now supposed to have made. Arent van Curler, an expert in Indian relations, had not heard of it in 1642, and considered his informal agreement of 1643 to be the first definite understanding ever reached with the Mohawks. No mention of it is found in all the Holland Documents, and no contemporary historian or commentator, and there were several, seemed to have known of it, although it would have been of the utmost importance. Perhaps the best evidence that it never existed is the fact that the English, searching for some ground older than the French treaty of 1624 upon which to base a claim to the Iroquois country, knew nothing of any such treaty made by the Dutch, and based their claim upon a supposed treaty of 1623 (a most convenient date), which claim must now be examined.[7]

In 1688, the year the English advanced their claim, England and France were on the brink of war. The Treaty of Dover, execrated from the first by the English people, had never represented any real connection with the French, and the Merry Monarch, pensioner of Louis XIV, had been more than three years gone. Within a year England was to be a member of the League of Augsburg opposing the expansion of France under Louis XIV, whose policy in Europe had its counterpart in America. The French claim to the Iroquois country, based upon priority and actual occupation by the Jesuits, was actively pushed by the Canadian governors.

The claim had been brought forward formally in 1684 and hotly

Colonies, 8; Fiske, Dutch and Quaker Colonies, 1:107; Joseph W. Moulton and John V. N. Yates, History of the State of New York (one volume in two, New York, 1824–26), 1:346; John R. Brodhead, History of the State of New York (2 vols., New York, 1853–71), 1:88; Edmund B. O'Callaghan, History of New Netherland, or, New York under the Dutch (2 vols., New York, 1855), 1:78–80; Albany Records, xxiv, 167; Heckewelder, Indian Nations Who Once Inhabited Pennsylvania, 47–59; Arnold J. F. Van Laer, ed., Minutes of the Court of Fort Orange and Beverwyck, 1652–1660 (2 vols., Albany, 1920–23), 2:211–219; New York Colonial Documents, 13:108–114; Osgood, American Colonies, 2:422; Beauchamp, New York Iroquois, 173.

[7] Arent van Curler to the Patroon, in New York Colonial Documents, 13:15, 112–113; Van Laer, Court Minutes, 213. The contemporary historians include Nicolaes Wassenaer and Johan de Laet, of whom De Laet became a Van Rensselaer partner in 1630. See Jameson, Narratives of New Netherland, 36–60. While these "claims" established and settled nothing, they were useful to governments as propaganda, both at home and abroad.

denounced by Colonel Dongan, the fiery Irish governor of New
York; unable to establish a post in the Iroquois territory, he sought
to establish an agreement older than the genuine French treaty of
1624. Beginning with nebulous statements about "a free and broth-
erly correspondence from the first settlement of this towne," Dongan found it desirable to produce something more substantial, for
the French not only had priests in the Iroquois towns, but had the
treaty of 1624, published more than fifty years before by Champlain. This treaty, though long since broken and never clearly understood, gave France an advantage on paper in respect to terri-
torial claims.[8]

The enterprising Dongan may not have known that there were
available at least two contemporary Dutch histories of the events
of the 1620's. If he did, it is not surprising that he failed to mention
them, for neither tells of any treaty. He chose to depend instead
upon a deposition by a person who claimed to have witnessed a
council and a treaty between the Dutch, the Iroquois, and the Ottawa sixty-five years before, and to remember with amazing clarity the terms of that treaty, which most conveniently antedated
the French treaty by one year.

The deponent, Catelina Trico, was eighty-three years of age.
She had already been used by Dongan as a deponent concerning a
claim to Delaware, in which deposition she had been unable to re-
call the year in which she had come to America, that fact having
been unimportant in 1685. She was probably a mid-wife, and her
only other appearances in the New York Colonial MSS are of a
slightly unsavory nature.[9] The argument need not be *ad hominem*,
however; her deposition is eloquent.

Within a little more than three years after her Delaware deposition Catelina's memory had improved to an extent that must have

[8] *New York Colonial Documents*, 3:512–532, contains representative arguments in
this controversy. Thomas Dongan, second earl of Limerick, was governor of New
York from 1682 to 1688, and was relieved by Andros. The Iroquois were notoriously
hostile to European posts in their territory because such posts would eliminate them
as middlemen. See also Wassenaer and De Laet, *ibid.*, 215, and Jameson, *Narratives of
New Netherland*, 36–60, 67–96.

[9] See Edmund B. O'Callaghan, ed., *The Documentary History of the State of New York*
(4 vols., Albany, 1850–51), 3:49, for a selection from the Doed Book relative to Catelina Trico; New York Colonial MSS, 2:61, 245, in the office of the secretary of state
of New York.

been disconcertingly gratifying to Dongan and Andros. She remembered now with surprising clarity all the necessary circumstances. She remembered that she had come to America in 1623; she remembered the name of the ship upon which she had come and the name of the captain of the ship; she remembered that in 1623

> . . . yᵉ Mahikanders or River Indians, yᵉ Maquase:Oneydes:Onnondages Cayougas, & Sinnekes, wᵗʰ yᵉ Mahawawa or Ottowawaes Indians came and made Convenants of friendship wᵗʰ yᵉ sᵈ Arien Jorise there Commander Bringing him great Presents of Bever . . . yᵉ sᵈ Deponent lived in Albany three years all which time yᵉ Indians were all as quiet as Lambs . . . in yᵉ year 1626 yᵉ Deponent came from Albany & settled at N:Yorke . . .
>
> WILLIAM MORRIS
> Justice of yᵉ pece[10]

Here is the familiar anachronism of the separate identification of the five Iroquois cantons, a distinction which the Dutch officials and traders could not have made until at least thirty-six years later.[11] Whether prompted or not, Catelina included in her deposition information she had acquired much later than 1623. But her memory was even more remarkable: she remembered the Ottawa at Albany, which is a much more serious anachronism. In 1623 the Ottawa had been visited by Champlain, but even he did not know them by that name; in fact, they were not so known until many years later. In 1623 they were a minor trading and fishing tribe living beyond the Hurons, a few on the shores of Georgian Bay and the rest on the islands of far northern Lake Huron.[12] It is probable that no Ottawa Indian came to Albany until 1696.

The appearance of the Ottawa at Albany in Catelina's deposition is not hard to fathom, however, if the suspicious eye can see the hand of Colonel Dongan in the testimony. Dongan had for more than four years been reaching out for the Ottawa trade at

[10] O'Callaghan, *Documentary History of New York*, 3:50–51.
[11] Frederick W. Hodge, ed., *Handbook of American Indians North of Mexico* (2 vols., Bureau of American Ethnology Bulletin no. 30, Washington, 1907–10), pt. 2, p. 503. The Dutch called all the western cantons Seneca. See the narratives of various western journeys in Jameson, *Narratives of New Netherland*, especially the "Narrative of a Journey into the Mohawk and Oneida Country, 1634–1635," pp. 135–162.
[12] See Champlain's *Works*. He called them *Cheveux Relevés*, and Radisson, in the 1650's, called them "stairing haires."

Mackinac, and in 1684 Duluth and Durantaye had caught two of his expeditions headed for the Ottawa.[13] The reader should at least keep this in mind when considering the validity of Catelina's deposition. It is safe to say that she never saw an Ottawa, and that in any event to have placed them at Albany in 1623 was an anachronism three-quarters of a century broad.[14]

Moreover, Catelina Trico concealed, perhaps inadvertently, a fact that has considerable bearing upon the likelihood of a treaty in 1623. She says that for three years the Indians were "all as quiet as Lambs" and that "in yᵉ year 1626 yᵉ Deponent came from Albany & settled at N:Yorke," but she omits to state why she left Albany, which reason may now be supplied. In 1626 the Dutch and the Iroquois were at war. Krieckebeeck, the Dutch commander, marched with the Mahicans west of the Hudson, and in an encounter with the Iroquois he was killed, with several of his men, and the allies utterly defeated. They retreated to Albany, and the civil population was evacuated to New York (then New Amsterdam, which Catelina did not remember), leaving only a garrison of sixteen soldiers.[15] Catelina did not remember this circumstance, or at least did not, for obvious reasons, insist upon its inclusion in her deposition. Who would believe, if that were included, that the Dutch and Iroquois had any treaty worthy the name in 1623? The whole affair, beginning with the date, seems to be a concoction of the artful Colonel Dongan.[16]

[13] These were known as the Roseboom and McGregory expeditions. For details see *New York Colonial Documents*, 3:436, 473; 9:287, 297, 309, 318, 320, 332, 348, 363; *Jesuit Relations*, 63:281–283; Francis Parkman, *Count Frontenac and New France under Louis XIV* (*France and England in North America*, pt. 5, Boston, 1877), 146–147. See also Tonty, "Memoir," in *Illinois Historical Collections*, vol. 1, pp. 151–152; Lahontan, *New Voyages*, 1:125–126.

[14] Compare Dongan's claim of February, 1688, that "yᵉ Ottawawaes have traded at this towne ever since it has been settled," with the statement made by Samuel York in 1700 that he had "often heard the Ottawas express a longing desire to trade with the English," in *New York Colonial Documents*, 3:510; 4:749. When the Ottawa did come, after 1700, they said that they had never been there before. Beauchamp, *New York Iroquois*, 173.

[15] Wassenaer, in O'Callaghan, *Documentary History of New York*, 3:43–44; also in Jameson, *Narratives of New Netherland*. See also Jonas Michaëlius' letter, *ibid.*, 131, and Brodhead, *History of New York*, 1:169–170.

[16] It has been necessary to present this detailed criticism of the Trico deposition because historians persist in accepting it, notably Adriaan J. Barnouw, in his "Settlement of New Netherland," in *Wigwam and Bouwerie* (*History of the State of New York*,

There is one more bit of evidence relative to the Iroquois status on the Hudson prior to 1626. In January, 1630, Kiliaen van Rensselaer wrote to his agent in America instructing him to purchase land from the Indians, and by August the purchase had been made and recorded. This purchase, a strip twenty-four miles wide, ran forty-eight miles west of the Hudson along the south bank of the Mohawk, and the names of the Indians selling it are not those of Iroquois but of Mahicans.[17] Incidental confirmation of the Iroquois exclusion from the Hudson prior to 1626 is not lacking. In 1609 Champlain, on or near Lake George, asked his Indian companions where the Iroquois habitations might be found. They replied that after reaching the Hudson they were two days' journey beyond.[18] The unknown author of the "Narrative of a Journey, 1634–1635," when returning to Albany in the spring of the latter year, passed a "ruined castle" about fifty miles from Albany, and was told that it marked the farthest eastern advance of the Mohawks that precipitated the war, and that it had been burned nine years before.[19] The cause of the war had evidently been the expansion of the Mohawks eastward toward the Hudson. Wassenaer's location of the Mahicans in 1624, "25 leagues on both sides of the river," is scarcely needed to mark the eastern boundary of the Five Nations. The case for Iroquois power on the Hudson now seems weaker than ever. If any of these treaties had been made, they must have been made in hostile country, and if Tawasentha was an ancient Mohawk townsite, the Mohawks who had built it had since been driven some distance west.[20]

edited by Alexander C. Flick, vol. 1, New York, 1933), 243. Beauchamp, in his *New York Iroquois*, 173, and Jameson, in his *Narratives of New Netherland*, 75, distrust the deposition, but neither details his distrust sufficiently to make a conclusive case against it. Jameson considers only the time that elapsed between the supposed event and the deposition.

[17] Arnold J. F. Van Laer, ed. and trans., *Van Rensselaer Bowier Manuscripts* (New York, 1908), 158–161, 166–169; *New York Colonial Documents*, 14:1–2, 12. The dimensions of the tract are given in O'Callaghan, *New Netherland*, 1:124.

[18] Champlain, *Works*, 2:93–96. The wording is not altogether clear, but this seems to be the best and most likely interpretation.

[19] Jameson, *Narratives of New Netherland*, 139–162. The most likely solution of the author's identity is in Van Laer, *Van Rensselaer Bowier Manuscripts*, 271n. Benjamin Sulte dismissed this war as one fought for vengeance alone. *Histoire des Canadiens-Française, 1608–1880* (8 vols., Montreal, 1882–84), 2:23.

[20] J. Grant Wilson, "Arent van Curler and His Journey of 1634–35," in American Historical Association, *Report*, 1895, pp. 81–101; Wassenaer, *Historisch Verhael*, in

The Iroquois and New England

The first mention of the Mohawks in the New England area is in Wood's *New England's Prospect, 1634*. Bradford does not mention them until 1637, when they aided the English colonists in the Pequot War, and Hubbard mentions that in the same year they cut off the Narragansetts. It is true that they did lay the Mahicans under tribute, but an interesting glimpse of their former status is afforded by the "Journal of New Netherland," which as of the year 1641 says that the Indians as far as the seacoast were forced to pay them tribute, "whereas, on the contrary, they were formerly obliged to pay tribute to these."[21]

The intertribal status of the Iroquois prior to 1626 now begins to assume its proper proportions. On the defensive against the French Indians, as evidenced by the expeditions of Champlain and others, humiliated by the Susquehannah, staved off from the Hudson, and perhaps under tribute to the Mahicans, they were very far from holding the position of conquerors. Archeological evidence also supports this view; they had retreated even from the Lake Ontario shore to the densely wooded highlands, from which, says Beauchamp, their towns did not emerge until after 1620.

The Iroquois Trade to 1640

Unfortunately the records of the Dutch West India Company, which may have recorded detailed information about the early Hudson River trade, are lost.[22] It is still possible, however, by put-

Jameson, *Narratives of New Netherland*, 67; Brodhead, *New York*, 1:8m. *Tawasentha* is said to mean "the place of the dead."

[21] *[William] Wood's New England's Prospect, 1634* (Publications of the Prince Society, Boston, 1865), 64; Bradford, *Plimouth Plantation*, 427, 430, 514; William Hubbard, *The History of the Indian Wars in New England*, edited by S. G. Drake (2 vols., Roxbury, Massachusetts, 1865), 1:38; Johannes Megapolensis, Jr., "A Short Account of the Mohawk Indians, 1644," in Jameson, *Narratives of New Netherland*, 172. The Mahicans tried to pass the tariff on down to the Wickquasgeck and the Tappans. See David P. de Vries, *Notes*, in Jameson, *Narratives of New Netherland*, 223; "Journal of New Netherland," in O'Callaghan, *Documentary History of New York*, 4:8. The tribute exacted by the Mohawks was a tribute from actually subject peoples and was truly commercial exploitation. See John W. DeForest, *History of the Indians of Connecticut* (Hartford, 1853), 34, 65n, 289n, 350n. This book is, unlike others of its vintage, written from sources.

[22] John R. Brodhead, agent for the state of New York, discovered in 1841 that they had been sold at auction twenty years before by the government of the Netherlands, and he was unable to locate them.

ting together what information can be gathered elsewhere, to arrive at a fair estimate of the volume of the trade, and to draw a few valid conclusions regarding the conditions under which it was carried on.

The Iroquois-Mahican war, while it spoiled the trade of Plymouth, far to the east, had a most salutary effect on that of New Netherland. The trade of 1626 amounted to more than 7,250 beaver and 800 otter, as compared with 5,295 beaver and 493 otter of the year before. No figures are available for 1627 other than De Laet's statement that it was "still more." In 1628 Wassenaer puts the trade at 10,000 skins. By 1633 it was probably nearing 30,000.[23]

This great and comparatively sudden increase in the trade indicates how important to the Dutch was the Iroquois seizure of the Hudson River trading center. It was also to be of great importance to the Iroquois, especially after their furs were gone, for the rapid increase in trade that enriched the Dutch traders was to exhaust the beaver of the Iroquois so much the sooner, and set them to carrying trade treaties and hatchets to the Canadian tribes. Although Lambrechtsen thought that their trade had from the first been largely in Canadian furs, it is certain that until about 1640 it consisted mostly of fur from their own territories. Interior New York, with its wooded highlands, was never an especially productive beaver ground, however, and the beaver, while probably fairly numerous about the lakes and in the small short streams running north into Lake Ontario, appeared to early observers to be an insignificant item in the fauna of the country. If the alarming pace set by the first decade of the Hudson trade continued, it

---

[23] On Plymouth see William Bradford's letter to Ferdinando Gorges, June 15, 1627, in *New York Historical Collections*, 2d series, 1:367. For the year 1625 in New Netherland see De Laet, *Jaerlyck Verhael*, cited in Jameson, *Narratives of New Netherland*, 82n. The whole trade for 1624 had been only 4,700 skins. As a result of the increase in 1626 the price went down two-thirds. See Van Laer, *Van Rensselaer Bowier Manuscripts*, 5n. For 1626 there are three sources: De Laet and Wassenaer, in Jameson, *Narratives of New Netherland*, 82n, 83, and an estimate in *New York Colonial Documents*, 1:37. These three are not identical, but they very nearly agree. For 1627 and 1628 see De Laet, *op. cit.*, 82n; Nicolaes van Wassenaer, *Historie van Europa*, in O'Callaghan, *Documentary History of New York*, 3:46. Regarding 1633, O'Callaghan's *New Netherland*, 1:139–140, quotes De Laet as saying twenty thousand pounds, which at current prices would approximate twenty-eight thousand skins. O'Callaghan adds that shortly afterward the trade on the North River alone amounted to fifteen or sixteen thousand beaver. See also Mason's letter in *New York Colonial Documents*, 3:17.

would not be long before the Iroquois country would be virtually exhausted of beaver.[24]

In 1640 the inevitable exhaustion of the Iroquois beaver occurred. In that year Kiliaen van Rensselaer wrote to Wilhelm Kieft, the director in New Netherland:

> I can not get over my surprise as to the changes which are said to have occurred in the fur trade at Fort Orange . . . That my people spoiled the fur trade can not by any means be true; they may have outbid and brought about the high price of the skins, but such outbidding . . . causes a greater supply. Now, as far as I can see, the trouble is not with the price of the skins but with the quantity, which is a great paradox to me that I can not understand.

There must have been an ulterior motive behind Van Rensselaer's apparent lack of penetration, for he certainly understood the "paradox" of high prices and no beaver very well. Seven years earlier he had written to the Council of New Netherland:

> Are not the contrary minded well aware that their course will never increase the trade because the savages, who are now stronger than ourselves, will not allow others who . . . live farther away and have many furs to pass through their territory . . . Yes, that the *Maquaas*, who will not allow the French savages who now trade on the river of Canada and who live nearer to us than to them to pass through to come to us, might through persuasion or fear sooner be moved to do so and that from these savages more furs could be obtained than are now bartered in all New Netherland?[25]

So Van Rensselaer was not entirely at a loss to understand, and had in fact known seven years before, the conditions which now limited the fur trade at Fort Orange. The Iroquois were out of fur,

---

[24] Sir Nicolaas Cornelis Lambrechtsen, "A Short Description of the Discovery and Subsequent History of the New Netherlands," translated from the Dutch by Francis A. Van der Kemp, in *New York Historical Collections*, 2d series, 1:92 (New York, 1841). See also "The Representation of New Netherland, 1650," in Jameson, *Narratives of New Netherland*, 297; *New York Colonial Documents*, 1:271, 318; and *New York Historical Collections*, 1:125–242. When Megapolensis says that "skins . . . are plenty in this country," he is speaking of skins used for clothing. See Jameson, *Narratives of New Netherland*, 173. Le Moine, while he speaks of the great numbers of other fauna, never mentions beaver. See the *Jesuit Relations*, 41:127–129. The Huron country was out of beaver by 1635, "the Hurons, who have not a single beaver, going elsewhere to buy the skins they bring." *Ibid.*, 8:57.

[25] Van Rensselaer to Kieft, May 29, 1640, in Van Laer, *Van Rensselaer Bowier Manuscripts*, 483–484; to the Council, *ibid.*, 248.

and would not permit the other Lakes tribes to come through them to the Dutch traders, nor would they permit the Dutch traders to go through them to the farther tribes. The Iroquois were savages, but by no means simple.

For the Mohawks the situation was much more pressing than for Van Rensselaer, and was becoming even desperate. They knew where the fur was, and for more than a decade had been angling for it by peaceful means. In the 1620's and again in 1633 they had tried to make a commercial treaty with the French Indians, particularly the Hurons, who held all the great trade of the north country and of the far Lakes, but both attempts had failed, the one having been foiled by Champlain's tactic, and the other by some unknown obstacle. Still a third treaty promised by the Hurons in this very year of 1640 also failed to materialize. The fur of the eastern Iroquois was gone, and shortly it was to be absolutely necessary to find somewhere a new supply.[26]

From the maze of alternatives, and of ways and means, that need stood out constantly and insistently; they must have fur by one means or another. After fourteen years of uninterrupted trade, it had become a necessity; they could scarcely renounce it now. Lahontan realized the unfortunate position of the Iroquois when he wrote that "by these means the Iroquese, being unprovided with Beaver-skins to be given in exchange for Guns, Powder, Ball and Nets, would be starved to death, or at least obliged to leave their country."[27] Corn they had in plenty, and game could be procured, but the white man did not want corn, and had not wanted it since the first hard years. A treaty with the French would do them no

[26] On the treaty of the 1620's see Charlevoix, *New France*, 2:34–35. Charlevoix says that the Hurons would have joined the Iroquois in that year had it not been for Champlain's instant dispatch of priests, who broke up the agreement. The priests many times served as emissaries to keep these two tribes hostile. Le Jeune and the writer of the "Narrative of 1634–1635," mention the affair of 1633. The projected peace of 1640 is mentioned by Kiotsaeton in his great speech to the Hurons. See the *Jesuit Relations*, 6:57; 27:263; and Jameson, *Narratives of New Netherland*, 150. In that year the eastern Iroquois were coming west to trade with the western cantons for beaver. The supply of the western cantons was not yet exhausted, and they did not become aggressive until it was. *Jesuit Relations*, 27:77.

[27] *New Voyages*, 1:227. These words were written at a date later than 1640, but the position of the Iroquois in relation to the Canadian trade had not changed, nor had the "condition of necessity," which did not permit a trading nation to renounce trade, lest it perish.

good; in fact, it would probably do them harm, since the French would not be party to any agreement which diverted the trade in northern furs, as Charlevoix clearly saw; yet to the Iroquois such a treaty was the only one worth having.[28]

Van Rensselaer was thinking along the same line. "I have not given up the hope," he wrote Muyssart in 1641, "if the Lord will grant me a few years more, of diverting to the colony a large part of the furs of the savages who now trade with the French in Canada . . . I hope that hereafter more attention will be paid to this."[29] Encouragement from the Dutch was hardly needed by the eastern Iroquois, who were already raiding and ambushing the trading fleets coming down the Ottawa. But these raids and ambushes, although they produced fur, produced only a meager supply, wholly insufficient for Iroquois needs. What they must have was a regular and peaceful commerce, and the wily Hurons refused to be snared by a treaty.[30] Another result of the raid and ambush procedure was that, paradoxically, the more effective these enterprises were the less they eventually yielded, for the Hurons and their allies of the Northwest could and did avoid them by using the safer though more circuitous route of the St. Maurice River, crossing to its headwaters far north and descending straight south to Three Rivers.[31]

Yet the Northwest seemed to be the only source of supply that they could tap. Northeast of them, in New England, there was no hope, for the New England Indians traded with the coastal settlements, and in any event their fur had been virtually exhausted long before. The Susquehannah, to the south, naturally traded with the near-by colony of New Sweden. Moreover, they were powerful

[28] "These Indians . . . could scarcely effect a reconciliation with us without excluding themselves from this precious mine of furs." Charlevoix, *New France*, 4:16.

[29] Van Rensselaer to Muyssart, June 6, 1641, in Van Laer, *Van Rensselaer Bowier Manuscripts*, 553.

[30] A trade treaty or agreement such as the Iroquois desired could hardly have been attractive to the Hurons, or indeed to any Indian nation. Even though the Dutch prices were higher, it would have resulted in the interposition of a middleman between themselves and the white man, and they were certain to come out of the transaction with less profit. They preferred to make their own deals with the whites and to deal with them directly, and could not have anticipated the disaster of 1649.

[31] The St. Maurice route, especially popular after 1650, is discussed further in the following chapter, which deals with the Huron trade.

and well armed, even having small cannon in their forts and being instructed in their use and in the use of small arms by the Swedes.[32] And thirdly, they were in an excellent position to cut the trade routes of the western Iroquois, should they be so minded.[33] There was little to be gained from falling upon the Susquehannah.

In the north and west there was, they knew, what appeared to be an inexhaustible supply of furs which came down the rivers in the summer and early fall in ever larger canoe brigades. To that empire of wealth the Hurons held the key.

[32] Clayton C. Hall, ed., *Narratives of Early Maryland, 1633–1684* (New York, 1910), 155, 371; Thomas C. Holm, "A Short Description of the Province of New Sweden," translated from the Swedish by Peter S. Du Ponceau, in *Pennsylvania Historical Society Memoirs*, vol. 3, pt. 1, 157–158; Ondaaiondiont, quoted by Ragueneau, in the *Jesuit Relations*, 33:133; "Report of Governor Johan Printz, 1647," in Albert C. Myers, ed., *Narratives of Early Pennsylvania, West New Jersey, and Delaware, 1630–1707* (*Original Narratives of Early American History*, New York, 1912), 123; Holm (*op. cit.*) describes the trade in small arms and the "small iron cannon." The reference to Swedish instruction of the Susquehannah, from Samuel Smith's *History of the Colony of Nova-Caesaria, or New Jersey* (Burlington, New Jersey, 1765), 24, is quoted by Robert Proud in his *History of Pennsylvania* (Philadelphia, 1797–1798), 1:111, and by John L. Bozman in his *History of Maryland* (Baltimore, 1837), 2:273. Smith cites a pamphlet published in 1648, which the writer has been unable to find. See also John G. Shea, "The Identity of the Andastes, Minquas, Susquehannahs, and Conestoques," in the *Historical Magazine*, 2:296 (New York, 1858).

[33] This actually happened later and was a primary cause of the great Iroquois-Susquehannah war. See below, Chapter 10. See also Lalemant, in the *Jesuit Relations*, 47:111.

IV. THE HURONS AND THEIR NEIGHBORS

THE HURONS, probably the most numerous of the Iroquoian tribes, occupied in the early seventeenth century the Georgian Bay–Lake Simcoe region of present-day Ontario. Their two score villages clustered close to the bay and spread fanwise toward the south, the most advanced being perhaps a hundred miles from the frontiers of the Neutral Nation above Lake Erie. The Hurons had apparently formed the northern wing of the Iroquoian migration, which bifurcated on Lake Erie, the Huron tribes passing north of that lake and of Lake Ontario, and finding a hospitable land east of Nottawasaga Bay. The Iroquois, as has been related, passed south of Lake Ontario, bifurcating again, perhaps, on the Susquehannah River, and pressing on across the St. Lawrence into the teeth of a consolidating Algonquin resistance. With the retreat from the Algonquins, the final division took place, the eastern end of Lake Ontario serving as a splitting wedge, the Algonquin warriors as a maul. Two tribes coasted the northern shore of Lake Ontario and finally moved into Huronia about 1589 and 1609 respectively, completing the four cantons identified there by Lalemant in 1639.[1] What is significant historically is that the Hurons were older in culture than the Iroquois and longer established

[1] Bushnell's *Tribal Migrations*, map 3, shows the migrations, which John Fiske, long ahead of his time, viewed correctly. See his *Discovery of America*, 44–45. For maps of Huronia and its townsites see Arthur E. Jones, "*8endake Ehen*," *or Old Huronia* (Ontario Bureau of Archives, *Report*, 1908); *Jesuit Relations*, vol. 34, which also has a map by Jones; "Identification of St. Ignace II and Ekarenniondi," in Ontario Provincial Museum, *Archaeological Report*, 1906, also appendix to the *Report* of the Minister of Education (Toronto, 1907); and François du Creux, *Historiae Canadensis* (Paris, 1664), which contains a contemporary map, as does Parkman, *Jesuits in North America*, iv. For Lalemant's description, see the *Jesuit Relations*, 16:227.

There are other theories of the prehistoric Huron migration, but little confidence may be placed in the sources upon which they are based, and they have been discarded

in their locale,[2] and that therefore their commercial economy, viewed in the next chapter, was a natural consequence not only of their environment but of their age and permanence as a separate and settled tribal entity.

The name "Huron" is a colloquialism made classical by time and repetition. Champlain called the Hurons *Ochateguins* or *Ochasteguins* from a chief of that name and confused them with the consanguine Iroquois.[3] They spoke of themselves as *Wendat* or *Ouendat*, which seems to have been derived from *Ah8enda*, "an island." They spoke of their country as an island, which indeed it was, being entirely surrounded by lakes and great water courses, and the French-Huron dictionary explains *Ahti8endo*, meaning *les Hurons*, with the words *quia in insula habitabant*.[4] The word survives in "Wyandot," the name of the descendants of the Petun or Tobacco Nation. Some early French soldier or sailor dubbed Champlain's Ochateguins *Hurons* (from *hures*, boars) because of their curious scalplock dressed in a ridge or roach down the middle of the scalp.[5] It was only one of many styles, and not even peculiar to the Hurons, but the name persisted.

They built their towns back from the shore to prevent a surprise attack by canoe, and to be near fresh spring water. Champlain found some of them with triple stockades thirty-five feet high, but Parkman's contention that the stockaded towns were those on the side exposed to Iroquois incursions is not true. The stockaded towns, from all accounts, seem to have been the larger ones wherever located, and they had in all probability been built against the Petuns in former years. There was formerly "cruel

as anthropological and archeological research has progressed. See Clarke, *Wyandotts*, 2–4; G. W. Bruce, "The Petuns," in Ontario Historical Society, *Papers and Records*, 8:34–39 (Toronto, 1907); Cusick, *Ancient History of the Six Nations*; David Boyle, "The Iroquois," in Provincial Museum of Ontario, *Archaeological Report*, 1905, pp. 146–158; and Hale, *Indian Migrations*. It is curious that Hale ridicules Cusick's chronology as "absurd" and then follows it absolutely, down to historic times.

[2] Horatio Hale, "Huron Folk-Lore," in the *Journal of American Folklore*, 1:178. Hale is here in his own field of philology and may be accepted as an authority. See also Thwaites, in the *Jesuit Relations*, 8:304n; Jones, *8endake Ehen*, 418.

[3] Champlain, *Works*, 2:68 ff.; Charlevoix, *New France*, 2:71. The Iroquets, a small Algonquin tribe of the Ottawa River, were named in a similar manner.

[4] *Jesuit Relations*, 15:21; 16:227; 33:237–239; Jones, *8endake Ehen*, 419, quoting the French-Huron dictionary.

[5] *Jesuit Relations*, 16:229–231; Charlevoix, *New France*, 2:71.

war" between these two, says the Relation of 1640, but they had long been united in a firm alliance.[6]

The number inhabiting Huronia has been a matter of great uncertainty and debate, but a compilation and fair estimate of the most reliable sources does not permit the Hurons to be calculated, previous to 1636, at less than thirty to thirty-five thousand. Champlain and all the Jesuits, including the observant Sagard, are in approximate agreement, and even conservative authors have ceased to question the Jesuit figures.[7] During the decade in which the plague raged in Huronia it is likely that this figure was cut in half. Lalemant, writing to Richelieu in March, 1640, estimated that the Huron population had been reduced from thirty thousand to ten thousand, but it must be remembered that he was drawing the darkest possible picture for the sake of an argument to support his appeal for aid, and would hardly have underestimated the Huron losses. Four days later he wrote to Vitelleschi at Rome informing him that during that one year of the plague the Jesuits had baptized "more than one thousand from among the dying,"[8] which argues a great total loss in three years. It is curious and important, we may note in passing, that in writing to Richelieu, Lalemant put the sole responsibility for the deaths upon the Iroquois, whereas in writing to Vitelleschi, four days later, he attributed them solely to the plague. This inconsistency should be remembered, for to understand Iroquois-Huron relations it is necessary to establish that Huron losses at the hands of the Iroquois did not begin until after the exhaustion of the fur supply of the Iroquois, about 1640.

[6] Andrew F. Hunter, *Notes of Sites of Huron Villages* (Toronto, 1899), p. 7; also appendix to the *Report* of the Ontario Minister of Education, 1898; Champlain, *Works*, 3:48; Parkman, *Jesuits in North America*, xxviii–xxix; *Jesuit Relations*, 20:43.

[7] Champlain gives 22,000 (*Works*, 4:302), but if he is taken literally, he means only the Great Bear Clan. He later increased his own estimate to 30,000 (*ibid.*, 302n). Sagard gives *environ trente ou quarante mille âmes en tout* (*Grand Voyage*, 80). Radisson, though he never saw the Huron towns, gives 20,000 to 30,000 (*Voyages*, 88). Le Jeune says 30,000 (*Jesuit Relations*, 6:59; 7:225). Lalemant gives 30,000 (*ibid.*, 17:223), and De Quen and Villeneuve give from 30,000 to 35,000 (*ibid.*, 42:221; 44:249; 70:205). Brébeuf has 30,000 (*ibid.*, 8:115), and Le Mercier, 30,000 (*ibid.*, 40:223). See also Brébeuf, *ibid.*, 7:224, and Mallery, "Former and Present Number of Our Indians," in American Association for the Advancement of Science, *Proceedings*, 26:340–366.

[8] Lalemant to Richelieu, March 28, 1640, in the *Jesuit Relations*, 17:223; to Vitelleschi, April 1, 1640, *ibid.*, 17:229.

The Huron economy, aside from trade, was almost purely agricultural, corn and fish being the principal articles of diet. They were extraordinarily provident, keeping on hand at all times a supply of corn sufficient for three or four years.[9] They used large quantities of fish, mostly as a meat seasoning for *sagamité*, a corn mush; they fattened bears for food, but game was scarce, as indeed it must have been in so heavily populated a land. Bressani said that the Hurons hunted only for pleasure or on extraordinary occasions, and Sagard complained that he touched no meat for six weeks or two months. Even with their maize culture they had no land title as did the Iroquois, which indicates the relative importance of agriculture and commerce to these two tribes.[10]

The Huron fraternal organization was not unlike that of the Iroquois, having, however, eleven gens and four phratries, and the tribe was not, as a whole, highly political. There were tribal councils and a national council, a crude standing army, and a police force, but the government, such as it was, was decentralized, and there was no absolute authority. Even at the solemn Feast of the Dead there was usually intratribal division and discord. There was no provision for the incorporation of conquered and immigrating peoples, and the only adoption ceremony seems to have been an elaborate mockery, prefatory to the most diabolically ingenious torture. The Huron government was engined chiefly for the purposes of preserving civil peace and, above all, the precious trade.[11]

The Huron mental capacity was undoubtedly great, their cranial capacity exceeding that of all other American aborigines, not excepting the highly civilized tribes of Mexico and Peru. Charlevoix characterized them as having a "solid, judicious, elevated mind,

[9] Parkman, *Jesuits in North America*, xxx. It is possible that Parkman exaggerated (a fault of which he was by no means incapable) a statement of Champlain's. See Champlain's *Works*, 4:328.

[10] Champlain, *Works*, 3:57. See Sagard, *Grand Voyage*, 92–99, 140, and Champlain, *Works*, 4:304–308, for their many ways of preparing corn; also Champlain, 4:309; *Jesuit Relations*, 38:245; Sagard, *Grand Voyage*, 92; Macleod, *Origin of the State*, 43.

[11] John W. Powell, in Bureau of American Ethnology, *Report*, 1879–80, pp. 59–63; Champlain, *Works*, 3:157–160; Le Sieur Gendron, *Quelques particularitez du pays des Hurons*, written in 1644–45 (Albany, 1868); Sagard, *Grand Voyage*, 137–138; *Jesuit Relations*, 10:279–281, 351; 14:17–21; Chaumont to Nappi, *ibid.*, 13:37–81. These pages provide an antidote to anti-Iroquois prejudice aroused by Iroquois cruelty.

capable of reflecting. . . . the most sedentary and laborious of all the nations yet known on this continent," and Le Jeune wrote, "I could not tell you how cunning this Nation is." After their wreck and dispersion they exerted upon the tribes about them an influence quite disproportionate to their numbers, and the Jesuits had chosen them as the field of their first missionary labors because of their position and acquaintance among many tribes. In 1640 Le Jeune had a map, made by the Hurons and given to him by Ragueneau, on which appeared the names and locations of twenty-nine tribes, "the greater part" of which, he said, "understand the Huron language."[12] It is significant that in 1634 Nicolet had Huron interpreters with him to the speak to the Winnebago.

The Hurons, popular and powerful within their own region, were dominant over the Iroquois, their only enemies. Far from being fearful of them, they were so careless in their attitude as to excite the comment of the priests, who remarked that the Hurons did not fear surprise and therefore did not enclose their villages with palisades. The fortified towns, which seemed so significant to Parkman and which he so far misplaced, were no longer being built. The power and influence of the Hurons "makes them more licentious," complained Le Jeune in 1630, "because they are better fed."[13]

The Petuns, or Tobacco Hurons, lived just west of the Hurons proper, on the Bruce Peninsula and just east of the Blue Mountains, about twenty-five or thirty miles from the center of Huronia. They were known both as Quieuenontatironons or "mountaineers" because of their locale, and as Petuneux or "tobacco people" because of their extensive cultivation of tobacco, but it was the former name, corrupted into many variants, that per-

[12] J. S. Phillips, *Admeasurements of Crania of the Principal Groups of Indians in the United States*, and Samuel G. Morton, *Crania Americana*, quoted in Parkman, *Jesuits in North America*, xliii–xlvi. Dr. Taché, of Laval University, also made many cranial measurements tending to support this view. See also Charlevoix, *New France*, 2:65, and *Journal of a Voyage to North America*, edited by Louise P. Kellogg (2 vols., Chicago, 1923), 1:286–287; 2:9–12; Le Jeune, in the *Jesuit Relations*, 5:73; 18:235; Ragueneau, *ibid.*, 34:205.

[13] *Jesuit Relations*, 10:95; 45:205; Radisson, *Voyages*, 91–92; Gendron, *Quelques particularitez*, 17. The Hurons had an alliance and trade relations of long standing with the Susquehannah of Pennsylvania. Ragueneau, in the *Jesuit Relations*, 30:85–88; Gendron, *Quelques particularitez*, 7. See also the *Jesuit Relations*, 6:254.

sisted.[14] They numbered nine or ten villages, which, on the basis of the proportions of the closely consanguine Hurons, would mean a population of about fifteen thousand. Champlain commented upon their sedentary way of life, their great crops of maize, and their production of hemp for thread, from which they manufactured fishnets.[15] They also cultivated, besides tobacco, hemp, and maize, beans and sunflowers. They were held in complete economic subjection by the Hurons proper, through whom they had their sole commercial contacts and with whom, despite a former hostility, they lived at peace.[16]

The Allumettes and Minor Ottawa River Tribes

The early traveler to Huronia by way of the Ottawa or, as it was then called, Grand River, encountered several small tribes living on or near its banks before reaching the dangerous rapids of Allumette Island. Of these the lower were the Iroquets, some of whom accompanied Champlain in 1613 on his trip with Vignau, when they set out for Hudson Bay and ended among the Allumettes. The Iroquets had once lived on Montreal Island, but after a brief period of independence following the outbreak of the Iroquois wars, they were for the most part incorporated into the ranks of the Iroquois, only a remnant remaining at the end of the century. The Noquets, likewise disintegrated and degraded, also disappeared as a tribal entity, as did also the "Petite Nation" of Algonquins.[17] There were a few more fragmentary tribes, such

[14] Gendron, *Quelques particularitez*, 6; Gabriel Sagard-Théodat, *Histoire du Canada* (new edition, 4 vols., Paris, 1866), 1:201. The most usual of the corruptions are "Tionnontaties" and "Dionnondadies." They are called Petuns in the Relations, but were never so known to the English. The modern name for them is Wyandot.

[15] Charlevoix, in his *Journal*, Letter XVII, calls them the "true Hurons," but this is a mistake. They were the only remaining Hurons, except the Hurons of Loretto. See also the *Jesuit Relations*, 20:42; 33:143; and Champlain, *Works*, 3:95–96, 136, for their way of life.

[16] Gendron, *Quelques particularitez*, 12; Lucien Carr, "The Food of Certain American Indians," in American Antiquarian Society, *Proceedings*, new series, 10:171–172 (1895); *Jesuit Relations*, 20:43, 51–53. A full account of the "Mission of the Apostles," with a fairly comprehensive study of the tribe, is given in Chapter 10 of Ragueneau, in the *Jesuit Relations*, 20:43–77. See also John G. Shea, in the *Historical Magazine*, 5:26.

[17] Champlain, *Works*, 3:65; Perrot, *Memoir*, in Blair, *Indian Tribes*, 1:42n; *Jesuit Relations*, 5:288–290; La Mothe Cadillac, "Relation," in *Wisconsin Historical Collections*, 16:360 (Madison, 1902); Daniel Greysolon Du Luth, letter dated April 12, 1684, *ibid.*, 117, 117n; Pierre Margry, *Découvertes et établissements des Français dans l'ouest et*

as the Katakououemi, but the aggregate importance of the lower
Ottawa River tribes was never great, and they soon vanished.
Their language, as probably their blood, was a mixture of Algonquin proper and Montagnais. No statement can be made concerning their number, except that it was not large.[18]

On Allumette Island, ruled by the sagacious and treacherous
Tesseouat, known later as Le Borgne, the "one-eyed," lived the
powerful and turbulent "Island Algonquins," called, after their
island, Allumettes. Around the island the river was obstructed
by dangerous rapids, and the passage involved a portage of canoes
and goods, a circumstance of which the tribe took the utmost advantage. It was their custom to charge all nations desiring passage
a heavy toll, and the volume of the river trade was sufficient to
enable them to live exceedingly well. They boasted only four
hundred warriors, yet the Hurons feared them, though perhaps
outnumbering them more than ten to one.[19] Feeling the power
of their position, they were the haughtiest, most arrogant, of all
the tribes known to the French, daring even, on several occasions,
to capture and abuse the priests to extort payment.[20] They desired to monopolize the trade of the upper nations, and to that end
attempted constantly to drive a wedge between the French and
the Hurons; they even tried to prevent Champlain from going on
upriver to the Nipissings in 1613. All their trade extended south and

dans le sud de l'Amérique Septentrionale, 1614–1754 (6 vols., Paris, 1876–86), 5:125.
The Petite Nation was also called "Ouaouechkarini." Arthur F. Hunter believes
that they were called "petite" because of their small size, but it seems more likely to
have been because of their small numbers. See the Jesuit Relations, 18:229, 258n.

[18] Jean B. A. Ferland, Cours d'histoire du Canada (2 vols., Quebec, 1861–65), 1:191;
Sulte, "Valley of the Grand River," in Royal Society of Canada, Proceedings and
Transactions, 2d series, vol. 4, sec. 2, p. 125. Sulte is almost always excessively con-
servative when estimating numbers. His assumption that all these tribes, including the
Allumettes, could muster no more than twelve hundred warriors is unwarranted.

[19] Thwaites, in the Jesuit Relations, 5:291n; Champlain, Works, 5:103; Sagard,
Grand Voyage, 88, 250, 252, 263; Perrot, Memoir, in Blair, Indian Tribes, 1:177; Sulte,
"Les Pays d'en Haut, 1670," in Royal Society of Canada, Proceedings and Transactions,
3d series, vol. 7, sec. 1, p. 83; Le Jeune, in the Jesuit Relations, 9:275. The Huron sub-
servience is easily understood. It would have required the entire Huron tribe, or more,
to force a passage, and the Hurons were always, when at the island, outnumbered.

[20] Sagard, Grand Voyage, 252; Le Jeune, in the Jesuit Relations, 9:247, 275; 14:271,
276; 16:43, 209–213; 20:155; 22:231; 25:249 ff. Regarding their treatment of priests,
see Perrot, Memoir, in Blair, Indian Tribes, 1:176–178, and the Jesuit Relations, 14:267;
15:151. Perrot is mistaken in the identity of the priest who was hung. It was Ragueneau, not Lalemant, as is shown by the Relation.

east, as far as Tadoussac and the land of the Abenaki in Maine. The Iroquets and the Petite Nation were their satellites, and about 1620 they forced a peace upon the Iroquois. In 1636 they sought alliance with both the Hurons and the Nipissings, but because of their extortionate tactics on the river were refused by both.[21] Feared by many, befriended by none, they were almost constantly in trouble with the French, and were not numerous enough to hold their own when their island was threatened by the muskets of the terrible Iroquois.

The Nipissings

The route to Huronia followed the Ottawa River highway above Allumette Island to the point where the Mattawan flows in from the west. It was by no means a land route, as is sometimes said, but ascended the Mattawan by many portages, through Plain Chaut Lake and Bouillon Lake, around the more than forty-foot drop of Talon Falls, and into Talon Lake. There two routes converged; the one ascended Antoine Creek by Lake Cahill and Perron Lake, and the other, the usual one, ran by the Pine Lake portage past Mud Creek and the Little Mattawan through Turtle Lake, where two other routes converged, each leading by easy stages to North Bay and Southeast Bay, respectively, of Lake Nipissing.[22] The journey from the Ottawa usually took two days.

The Nipissings, who inhabited the shores and islands of the lake, were the chief rivals of the aggressive Allumettes, with whom they were not at all friendly. Their trade contacts, unlike those of the Allumettes, extended north and west, the intermediate Mattawan River being the commercial watershed between the St. Lawrence and Hudson Bay. They were variously known to

[21] *Jesuit Relations*, 5:239–241; 6:18; 9:275; Champlain, *Works*, 2:284–286; Sulte, "Valley of the Ottawa," in Ontario Historical Society, *Papers and Records*, 13:32. On their trade see Vimont, in the *Jesuit Relations*, 22:231, and Le Jeune, *ibid.*, 16:10. They did not even know the north country, but retreated to the French when threatened. On the peace with the Iroquois see Vimont, *ibid.*, 33:277. Young Jean Nicolet was with this "peace deputation," which doubtless was, to judge from its size, a war party. The refusal of the Hurons and Nipissings is discussed *ibid.*, 10:75–77.

[22] Ida A. Johnson, *The Michigan Fur Trade* (Lansing, 1919), 2; detailed map in Ontario Provincial Museum, *Archaeological Report*, 1916, frontispiece and explanatory article by T. W. E. Sowter.

the Hurons and Algonquins as "Nebicerini," "Sorcerers," and "Gens de Puant."[23] In 1637 they inhabited nearly the whole coast of the lake, which was one of rare beauty and swarming with fish. Perhaps because of their abundant supply of fish, they cultivated the land very little but traded widely, making use of the waterways running in all directions from their lake. They traded a six weeks' journey to the west, they told Sagard, with a people who dwelt by a lake and a river, and even in the days of Champlain they traded a forty days' journey north.[24] Charlevoix thought them the original Algonquins or Algoumequins, and Sulte believed them to be practically the same people as the Allumettes. They probably were merely a tribe of the Algonquin peoples which had reacted inevitably to its peculiar environment.[25]

Their relations with other tribes, except the Allumettes, were very friendly, and even with the Allumettes they never waged war. They had a positive treaty with the Amikoue, an Ottawa tribe, and often wintered, as did other Algonquin tribes, near the Hurons. Their proximity to Huronia, their constant contact with the Hurons, and their docility made them desirable allies. They were a wealthy people: their presents to other people, at the Feast of the Dead in 1640, were valued by the priests at forty to fifty thousand francs. Their Mission of the Holy Ghost was not a permanent one, but was conducted from Huronia as a base. Pijart and Raymbault stayed with them there during the summer of 1640, and Pijart and Ménard during the winter of 1642–43. Illness and misfortune seemed to stalk the mission. Raymbault contracted his fatal illness there, and Gareau nearly died of fever and dysentery. Much that is known about them after 1633 prob-

[23] Usually translated freely as "people of the sea." *Puant* means a bad taste or odor. The Winnebago of Green Bay were also known by that name. For a discussion of the name see the *Jesuit Relations*, 10:322n; 38:187, 194; Sagard, *Grand Voyage*, 50–55; Benjamin Sulte, "Découverte du Mississippi en 1659," in Royal Society of Canada, *Proceedings and Transactions*, 1902 (2d series, vol. 9), sec. 1, p. 5; Champlain, *Works*, 2:260.

[24] Ragueneau, in the *Jesuit Relations*, 35:201; Sagard, *Grand Voyage*, 74, 75, 243; Champlain, *Works*, 2:40. The people of the lake and river were undoubtedly the Winnebago of Green Bay. See also Champlain, *Works*, 3:105. The journey of forty days north was probably to Hudson Bay. Their trade there is discussed in the next chapter.

[25] Charlevoix, *New France*, 2:95, 95n; Sulte, "Les Pays d'en Haut," in Royal Society of Canada, *Proceedings and Transactions*, 3d series, vol. 7, p. 78.

ably came from the pen of Nicolet, who had lived among them. Le Jeune had the written memoirs of Nicolet, from which the fathers undoubtedly acquired much of their knowledge.[26]

The Ottawa

Leaving Lake Nipissing by the French River, the traveler to Huronia found, in 1615, the easternmost settlements of an Algonquin tribe little known to the whites of that century, called by Radisson the "Cheveux Relevés" or "raised hairs" because of their roached scalplock and known in later years as Outaoua or Ottawa, the ancestors of the great Pontiac.

Their traditional history pictures a probable origin on the Atlantic seaboard and successive migrations westward—not "swarmings of the hive"; that is, not movements prompted by increase in numbers and prosperity, but migrations necessitated by economic disaster and starvation. The westering tribe split, seemingly, upon the Strait and Peninsula of Upper Michigan and the eastern end of Lake Superior. It split into the Chippewa, who moved west on both shores of Lake Superior; the Potawatomi who, as "keepers of the fire" and the vanguard, pushed south into Michigan; and the more or less residual Ottawa, who remained in northern Michigan and inhabited the islands of northern Lake Huron. These three tribes were always associated in a loose confederacy and were still in league in the days of the Prophet. The great similarity of their pictographs alone indicates a close kinship.[27]

Those whom Champlain met at the mouth of the French River were agricultural, but were already veteran traders, claiming trade relations four or five hundred leagues distant. They were in

[26] *Jesuit Relations*, 9:215–217; 10:83; 18:55; 30:109–125.

[27] Andrew J. Blackbird, *History of the Ottawa and Chippewa Indians of Michigan* (Lansing, 1887); Garrick Mallery, "General Field Studies," in American Bureau of Ethnology, *Report*, 1888–89, pp. 566–567, which contains a pictographic record of westward migration; *Jesuit Relations*, 67:153–157. Lewis Morgan, in his *Ancient Society*, 108–109, includes the Cree in the original family, as does also Louis A. Prudhomme in his "La Baie d'Hudson," in Royal Society of Canada, *Proceedings and Transactions*, 1909 (3d series, vol. 3), sec. 1, p. 5. On the late alliance see William Henry Harrison's letter to the secretary of war, September 5, 1807, in the *Annals of Congress*, 10 Congress, 1 session, 1:16. For further remarks on pictographic similarity see Mallery, *op. cit.*, 350.

alliance with the Neutral Nation against the "Fire Nation" across Lake Huron, and were friendly with the Hurons. Champlain's map can hardly be trusted for their location, for he placed the parent tribe in a spot on the Bruce Peninsula, which he knew only by hearsay. The parent tribe was undoubtedly on Manitoulin Island, and the French River Ottawa a migratory fragment.[28] They did certainly trade as far west as Green Bay, and early worsted the Winnebago in a commercial war to force them to take French trade goods. In 1633 a fleet of Ottawa canoes came to Quebec, the first of the peoples of the upper Lakes to visit the French habitations. Hence the whole of the upper Lakes country was known to the French as the Ottawa country, and "Ottawa" became, incorrectly, a very inclusive name.[29]

After the fall of the Huron nation in 1649, the great fleets that came down the river were invariably manned by the Ottawa or other upper Lakes peoples, and the river which had been known as the Grand River and the River of the Prairies came to be known as the River of the Ottawa, the name which has persisted to the present day.

These Ottawa, though a clever people, adept at intrigue and business, bore among the white men who knew them a reputation for brutal ferocity and utter cowardice.[30] Lahontan, who led them toward battle but could never lead them into it, despised them. Radisson wrote, "They are the coursedest, unablest and the unfamous and cowarliest people that I have seene among fower score nations that I have frequented." He noted that they were perfidious and brutal, and thought that "those yᵗ liveth on fish

[28] Champlain, *Works*, 3:43, 43n; 4:280–282; Sagard, *Histoire du Canada*, 1:192; Thwaites, in Lahontan, *New Voyages*, 1:153n; *Jesuit Relations*, 18:231; 51:21. Their enmity to the "Fire Nation" shows their connection with the Ottawa of Michigan, who were for long at odds with these southerners.

[29] La Potherie, "History of the Savage Peoples Who Are Allies of New France," from his *Histoire de l'Amérique Septentrionale*, in Blair, *Indian Tribes*, 1:293; *Jesuit Relations*, 1:32; 5:203 ff., 288; 55:207.

[30] [Rowland B. Orr], "The Ottawa," in Ontario Provincial Museum, *Archaeological Report*, 1914, p. 22; John G. Shea, "Indian Tribes of Wisconsin," in *Wisconsin Historical Collections*, 3:135. Mooney and Hewitt, in Hodge, *Handbook of American Indians*, claim that "Ottawa" came from *adawe*, meaning "to trade." Orr thinks that this is far-fetched, and that the word is derived from *Outaoua*. Orr's point is difficult to see, for *Outaoua* might easily have come from *adawe*. Sagard's version of the name is "Andaah-ouata," and the tribe, Orr admits, was already an important middleman.

uses more inhumanities then those that feed upon flesh." Perrot, a keen and impartial observer, had a similar opinion of them, and Denonville, governor of Canada, wrote to his minister that although the Hurons did very well, "our rascally Otaoas distinguished themselves by these barbarities and by their poltroonery, for they withdrew from the battle." It was probably the only battlefield the Ottawa observed, voluntarily, in the seventeenth century, and their services consisted of opening the warm bodies of their enemies, slain by others, and drinking the blood.[31] As late as 1757 a sort of cowardly and shrinking ferocity in dealing with prisoners seemed to be their chief characteristic in war and almost their sole participation in it.[32] But if they were not brave they were very wise, having always an eye to the main chance; and with the fall of the Hurons they acquired a power out of all proportion to their military ability, becoming the Phoenicians of the upper Lakes. Adario and Pontiac are still great names in Indian history, but it is significant that Pontiac did not include his own tribe in his conspiracy.

Closely associated with them were a few separate and subsidiary Ottawa bands, such as the Amikoue, or Beaver People, sometimes called the Nez-Perce, who, like the Ottawa, warred with the Winnebago. The Kiskakon, or Kichegoueiak, were merely the Short-tailed Bear clan of the Ottawa; with the Sinago and the Rasaoua-Koueton, or People of the Fork, they were eventually incorporated into the Ottawa proper, from whom they had originally sprung. The Mississaga remained separate, and attained some prominence in the American border wars of the eighteenth century.[33]

The Neutrals

The Neutral Nation, so called because of its neutrality in the great war between the Hurons and the Iroquois, was located in southwestern Ontario. Its boundaries were, roughly, the Niagara

[31] Lahontan, *New Voyages*, 1:159–160, 163; 2:503; Radisson, *Voyages*, 203, 222; Perrot, *Memoir*, in Blair, *Indian Tribes*, 1:154, 210–214; Denonville to Seignelay, in *New York Colonial Documents*, 9:338.

[32] See *Lettres Edifiantes* (Paris, 1842), quoted in Orr, "The Ottawa," in Ontario Provincial Museum, *Archaeological Report*, 1914, p. 24.

[33] De Quen, in the *Jesuit Relations*, 42:75; Thwaites, *ibid.*, 295; Perrot, *Memoir*, in Blair, *Indian Tribes*, 1:62–63; Radisson, *Voyages*, 90–91; Sulte, "Découverte du Mis-

River on the east, Lake Erie on the south, Lake St. Clair on the west, and a hazy Huron-Neutral frontier on the north, about seventy-five miles from Huronia.[34] They were known to the Hurons as the "Attiwandaronk," and to the French, because of their neutrality, as "Neuters." They were an Iroquoian people who had, as the rear guard of the Iroquois migration, moved in from the south, and they remained affiliated with their brethren the Erie, with whom they were sometimes confused.[35]

Their numbers are at best a guess. De la Roche Daillon, who visited them in 1626, estimated that there were twenty-eight towns like those of the Hurons, which would give a population of more than forty-two thousand. Daillon, however, saw little of the Neutral territory, and Sagard, who saw none of it, was quoting Daillon in his estimate of *cinq ou six mille hommes*. The most likely estimate, and probably a reliable one, is that of Brébeuf and Chaumonot, who passed through eighteen villages, making stays at ten. They estimated three thousand persons in the ten villages, and thought that there were about forty such villages in the nation.[36] This would give a population of about twelve thousand, and there is no reason to suppose that it was any greater. Huron proportions cannot be used in calculating Neutral population, for the economy of the two nations was very different.

The chief product of the Neutrals was tobacco, which they raised in great quantities for the trade with their neighbors. Their country appeared to the French to be a terrestrial paradise, its rivulets filled with fish and beaver, and its woods with fruits, deer,

sissippi," in Royal Society of Canada, *Proceedings and Transactions*, 2d series, vol. 9, sec. 1, p. 5; *New York Colonial Documents*, 9:171, 173, 176–183, 197–198; *Jesuit Relations*, 33:149, 151, 151n.

[34] For discussions of the eastern boundary see Orsamus H. Marshall, in the *Magazine of American History*, August, 1878, and William M. Beauchamp, "Origin of the Iroquois," in the *American Antiquarian*, 16:194, 196, 200 (March, 1894).

[35] Gendron, *Quelques particularitez*, 7; *Jesuit Relations*, 21:193. The Relation says that *attiwandaronk* means "neutral," but Beauchamp translates it as "those who speak a little differently," which, according to Indian usage in nomenclature, is the most remarkable conjecture, since the Neutrals were, like the Hurons, an Iroquoian people. See also Bushnell, *Tribal Migrations*, maps 3 and 4, and Drake, *Indian Tribes*, 1:403–404.

[36] Letter of Daillon in Chrétien le Clercq, *First Establishment of the Faith in New France*, edited by John G. Shea (2 vols., New York, 1881), 1:265–268; *Jesuit Relations*, 8–115; 21:189, 223. Sagard, *Histoire du Canada*, 2:417.

and fat bears, which were "fatter and of better flavor than the most savory pigs of France." An Iroquet chieftain took over five hundred beaver there on one hunting trip.[37] In this land of abundance the Neutrals had no immediate need of direct trade, and could not have taken advantage of the opportunity had it offered, since they were unskilled in either the manufacture or the use of canoes, which were indispensable in a trading economy.[38] Despite the frantic efforts of the Hurons to prevent it, many a Frenchman penetrated the Neutral country for furs, but the Neutrals usually sold their furs to the Hurons. Had the Hurons lost the Neutral trade it would have been a severe blow to them, as they well knew.[39]

The intertribal relations of the Neutrals were an odd combination of neutrality and oppression. They were at war with the "Fire Nation" of southern Michigan, in cooperation with the Ottawa, and friendly to the Hurons, though Sagard tells of an occasion when the Hurons seemed quite ready to fall upon them. They were successful in their Michigan war in 1644, but so far as is known it was their sole military venture, and toward the Hurons and the Iroquois they kept the strictest neutrality.[40]

Only one convincing reason has been advanced for this neutrality, and that is that in the Neutral country lay the great flint beds

[37] Champlain, *Works*, 3:99; 4:282–283; Sagard, *Histoire du Canada*, 3:803, 806' 810; *Grand Voyage*, 148; Galinée, "Narrative," in Kellogg, *Early Narratives*, 197, and in Ontario Historical Society, *Records and Papers*, 4:53–55; Daillon, letter in Le Clercq, *Establishment of the Faith*, 1:266.

[38] Galinée, "Narrative," in Kellogg, *Early Narratives*, 172; Sagard, *Histoire du Canada*, 807. The elm bark, which alone was available to them for canoes, was unsatisfactory, and their land was too far south for the birch. See Tonty, "Memoir," in *Illinois Historical Collections*, 1:134, 151; *Relation of the Discoveries and Voyages of Cavelier de la Salle*, edited by Melville B. Anderson (Chicago, 1901), 163–165; and Cadillac, "Relation," in *Wisconsin Historical Collections*, 16:304. No use of canoes meant no trade. In an economy consisting of farming and hunting alone, communication is unnecessary. See Diron Dartaiguiette, "Journal," in Newton D. Mereness, *Travels in the North American Colonies* (New York, 1916).

[39] The Hurons feared a direct communication which would threaten their own middleman status. See Chaumonot's letter to Nappi in the *Jesuit Relations*, 18:39–45; Daillon's testimony, in Le Clercq, *Establishment of the Faith*, 1:260–271; *Jesuit Relations*, 21:203; and Orr, "The Attiwandarons or Nation of the Neutrals," in Ontario Provincial Museum, *Archaeological Report*, 1913, pp. 7–20.

[40] Champlain, *Works*, 3:43; Sagard, *Histoire du Canada*, 1:192; 2:408, 416–417; *Jesuit Relations*, 21:195–197, 201; 27:21–27; Orr, "The Attiwandarons," in Ontario Provincial Museum, *Archaeological Report*, 1913, p. 17.

mentioned earlier, the source of the flint which they bartered to other nations. It is thought by many that since flint was necessary in aboriginal economy, both Huron and Iroquois preferred to have access to it on a basis of neutrality and "fair competition."[41] To this writer the wonderment over Neutral neutrality is considerably stranger than the fact of their neutrality. If Indians are regarded as at all a rational people, it is hard to see what there is about their neutrality that is abnormal. Orr's statement that the Neutral position is without parallel in aboriginal history is contradicted by Radisson and many others, and the Neutrals could have had no possible reason for warring on either tribe. Neither would either tribe have wished war with the Neutrals until the principal issue between them should be settled.[42] The Seneca, eastern neighbors of the Neutrals, were completely at peace with the Hurons until after 1639, and as they were the most numerous and most powerful of the Iroquois cantons, and as the Hurons outnumbered the Neutrals three to one, an assault upon either would have been a piece of unparalleled stupidity. By the 1640's the supposedly marvelous state of neutrality was wearing thin, and a Huron was no longer as safe in a Neutral lodge as was an Iroquois.[43] In the meantime the Neutrals traded their flint, their tobacco, and their furs to the Hurons, and lived at peace and at ease. It appears that those who have marveled at this status have not considered the obviousness of the Neutral position up to 1640.

Briefly, for either Hurons or Iroquois to have forced a belligerent status upon the Neutrals would have meant one more enemy for the nation foolish enough to do so. For the Neutrals to have gone to war would have meant participation in a terrible struggle which did not concern them. Therefore they stayed at home, and that is not unparalleled, nor even strange.

[41] Champlain, *Works*, 3:96; Gendron, *Quelques particularitez*, 8; Orr, "The Attiwandarons," in Ontario Provincial Museum, *Archaeological Report*, 1913, p. 17; Harris, in Buffalo Historical Society, *Publications*, vol. 4; *Jesuit Relations*, 8:297n.

[42] See Radisson, *Voyages*, 226–227. Here is found an Indian tribe absolutely neutral in a war between Assiniboine and Cree. The truth is that Indian nations did not war simply for the sake of fighting; they were more often neutral than not. The Seneca were neutral even in the wars of their own brethren of the League. Until after 1650 this situation was very common within the League of the Iroquois.

[43] *Jesuit Relations*, 21:193. On Seneca-Huron relations to the year 1640 see Lalemant, in the *Jesuit Relations*, 17:111.

V. THE HURON TRADING EMPIRE

THE THEORY THAT the Hurons proper, the Petuns, and the Neutrals were confederated in a sort of loose union similar to the League of the Iroquois[1] is of doubtful validity; but even if it were not, the combined numbers of these three nations and the influence that any such shadowy alliance could have exerted would still be a comparatively unimportant fact in Huron history. The great importance of the Hurons hinges upon their intertribal function, which neither required nor recognized political considerations; the function of intertribal commerce, in the course of which they gathered up and delivered to the French at Three Rivers and Montreal the entire accumulation of furs of an immense territory, reaching from the Saguenay and Lake St. John on the east to Lake Nipigon on the west, and from Lake Erie to James Bay. Before the fall of the Hurons there was a little independent trading down the Saguenay and across to Tadoussac, and the Attikamegue or Whitefish nation traded down the Gatineau and St. Maurice rivers to the French, but for the most part the Hurons had it all. The Tadoussac trade was mostly from the south side of the St. Lawrence, and the Attikamegue came to the French not oftener than one year in five. In the following pages are outlined the means and the routes by which this trade was carried on. It is perhaps unparalleled in aboriginal history, and in it appears to lie both the genesis and the continued motivation of the great wars of the Iroquois.

The motivation of the wars of the 1680's against the Illinois and the participation in King William's War is generally con-

[1] William M. Beauchamp, "Origin of the Iroquois," in the *American Antiquarian*, 16:193.

ceded to have been commercial.[2] But the characterization of the
Iroquois as the "furbearing Indians" dates from that point, by
which time the real wars of the Iroquois were over. Pushed by
necessity, they had played a desperate game for forty years, and
lost the thing they had been striving to achieve, though influencing,
it may be said parenthetically, the whole course of American
history. The fall of the Hurons, the rise to affluence and power of
the Ottawa, the depopulation of western Ontario and Michigan and
the repopulation of Wisconsin, the conquest of Pennsylvania and
Ohio—all these were the results of the efforts of the Five Nations
to get furs and assume the position held by the Hurons before
1649. The Hurons had the furs, they refused to give them up
peaceably, therefore they were destroyed. Before proceeding to
the conflict and its results it may be well to consider that empire
of trade for which the Iroquois strove.

Champlain noted the Huron's penchant for trade and their extreme avarice, and remarked upon their commerce with the Algonquins of the north and the Nipissings, with whom they exchanged corn and meal for furs. He spent the winter of 1615 in the
Huron towns and found that the season was largely given over
to preparation for the summer trade. "The women," he wrote,
"grind corn for summer traveling for their husbands, who go to
trade with other tribes according as they have decided in their said
councils."[3] He had noticed that each tribe along the Ottawa had
tried to prevent his passage to the one farther on. The Allumettes
had warned him against the Nipissings two years before; now the
Ottawa (Cheveux Relevés) tried to dissuade him from proceeding
to the Neutral Nation, who, they said, were sullen and revengeful,
and especially angry with the French. Though some of the tribe

---

[2] Even Parkman admits that an economic motive is discernible. See his *La Salle*
(1892 ed.), 203, 204.

[3] *Works*, 3:52–53, 166. It is unlikely that the Huron commerce reached far to the
south in great volume. Despite an alliance with the Susquehannah, it is doubtful
whether the furs of the Lakes region found their way to Virginia, or Virginia tobacco
to Huronia, as Brinton and Sulte have said. Brinton thinks that the Hurons had considerable commercial intercourse with the tribes south of Lake Ontario, but his
reference to the *Jesuit Relations* makes it evident that he had missed their true import.
The words are *car aussi tost que la glace est assez forte, ils portent des bleds aux Algonquins, & en rapportent force poisson*. From the context it is clear that the Algonquins
of Lake Huron are meant. There were no Algonquins on the south shore of Lake

assured him that it was not true, Champlain turned his back upon the Neutrals, and instead revisited the Nipissings.[4] The whole affair was a repetition of the situation that Cartier had found eighty years before at Stadacona, the desire of each tribe for the middleman status in relation to other tribes, but Champlain apparently did not recognize it for what it was. Not until after the English occupation and the coming of the astute Jesuits, who lived among the Hurons and studied their institutions carefully, was the Huron trading economy thoroughly understood.

The Hurons at first distrusted the priests, fearing that they were interested in their *castors et pelleteries* (a fear that was not altogether unjustified), and hesitated to take them into Huronia lest they appropriate some share of the trade.[5] With the establishment of the Jesuit missions the reason for their apprehension became clear to the priests, for it appeared that trade was the principal means of Huron livelihood. Their occupation, Du Peron wrote to Joseph, was trading with neighboring nations, the Petuns, the Neutrals, the Ottawa, and even the Chippewa and the distant Winnebago.[6] Brébeuf reported that an enemy would find no one at home in the Huron towns in the summer, "as then the Country is stripped of the men, who have gone trading, some one way, some another."[7] Bressani commented upon their skill with the birch canoe, and the "somewhat long and dangerous navigation which they conduct, on rivers and enormous lakes, with very distant nations," and added that "because of their trade and excellent devisings" they were "hardly Barbarians, save in name."[8] It is obvi-

---

Ontario. See the *Jesuit Relations*, 13:250. Sulte has Virginia Indians trading their tobacco in Canada for northern skins, but the Canadian Indians raised their own tobacco in exportable quantities, and from Smith's account it would appear that the Lakes region was unknown in Virginia except by hearsay through the Susquehannah. See Sulte, "Valley of the Grand River," in Royal Society of Canada, *Proceedings and Transactions*, 2d series, vol. 4, sec. 2, p. 119. Examination of the Huron bonepits has revealed that some of them contained articles of aboriginal Mexican manufacture, and that large conch shells from the Gulf or the southern coast were numerous in Huronia. All but one contained pipes from the Minnesota River country, a thousand miles west. There is a fine collection of these things to be seen in the Taché Museum at Laval University in Quebec.

[4] Champlain, *Works*, 2:284–286; 3:100, 101; Sulte, "Valley of the Ottawa," in Ontario Historical Society, *Papers and Records*, 13:32.

[5] Sagard, *Grand Voyage*, 154–156.   [6] *Jesuit Relations*, 10:51–53.

[7] *Ibid.*   [8] *Ibid.*, 38:247–257

ous that a population so huge, in so small a territory, could hardly be supported without trade, and it is peculiarly significant that the Huron population of the 1630's equaled the white population of the same territory of so late a year as 1906.[9] Before considering the expeditions of the Hurons to distant nations, it may be profitable to observe their trade relations with the nations nearest to them, the Petuns and the Neutrals.

The great Petun crops of corn, tobacco, and hemp were entirely monopolized by the Hurons, and so jealous were they of their control that the priests found it difficult to make any progress in the Mission of the Apostles. Garnier and Jogues were villified, abused, and endangered there because "Hurons, who went thither from time to time to effect some trades, incensed minds against them, and even did their utmost to the end that they be got rid of as soon as possible."[10] The Petuns could give no reason for their own enmity except the hostility of the Hurons to the mission, and the difficulty of the priests was the greater in that the Petuns never went to the French settlements to trade, "those who claim the trade for themselves *not permitting it*."[11] The mission was never very successful, and the Hurons kept their monopoly of the Petun corn, tobacco, and hemp to the end, no Petun ever visiting the French at Montreal or Three Rivers until after the Hurons had been dispersed.

An equally profitable monopoly of the great crops of the Neutrals was enjoyed by the Hurons, and they were equally reluctant to lose any of its profits. Father de la Roche Daillon, a Recollect priest, was the first missionary among the Neutrals, but when he spoke of trade, the Hurons slandered the French as sorcerers and lycanthropes, and Daillon had not the slightest success.[12] When Brébeuf began the Mission of the Angels there, the Hurons spread the rumor that he was in league with the Iroquois, and a deputy from the "elders" of Huronia offered the Neutrals a rich bribe to slay him.[13] Yet in spite of all this intrigue of the Hurons

---

[9] Charles C. James, "The Downfall of the Huron Nation," in Royal Society of Canada, *Proceedings and Transactions*, 1906 (2d series, vol. 12), sec. 2, p. 317.
[10] Lalemant, in the *Jesuit Relations*, 20:51, 53.   [11] *Jesuit Relations*, 21:177.
[12] Letter, in Le Clercq, *Establishment of the Faith*, 1:265–268.
[13] Lalemant, in the *Jesuit Relations*, 23:35, 37; Ragueneau, *ibid.*, 34:173. Ragueneau's testimony is in reminiscence, seven years after the event.

against the priests among the Petuns and Neutrals, the same priests were welcome and safe and enjoyed great influence in Huronia. It was only their contact with the Petuns and the Neutrals that the Hurons feared. Chief Iroquet, prompted by the Hurons, refused even to tell Daillon the route to Montreal, and so far as is known no Neutral ever visited the French settlements until after 1652. Lalemant spoke of this as a constant Huron policy with near-by tribes, but particularly with the Petuns and the Neutrals. They never attempted, however, to intrigue against the Jesuits among the Nipissings or the Ottawa, thus showing the value they placed upon the crops of the Petuns and Neutrals as trading material for their commerce in northern furs.[14] The countries of the Neutrals and Petuns were little more than great Huron farms, carefully guarded against possible competitors. The easy conditions of life in those regions, and the fact that the Neutrals, particularly, had no knowledge of canoe travel, made the monopoly relatively easy to maintain.

Going farther afield, the Hurons had also a tremendously important trade connection with the Nipissings, who next to the Hurons were the greatest travelers and traders of the region. Champlain had noticed that they were not agricultural, an observation that was confirmed by the Jesuits, and that their chief business seemed to be trade rather than hunting—the exchange of the furs which they obtained somewhere in the north for the corn and meal of the Hurons, eliminating the necessity for food crops. The only details he discovered were that at one rendezvous (the Sault Ste. Marie) they obtained buffalo robes and found excellent fishing, and that another (James Bay) was a forty days' journey distant. Sagard, listening to their tall stories a decade later, anticipated Nicolet by dreaming of China, but the later priests of Huronia, intrigued by the great quantity of furs accumulated by the Nipissings,[15] worked out a plan of their whole economy, which, they

[14] *Jesuit Relations*, 23:179, 181; *ibid.*, 207 ff., on Pijart's and Raymbault's Mission of the Holy Ghost among the Nipissings. Of course French contact with the Petuns and Neutrals would not have been for the sake of their products, which the French did not want, but it would have turned them swiftly to the fur business, spoiling the Huron set-up.

[15] Champlain, *Works*, 3:40, 41, 53, 105; 4:287–288; *Jesuit Relations*, 21:241; Sagard, *Grand Voyage*, 74–75. "One savage alone, having his supply of grain, had besides,

found, not only took advantage of each season in cyclical fashion but divided the labor of trade between different parts of the tribe.

In middle or late winter the Nipissings journeyed to the great Northwest rendezvous at Sault Ste. Marie, where the far tribes came to winter, attracted by the numberless whitefish which could be speared in the rapids. With the coming of spring the tribe divided. "A part of them remain for fishing," says the Relation, "a part go away to trade with the tribes which gather on the shore of the North or icy sea, upon which they voyage ten days." In the meantime those who had remained at the Sault returned to Lake Nipissing and made ready for the autumn expedition to Huronia, and in middle or late autumn the traders returned to Lake Nipissing from the north. "About the middle of Autumn," continues the Relation, "they begin to approach our Hurons . . . but, before reaching them, they catch as many fish as possible, which they dry. This is the ordinary money with which they buy their main stock of corn, although they come supplied with all other goods, as they are a rich people and live in comfort."[16] So highly was the Huron connection valued by the Nipissings that they gave the Hurons a special ceremony and the highest place at the annual Feast of the Dead, though a single ceremony sufficed for all their Algonquin allies.[17] The connection was truly advantageous to both, the Nipissings receiving their year's supply of corn, for food and trading, and the Hurons their supply of dried fish and northern furs in exchange for corn supplied them by their Neutral and Petun "farms."

The enterprising Ottawa traders supplied the Hurons with the western fur, and the Hurons, with their allied tribes, forcibly imposed their trade upon the Winnebago of Green Bay.[18] The Hurons themselves were well acquainted in the West, and traded with the Potawatomi of Michigan.[19] It may be seen that the canny Hurons enjoyed an enviable position, merely exchanging

300 beaver, which are the best money of the country." *Jesuit Relations*, 21:123. See also 11:197, 199.

[16] *Ibid.*, 21:239.   [17] *Ibid.*, 23:221.

[18] Sagard, *Grand Voyage*, 51; Champlain, *Works*, 4:281; *Jesuit Relations*, 15:248; La Potherie, "Savage Peoples," in Blair, *Indian Tribes*, 1:293.

[19] Kellogg, *French Régime*, 69; *Jesuit Relations*, 33:151; Wrong, *Rise and Fall of New France*, 1:220; Parkman, *Jesuits*, xxx; Champlain, *Works*, 4:238.

the products of the economically captive Petuns and Neutrals for the true riches of the region. In this position, it is not strange that they should have allowed their agricultural production and provision for the future to wane, that they should have come to depend less and less upon their own crops for a food supply and to put by less against a day of want. Such an economy would function very well so long as the complex and intimate tribal relationships upon which it depended were undisturbed, but the complexity of the mechanism made it fragile, and if it were to be shattered, the result would be catastrophic. The phenomenon of a nation's or a section's dependence upon a single "cash crop" or solely upon exchange, and the result of that dependence, is too familiar to require citation. The result has often been catastrophe, and such a fate awaited the Hurons in 1649 and 1650, when the finespun fabric of their commerce was torn apart by the storming Iroquois and, though losing few in battle, they starved by thousands.

The independent trade of the Hurons in foreign territory was probably even more extensive than that brought to them in Huronia. After the departure of the Nipissings, when the Lakes had frozen sufficiently to bear parties, they trafficked with the Ottawa living on the islands of Lake Huron, trading them corn for fish. With the coming of summer began the exodus from the Huron towns mentioned by Champlain and Du Peron. For their summer trading the Hurons had more than corn and tobacco, for in a small way they were manufacturers during the winter. They wove collars of nettles, they made sacks, and from the hemp raised for them by the Petuns they made fishnets.[20] With these things, and with heavy loads of cornmeal prepared during the winter and bales of tobacco, they set out, some for the lower Ottawa, where they had a yearly rendezvous with the Algonquins at Cap Victoire,[21] and others, turning north at the mouth

[20] *Jesuit Relations*, 13:239; 15:155; Champlain, *Works*, 3:131, 136, 166; Radisson, *Voyages*, 90–91. The Petuns also manufactured fishnets, and the Hurons traded for them.

[21] Sometimes called Cap de Massacre. It was here where Champlain first met the Iroquois, and Father la Noue froze to death. See Sagard, *Grand Voyage*, 224; *Jesuit Relations*, 29:23.

of the Mattawan or another river a few leagues above Allumette Island,[22] began the northern arc of a great circle, which would bring them home in the fall in time for the Nipissing trade.

No exact route followed by the Hurons in their journey northeast can be given, and it is probable that there were many routes. A likely one led up the Ottawa past Lake Temiscaming, turning east to Grand Lake, where furs abounded. Turning south here, the Hurons could easily reach the headwaters of the Gatineau if they were already loaded with fur, and this Gatineau highway was already an old road in 1613. If the traders wished to continue, they could cross from Grand Lake to the headwaters of the Bell River and, following it to Lake Mattagami, take a chain of lakes eastward to any of the tributaries of Lake St. John. Here were easily available the waters of the upper Trenche River, which led to the St. Maurice,[23] the country of the Attikamegue, and flowed south to Three Rivers. The Attikamegue could also be reached by the Gatineau road, and Champlain was told that it was the usual route.[24]

The Attikamegue inhabited the country north of Three Rivers, about the headwaters of the St. Maurice. They must have been fairly numerous, for on their expedition of 1648 to the French settlements they came in three bands, the last of which alone contained forty canoes. They kept a regular yearly rendezvous with the Hurons, who brought them "corn and meal from their country, Nets, and other small wares" in exchange for fur, the Attikamegue being solely hunters. Buteux penetrated to them in 1651 and reported that back of them lay still other tribes who had had no

---

[22] Sagard, *Grand Voyage*, 247–248. This river was about twenty-five or thirty miles above Allumette Island, and Sagard rejoiced that he had discovered the secret of the Huron coming and going, so bewildering at Quebec. The French were at a loss to discover the route of the Hurons, who apparently crossed through the north, appearing at Quebec from the east.

[23] Bressani, in the *Jesuit Relations*, 38:237; Champlain, *Works*, 1:119; 2:18; 4:165–166. Sulte believes that the Dumoine River was utilized to reach the St. Maurice. See his "Valley of the Grand River," in Royal Society of Canada, *Proceedings and Transactions*, 2d series, vol. 4, sec. 2, p. 128.

[24] Champlain, *Works*, 4:165–166. The routes into and across the north country were numerous, and Dreuillettes described a number of them. See the *Jesuit Relations*, 44:217–233. The St. Maurice route was used in 1653 by envoys from Lake Michigan, who had gone by the circuitous route of Lake Nipigon. See Kellogg, *French Régime*, 96–97; *Jesuit Relations*, 38:181.

intercourse whatever with the French, and from whom the Hurons had also obtained fur. The Huron expeditions to this country, more than a thousand miles from Huronia, were so regular that the priests in Huronia used them for a postal service, the letters being delivered to Three Rivers from the north. It was circuitous, but it was safe; and, being as much or more a part of the Huron economy than their corn crop, it was regular. Father Pijart even came in person by this route, arriving at Three Rivers on August 6, 1647.[25]

But the northern arc of the Huron trading circle was by no means completed in the country of the Attikamegue; east and north of them were the numerous small tribes of the Saguenay River, who were also regular customers of the Hurons.[26] De Quen had penetrated to Lake St. John in 1647, but the French had no knowledge of the tribes above except through the Hurons.[27] About a hundred miles above Lake St. John was the great yearly rendezvous of Nekouba, to which came the tribes from near the Bay. Here came the Papiragaw (Papinachois) to obtain birchbark for their canoes (it being too cold in their country for the birch tree), the Outakwamick, and the Porcupine.[28]

Descending the Saguenay, the Huron traders came to the indeterminate frontiers of the Montagnais, who traded mooseskins, of which the Hurons had none, for cereals and tobacco. The Montagnais were far from ingenuous themselves in commercial matters; they charged the Abenaki of Maine a stiff tariff for permission to trade beyond them, as the Allumettes did the upper Algonquins and Hurons who passed their island.[29] Ascending the St. Lawrence to Quebec, the Hurons were on the last lap of their

[25] Lalemant, in the *Jesuit Relations*, 30:221, 223; 31:209; 32:283, 289; Vimont, *ibid.*, 23:289; Buteau, *ibid.*, 37:65; Thwaites, *ibid.*, 9:307; *Journal des Jesuites*, *ibid.*, 30:189.

[26] Sagard, *Grand Voyage*, 243; Champlain, *Works*, 4:231; Vimont, in the *Jesuit Relations*, 30:75, quoting Ragueneau. Sagard, descending the river in the fall, met the Hurons returning to their towns.

[27] *Jesuit Relations*, 30:67.

[28] Dablon, *ibid.*, 18:115–117; 46:257–277; Sulte, "Valley of the Ottawa," in Ontario Historical Society, *Papers and Records*, 13:27, 32.

[29] Sagard, *Grand Voyage*, 218; Le Jeune, in the *Jesuit Relations*, 12:189. The Montagnais were also called Montagnards, and the name was used generically for the Algonquins inhabiting the highlands north of the lower St. Lawrence River and the lower Saguenay River.

journey. Having delivered their accumulated furs to the French and received a stock of goods, they pulled away up the river in the fall. Sagard, descending, met them on their way back to meet the Nipissings for the fall trade, replenish their stores of corn, tobacco, and "small wares" from the Neutrals and Petuns, attend to the winter business across the ice with the Algonquin islanders, and, with the summer, be ready for the road again.

The trading economy of the Hurons was naturally reflected in their government, which made provision for personal, family, or clan monopoly of small trading areas and for distribution among the entire tribe of such trade as was too large to be handled by a clan. Le Jeune, making a study of their civil government, wrote in 1636:

There is also a certain order established as regards foreign Nations. . . . several families have their own private trades, and he is considered Master of one line of trade who was the first to discover it. The children share the rights of their parents . . . as do those who bear the same name; no one goes into it without permission, which is given only in consideration of presents; he associates with him as many or as few as he wishes. If he has a good supply of merchandise, it is to his advantage to divide it with few companions, for thus he secures all that he desires, in the Country; *it is in this that most of their riches consist* [italics mine]. But if any one should . . . engage in a trade without permission from him who is Master, he may do a good business in secret and concealment; but, if he is surprised by the way, he will not be better treated than a thief,—he will only carry back his body to his house . . . there will be some complaint about it, but no further prosecution.[30]

The Relation of 1641 recounts that the Great Bear clan of the Hurons (the Arendaronons) were the first to encounter the French trade, which belonged to them exclusively according to the laws of the country. It was too big a trade for them to handle alone, however, and "they found it good to share it with the other nations [clans]" of Hurons.[31]

The importance of trade was reflected also in their laws concerning murder, which, when intratribal, was usually atoned for by "presents," the penalty for the death of a man being thirty "presents" and for that of a woman, forty. But if the murdered should be "an alien, they ask more, because, otherwise . . . trade would be ruined."[32]

In summary of the Huron trade, it does not seem too much to say that the Hurons had become almost exclusively a trading nation. Using the Petun and Neutral nations as sources of food-stuffs and trading material, they spent the entire year in the act of trade or in preparing for it, in consequence of which their own production of foodstuffs declined, with disastrous result, as they were to discover in 1649. Nor did they get from their own area even a portion of the furs they sold to the French—"the Hurons, who have not a single beaver, going elsewhere to buy the skins they bring," says the Relation of 1635.[33]

Not alone among the Hurons, but among all the tribes participating in the trade, was the basis of intertribal relations an economic one; the middleman status was desperately sought and maintained, each tribe attempting to prevent, by all the means that offered, any commercial intercourse between the peoples on either side of it. The Allumette-Nipissing rivalry, the determination of the Hurons to prevent the establishment of missions in the countries of the Neutrals and Petuns, the Allumette and Montagnais tariffs, and the Ottawa-Winnebago war have already been mentioned, and there are many other illustrations. Iroquet, a lower Algonquin chief, refused to tell either the Neutrals or Father Daillon the route from the country of the Neutrals to the St. Lawrence, and the Nipissings refused to take Frenchmen to the Winnebago, *de peur de descovrier leur bonne et meillure traicte et le pays ou ils vont amasser quantité de pelleteries.*[34] Du Chesneau wrote to Seignelay that the Far Indians rarely came to Montreal "because the other Indians intimidate them, in order to be the carriers of their Merchandise and to profit thereby." The tribes of the Sagné (Saguenay) were even very jealous of their trading preserves, refusing to take even a priest with them until he proved that he carried no trade goods, and absolutely refusing to take any

[32] Bressani, in the *Jesuit Relations*, 38:285; Ragueneau, *ibid.*, 245; Sagard, *Histoire du Canada*, 2:407, and *Grand Voyage*, 153–154.

[33] *Jesuit Relations*, 7:57.

[34] Le Clercq, *Establishment of the Faith*, 1:266; Sagard, *Histoire du Canada*, 3:803, and *Grand Voyage*, 75.

other man. The trade at Tadoussac was with the lower Saguenay tribes, who permitted no commerce through them, save that of the Hurons. The volume of the intertribal Canadian trade is interestingly portrayed by Le Jeune, who, in the Relation of 1640, quotes an Algonquin who had been to the far lakes: "We have been told this year that an Algonquin, journeying beyond these peoples, encountered nations extremely populous. 'I saw them assembled,' said he, 'as if at a fair, buying and selling, in numbers so great that they could not be counted.' "[35]

It is interesting to note here that the situation was exactly the same south of the St. Lawrence among the Iroquois, where the Mohawks, by reason of their location not far west of Albany, held a monopoly of the Dutch trade and imposed onerous conditions upon the other four Iroquois nations desiring access to the Dutch. First they attempted to prevent commercial intercourse between the French and the upper (western) cantons for economic reasons, and it will be seen later not only that they were the most implacably hostile of all the Iroquois nations but that they tried to prevent peace and deliberately fractured negotiations for peace between the French and their brethren. When the French appeared about to make a settlement among the Onondaga, they "manifested a jealousy almost verging on fury, because we wished to dwell with those people; for it was greatly to the benefit of their trade, that the Onnontoeronnons should always be compelled to pass through their country. . . . They illtreated the Onnontoeronnons, both by word and deed, for they could not brook our alliance with them . . . could not bear to see our alliance with those tribes." So tense was the situation nearly a decade before those words were written that the Onondaga withdrew from the Huron war and even considered allying themselves against the Mohawks because of the indignities and disadvantage they suffered in the trade.[36] The middleman status, in those years, very nearly disrupted the League of the Iroquois, which would not for a moment have survived a fundamental conflict of eco-

---

[35] New York Colonial Documents, 9:161; Le Jeune, in the Jesuit Relations, 18:233; 21:101; Ragueneau, ibid., 35:273–275.

[36] Ragueneau, ibid., 33:123; Le Mercier, ibid., 41:207–219; Le Jeune, ibid., 43:129, 137, 165; ibid., 44:149–151; Charlevoix, New France, 2:259–260, 264–266.

nomic interests. The situation was saved for the League by the fact that the economic clash of all the Iroquois cantons with the Hurons was far more serious than was the intratribal clash of Mohawks and Onondaga. The matter has been mentioned here only to illustrate again the universality of the economic basis in intertribal relations. It will be taken up in detail in succeeding chapters.

The Huron trading empire included all the nations of the north country above the St. Lawrence, from whom the Hurons extracted the furs which they poured, as through a funnel, into the French warehouses at Montreal and Three Rivers. Buffalo and beaver from the innumerable tributaries of the lakes and even seal from Hudson Bay[37] floated in thousands down the Ottawa in the Huron fur brigades through the summers. Upon this wealth the Iroquois, lacking furs and being unable to supply the lack from any of the nations to the east, south, or west, looked with envious eyes. Furs they must have, and here were furs enough to satisfy their wildest desires.

[37] Champlain, *Works*, 2:119.

VI. IROQUOIS AND HURONS

THE NUMBER OF the Iroquois was never very large as compared with that of any of the tribes they conquered. Morgan, impressed by their conquests and unfamiliar with historical sources, estimated them at 25,000, but later revised his own estimate, agreeing with Bancroft that they could not have numbered more than 17,000. Even this revised figure seems entirely too high, for no such figures are given in any documents, either contemporary or modern, with the sole exception of a ridiculous figure given by Lahontan, who knew nothing at all about the Iroquois. The Jesuits never estimated them at more than 2,350 warriors, and other contemporary estimates fall between 2,000 and 2,150, of which a large proportion were adoptions. Parkman, Sulte, and Lloyd all agree upon 12,000 or thereabouts as the total population, and there appears to be no reason for increasing the figure.[1]

To the political organization of the five cantons, the celebrated League of the Iroquois, historians have in large measure ascribed the Iroquois ascendancy. Channing says that "so far from being an ordinary tribe the League of the Iroquois . . . was the strongest and most formidable organization in North America," and Livingston Farrand regards it as the reason for Iroquois dominance. Morgan thought, strangely, that the real intention of the League was universal peace, and that the dispersion of the tribes resulted from their particularistic refusal to join the confederacy. Another historian of the Iroquois, Horatio Hale, writes that "the regard of Englishmen for their Magna Charta and Bill of Rights, and that

[1] Morgan, *League of the Iroquois*, 25, and "Indian Migrations," in Beach, *Indian Miscellany*, 177; Bancroft, *United States*, 3:253; Lahontan, *New Voyages*, 1:58; Wentworth Greenhalgh, "Journal," in *New York Colonial Documents*, 3:250–252; *ibid.*, 9:162, 196, 321; Parkman, *Jesuits in North America*, lxvi; Benjamin Sulte, "Les Cou-

of Americans for their Constitution, seem weak in comparison with the intense gratitude and reverence of the Five Nations for the Great Peace."[2]

These exaggerated estimates of the power and purpose of the League are probably to be explained by the fact that when it was first carefully observed by Lafitau in the eighteenth century and by Morgan in the nineteenth, it seemed to them to be an organization which must have been tremendously effective in the seventeenth century. Accepting with amazing credulity the testimony of tradition regarding the age and history of the League, and making no study of its actual operation during the period of the Iroquois wars, they probably assumed that the organization which stormed among the Lakes peoples in the fifth decade of the seventeenth century must have been the same they were observing a century and two centuries later. What they failed to take into account was the mutability of political institutions, particularly aboriginal ones.

The tendency of successive historians of the Iroquois has been to assign later and later dates to the origin of the League. Fiske, Hale, and Morgan, perhaps following Cusick or similarly fanciful traditional accounts, placed it in 1450. Beauchamp believed the true date to have been about 1600, and Sulte, about 1630.[3] There is reason in this advance of the date. The confederacy may have had its genesis in very remote times, but that does not seem to have any importance historically except possibly to the antiquarian. As a mere confederacy it had its duplicates in many places, probably all over the continent. Its importance depends upon the things it did, its effectiveness in action; and the effective-

reurs des bois au Lac Superieur, 1660," in Royal Society of Canada, *Proceedings and Transactions*, 1911 (3d series, vol. 5), sec. I, p. 250; Lloyd, in Morgan, *League of the Iroquois*, Preface. See also La Salle, *Relation*, 189; Henry R. Schoolcraft, *Notes on the Iroquois* (New York, 1846), 23.

[2] Edward M. Channing, *A History of the United States* (6 vols., New York, 1905–25), 1:104; Farrand, *Basis of American History*, 165–166; Morgan, *Ancient Society*, 153; Horatio E. Hale, ed., *Iroquois Book of Rites* (Philadelphia, 1883), 33–34. Hale, again out of his field of philology, also thinks that the Iroquois were "hospitable" to the Mahicans and asserts that the Iroquois never burned women. See pages 33 and 97.

[3] Fiske, *Discovery of America*, 1:45–46; Hale, *Iroquois Book of Rites*, 36, 180–183. Beauchamp gives an excellent survey of the theories of origin in his *New York Iroquois*, 153–167. See also Sulte, "Valley of the Ottawa," in Ontario Historical Society, *Papers and Records*, 13:33.

ness and unanimity of decision emphasized by historians certainly did not exist until much later than 1630. That the League made provision for unanimity of decision is not very important so long as it did not achieve it. It may be here remarked, in anticipation of what is to follow, that unanimity of action first begins to appear in the Neutral and Erie wars of 1660–65, that it was stimulated by the great Susquehannah war of 1660–75, and that by 1690 the League was acting as a political entity in commerce, peace, and war.[4] It could not, however, have been responsible for the great successes of the Iroquois before 1660, for in practical application it did not then exist.

The great advantages which the Iroquois had were their insistent motivation, already mentioned, and the fact that they occupied perhaps the best military position on the continent, a position that was not only strong in itself but admirable in relation to the French and their trade, lying as it did away from the French settlements and near the great water highways of the French to the interior, the St. Lawrence River and Lake Ontario. If New France was to preserve its communication with the interior, it must either exterminate the Iroquois, move them out, or placate them, all of which it failed to do. Throughout the century this was the fundamental weakness of the position of New France.[5]

The position of the Iroquois was equally strong for conquest in all directions. The Ohio and Susquehannah valleys led south and west away from their highland, offering easy access to enemy country and making possible the sudden assaults for which the Iroquois became notorious. The whole central Appalachian system, opening upon their southern borders, was in effect a great valley between the Blue Ridge and the Allegheny front, to which the lower waters of the Susquehannah gave access.[6] The Potomac

[4] According to Morgan, these wars were decided upon in unanimity. See his *Ancient Society*, 143. There is no evidence for this conclusion, and much against it. The drawing together of the League in action was not an act of conscious legislation, but an evolutionary response to a situation requiring cooperative effort. See Lloyd, in Morgan, *League of the Iroquois*, 1901.

[5] Winsor, *Narrative and Critical History*, 4:xxi; *New York Colonial Documents*, 9:165; 14:124.

[6] Bailey Willis, "The Northern Appalachians," in *The Physiography of North America* (National Geographic Society, New York, 1895), 172–173.

led east from the upper valley, and the James farther down. West
of the valley of Virginia, the "Warriors Path" led from the homeland of the Iroquois through western Pennsylvania to the Cumberland, a deep, wide, hard trail "flanked by a thousand secret
hiding places."[7] With Lake Ontario on their northern border they
were fairly safe from attack.

Before the very definitive years of 1640 and 1641 the conflict was
not, comparatively, serious; the issues were not clear to the
Iroquois, and the French-Huron alignment against them was not
necessarily permanent. The war, such as it was, went on much as
in the days of Champlain, by sudden onfall and skirmish, with
few or no predetermined plans and no noteworthy results. As late
as 1617 eight hundred Hurons gathered at Three Rivers and contemplated cutting off the French, and in 1634 French traders were
still journeying freely to the country of the Iroquois, doing business there, and offering serious competition to the Dutch. They
were accompanied by French savages, who seem also to have
come and traded independently.[8] The lines of the conflict were
not only undrawn, but hardly sketched.

In those years the Iroquois, who were led later by the Mohawks,
were not conquerors. Being at a disadvantage in intertribal warfare, they tried ceaselessly to make a permanent arrangement by
treaty, and nothing could be farther from the truth than the ancient assumption that Champlain's skirmishes produced a lasting
enmity. On June 2, 1622, Iroquois deputies arrived at Three
Rivers to arrange a peace with the French, which was confirmed,
after an interval to allow for its ratification in Iroquoia, in 1624.[9]
This peace was only with the Mohawks, for the upper nations
were not yet interested. On the side of the French, the peace

[7] Archer B. Hulbert, *Indian Thoroughfares* (*Historic Highways of America*, vol. 2,
Cleveland, 1902), 48–50; P. Camille de Rochemonteix, *Les Jésuites et la Nouvelle-France
au XVII siècle* (2 vols., Paris, 1897), 2:11.

[8] Sagard, *Histoire du Canada*, 1:54; Charlevoix, *New France*, 2:30; Jameson, *Narratives of New Netherland*, 139, 149, 150.

[9] Champlain, *Works*, 5:73–80; Ferland, *Histoire du Canada*, 1:206–207; Beauchamp,
New York Iroquois, 174; Sulte, *Histoire des Canadiens-Français*, 2:23. According to one
authority, a peace was concluded in 1621, but this is doubtless an error, since he refers
to the same peace. See the "Memoir touchant le pais des Iroquois," in *Collection de
manuscrits contenant lettres, mémoires, et autres documents historiques relatifs à la Nouvelle-
France* (4 vols., Quebec, 1883), 1:19.

seems to have included their Indian allies,[10] and here may first
be noticed what was to become their settled technique of negotiation, namely, that they would countenance no peace between their
Indian allies and the Iroquois which was not made through French
offices. Hearing, at about this time, that the Hurons were considering an independent arrangement for peace with the Iroquois,
Champlain was obliged to send Father Joseph le Caron, who had
accompanied him to Huronia in 1615, and with him Father Gabriel
Sagard, to the Huron towns with instructions to break up any
such negotiations.[11] This appears to have been the occasion for the
journey of Sagard to the Hurons which resulted in his books. The
trip is particularly significant in view of Sagard's remark that he
would have liked to arrange a peace, and could have done so had
he not received instructions to the contrary. He was told that if
such a peace were permitted, the Iroquois would divert the Huron
trade in furs to the Dutch.[12] Thus the true situation appears: the
Iroquois were eager for peace and the Hurons willing, but the
possibility was frustrated by the intriguing French, who, with the
priests as their envoys, put a stop to any negotiations that might
divert the trade.

Nor is this the only time that the French prevented peace, or
that the priests became their willing instruments in fostering intertribal war. On the orders of the governor they stirred up
hatreds and prevented accord; occasionally the governor gave a
special word of praise to the priest who was especially adept at
this business, as did Denonville to Father Enjalran.[13] As the priests
well knew, French trade and French missions could hardly be
separated, and the most effective way to serve the missions was

[10] Perrot, *Memoir*, in Blair, *Indian Tribes*, 1:148; La Potherie, "Savage Peoples,"
ibid., 2:51; Ferland, *Histoire du Canada*, 1:206; Champlain, *Works* (Laverdiere ed.),
6:80.

[11] Charlevoix, *New France*, 2:34-35. Champlain and Sagard, perhaps naturally, do
not mention this reason.

[12] *Ie m'estois autrefois voulu entremettre d'une paix entre les Hurons & les Hiroquois
pour pouvoir planter le S. Euangile par tout & faciliter les chemins à la traicte à plusieurs
nations qui n'y ont point d'accez, mais quelques Messieurs de la Société me dirent qu'il
n'estois pas expedient & pour cause d'autant que si les Hurons avoient paix avec les Hiroquois, les mesmes Hiroquois meneroient les Hurons à la traicte des Flamands & les diver-
toient de Kebec, qui est plus esloigné.* Sagard, *Histoire du Canada*, 3:811.

[13] *New York Colonial Documents*, 9:84-85, 228, 313.

to serve the trade. As Ragueneau pointed out, such a condition and such an attitude was "necessary for the maintenance of the Faith in all these regions, for the good of the French colonies, and for the support of New France."[14] The Fathers were patriots as well as Catholics; Ignatius had written that "Prudence of an exquisite quality, combined with average sanctity is more valuable than eminent sanctity and less of prudence." However that may be, it appears that the failure of the Hurons and the Iroquois to come to an agreement is to be explained in terms other than Iroquois ferocity, and that the distress of the Jesuits in later years was over a situation that had been partly of their own making, and for their own purposes. Even if we allow fully for the good intentions of the priests, we cannot wonder that the Iroquois considered them "the chief clerks of the fur trade." Viewed in the light of these circumstances, the familiar accounts of the basis for the wars of the Iroquois begin to appear more and more fanciful.

There were some difficulties between the Hurons and the Iroquois in 1627, but the cause of it, as given by Champlain, involved not the Mohawks, who alone had made the treaty with the French, but the Onondaga, who had nothing whatever to do with it. The dispute took place in the Onondaga towns, and the whole affair is said by Faillon to have been the fault of the Hurons. The entire matter is incidental, however, and, as has been seen, did not affect the Algonquin and French commerce with either the Mohawks or the Onondaga in Iroquoia.[15]

During the brief English occupation from 1629 to 1632 the Hurons had little connection with Quebec, and that little was unpleasant. No record of intertribal negotiation for those years is available, but in 1633 the Iroquois were again seeking an alliance with the Hurons, which met with only partial success. In 1635 they did manage to effect a friendly understanding with the Montagnais, but Le Jeune, seeing in it "a ruse . . . to divert,

[14] Ragueneau, in the *Jesuit Relations*, 34:205.
[15] Champlain, *Works*, 4:221–232. It is noticeable that Champlain could not yet distinguish the Iroquois cantons from one another, which is itself a tacit commentary upon the deposition of Catelina Trico, mentioned in a previous chapter. See Étienne M. Faillon, *Histoire de la colonie française en Canada* (3 vols., Paris, 1865–66), 1:215–2:6; and "Narrative of 1634–1635," in Jameson, *Narratives of New Netherland*.

through their agency, the Hurons from their commerce with our French," predicted, with an air of authority, that the understanding would not last long.[16]

Until 1637 there was a definite peace of some years' standing between the Hurons and the Seneca, the most westerly of the Iroquois cantons, the breaking of which seems to have been entirely the fault of the Hurons. Charlevoix, apparently feeling that in the ensuing wars the Iroquois were motivated by little more than a desire for conquest and vengeance upon an enemy, thought that the Iroquois played a very deep game in the 1630's, treating for peace with the body of the Huron nation in order to lull possible alarm, and in the meantime vindictively assaulting exposed portions. In 1636, he says, the Iroquois "threw off the mask and appeared in arms in the midst of the country."[17] Aside from the fact that the records furnish no justification whatever for this characterization of Iroquois policy, the phrasing of Charlevoix gives a distinctly erroneous impression, since there was no invasion of Huron territory by the Iroquois in the whole decade.

Examining the records of the priests in Huronia for those years, one finds, in the Relation of 1636, Brébeuf's account for the very year mentioned by Charlevoix. "We have had this year two alarms," wrote Brébeuf, "which resulted, thank God, in nothing more than the fear aroused by the apprehension of enemies." Charlevoix's "invasion" shrinks to a small group of Iroquois skulkers, at the very most, who vanished in the dark before the astonished eyes of a troop of Hurons a day's journey from Huronia. It is not even certain that they were Iroquois.[18] But, Charlevoix continues, citing the Relation of 1636, "the few French who had followed the missionaries to those parts presented so bold a front that the enemy judged it proper to retire." The source he quotes says nothing about any Frenchmen in Huronia.[19] Le Mercier

[16] Le Jeune, in the *Jesuit Relations*, 5:205, 211; 6:57; 8:59–61; Charlevoix, *New France*, 2:66; John G. Shea, *ibid.*, 66n.

[17] *Jesuit Relations*, 13:45; Charlevoix, *New France*, 2:93–94.

[18] *Jesuit Relations*, 10:49, 95.

[19] Charlevoix, *New France*, 2:94. Charlevoix may have confused his dates, since a circumstance similar to the one he recounts did occur in 1644. If so, the confusion is a vital one, for 1640 is an important turning point in Iroquois-Huron policy and relations.

wrote in April, 1637, that there had been alarms, "which are so much the less credible that they are so common, and all the more to be feared since our Savages give themselves so little concern thereat." He said that the rumors were commonly started by old men "in order to keep always in the villages a good part of the young men and of those capable of bearing arms, and to prevent them from going away, all at the same time, to do their trading."[20] It is quite evident that the Iroquois, far from "throwing off the mask" and invading Huronia, were remaining religiously at home, and that the Hurons, far from being forced to a desperate defense, were fearless and even contemptuous of them.

What engagements there were during this decade favored the Hurons, who, confident, as Le Mercier said, were invading Iroquoia rather than themselves being invaded. In 1637 they brought in twelve Iroquois whom they had captured while fishing on Lake Ontario. In May, 1639, Du Peron saw twelve more burned, and later in the summer a large body of Iroquois were defeated, of whom one hundred were taken prisoners and brought to the Huron towns to be burned. Another stray prisoner had been caught "on the frontiers of that country." The only effective retaliation possible to the Iroquois seemed to be ambuscades on the lower Ottawa, past which the Hurons came for trade. Throughout the decade, despite the occasional success of such an ambush, the Iroquois seemed to fear the savage allies of New France even when at home, and this fear was reflected in the overweening confidence of the Hurons, their disregard of precaution and fortification, and their whole-hearted devotion to the trade.[21]

Throughout 1640 the situation remained the same. Although Chaumonot, writing to Nappi at Rome, complained that several Hurons were killed each year on the lower Ottawa, and although Lalemant reported to Vimont that a Huron had been killed in Huronia by skulking Iroquois, the Huron raiding expeditions on Lake Ontario were not without some small success.[22] In this

[20] *Jesuit Relations*, 14:39. This is another significant reference to the Huron summer commerce treated in the preceding chapter.

[21] Du Peron to Joseph, in the *Jesuit Relations*, 15:185–187; 17:63–77, 101. On the Iroquois fear of the Hurons see Jameson, *Narratives of New Netherland*, 149–151.

[22] Chaumonot to Nappi, in the *Jesuit Relations*, 18:33; Lalemant to Vimont, August 3, 1640, *ibid.*, 19:79; 20:167–169.

year the Iroquois again made advances to the Hurons in the matter of peace, and the Hurons were ready to go on the mission, but some influence detained them and they never went.[23] It is not unreasonable to suppose that Jesuit diplomacy may again have intervened.

By 1641 the Iroquois were in straitened circumstances. The failure of their own beaver supply and the legislation of the Dutch against the sale of firearms put them in the unenviable position of having none of the material for a commerce that was now necessary to them, and no means of getting it.[24] The failure to negotiate a Huron treaty the previous year shut off all possibility of supply from that direction, and they came to the French settlements petitioning for peace.

A band of five hundred Iroquois came to Three Rivers bringing a French captive, one Marguerie, as spokesman. Marguerie testified that they needed arms, for the whole Iroquois band had but thirty-six muskets.[25] In fact, firearms seemed to be the one thing they wanted, and when negotiations opened with two exchanges of presents in which the French offered no arquebuses, "they offered a third one [belt] . . . that their uncle Onontio, the great Captain of the French, might present to them some arquebuses." They wanted, moreover, a peace on their own terms. But their flint found steel in Montmagny. He not only insisted that the peace should include his Indian allies but that it be exactly such a peace as the French wanted, and his assurance of friendship toward the Iroquois was couched in terms so vague as to give the Iroquois no privileges at all. After the Indians had voiced their reproaches because "Onontio had not given them arquebuses to eat," the council broke up, nothing having been accomplished save further alienation, which was inevitable as the issues became more and more clearly understood.[26] The next summer the

---

[23] Kiotsaeton to the Hurons, *ibid.*, 27:263, where he recalls in 1645 the attempt of 1640, without contradiction from the Hurons.

[24] See below, Appendix A, for the Dutch trade in and legislation on firearms.

[25] *Jesuit Relations*, 21:37. This testimony has apparently been overlooked by historians who picture them as loaded with firearms and seeking nations to exterminate.

[26] *Ibid.*, 43–65, a record of the whole council. *Onnontio* means "Big Mountain" in the Iroquois tongue, a fair literal translation of Montmagny, the name of the French governor. Thereafter all French governors were known to them as *Onnontio*, even

war broke out in earnest, the true beginning of the long and desolating wars of the Iroquois.

During this summer of 1642 the Iroquois raided the Iroquets on the Ottawa River, captured Father Jogues, and attacked what Lalemant called a frontier town of the Hurons, from which only a score escaped. Actually, the town was far separated from Huronia proper, and the reports of the priests in Huronia give no hint of an invasion. The incursions and onfalls along the Ottawa, though petty, were more numerous than before. On the other hand, the Hurons were almost equally successful. Lalemant described a Huron invasion of Iroquoia across Lake Ontario, and another occasion on which fifty Hurons put five hundred Iroquois to flight. Vimont wrote of another Huron invasion of the Iroquois country, and of fortifications begun by the French along the River Richelieu as a move toward relieving the annoying series of Iroquois ambuscades. Vimont was impressed with the effectiveness of the Ottawa blockade, but the letters from Huronia were cheerful, even optimistic.[27]

In the following year, 1643, the Iroquois, reinforced by their first treaty with the Dutch, redoubled their efforts. It seemed to Vimont that they had changed their tactics, haunting the Ottawa River in small bands which relieved one another with such mechanical regularity that the river was never open. That this was a change in Iroquois policy is doubtful, however, for Vimont had described an almost identical policy the year before. In that same year Megapolensis, a Dutch preacher in New Netherland, observed that his Indians "got great booty from the French on the River," and the priests observed that Iroquois ambushes had increased and that the Huron parties going into Iroquoia were annihilated.[28] "God regards you as his children," said the priest

as Dutch and English governors were known to them as *Corlaer*, derived from Arent van Curler, whom the Dutch sent among them as an envoy.

[27] *Jesuit Relations*, 22:247, 269, 277–281, 305–307; 23:25; 26:175; Vimont, letter of October 4, 1642, *ibid.*, 22:31–37. The fortifications on the River Richelieu were the result of a trip by Le Jeune to France, where he had succeeded in interesting the Duchesse d'Eguillon, who in turn interested Cardinal Richelieu.

[28] For the Dutch treaty see Arent van Curler to the Patroon, June 6, 1643, in *New York Colonial Documents*, 13:15; O'Callaghan, *History of New Netherland*, 1:463–464. See also Vimont, in the *Jesuit Relations*, 24:273, and his letter of October 4, 1642, *ibid.*, 26:31–37. Sulte and Wrong accept Vimont's version as significant, though no

to the Hurons regarding their misfortune. "He uses the Iroquois as a whip, in order to correct you." "Alas!" replied the despondent Hurons, "why did he not begin with the Iroquois?"[29] In March, 1644, Lalemant wrote that the river was completely closed as far up even as Quebec, and that summer only one Huron fleet out of four escaped capture. The Algonquins of the St. Lawrence, including the now dispossessed Iroquets, wintered among the Hurons for safety, and escaped prisoners said that ten Iroquois bands lurked on the St. Lawrence. Nevertheless a Huron chieftain rejected a new offer of peace from the enemy.[30]

The only effort ever made by the French to give military aid to Huronia was in 1644, when twenty soldiers ascended the river to the Huron towns, protesting to Vimont that they desired only to ply their trade for the good of the faith. They returned from Huronia the next year, said Vimont, "better supplied with virtue and with knowledge of Christian truths than when they embarked to leave France." Lalemant viewed their supply of Christian truths and virtue with frank pessimism, noting that they had returned with thirty to forty thousand francs' worth of beaver, and were immediately engaged in a wrangle over it.[31] One service they did perform, unwittingly. An Iroquois band which invaded Huronia, learning of the presence there of French soldiers, turned back without striking a blow.[32] There were many small incursions around Montreal that winter, and Maisonneuve, governor of Montreal, killed an Iroquois captain with a pistolet. The Hurons captured a few Iroquois, whom they carefully preserved as possible trading stock in a peace, for which by now they were earnestly hoping. But the new fortifications on the River Richelieu were abandoned, and the future did not look encourag-

difference in policy is discernible in further reading. Sulte, "Valley of the Grand River," in Royal Society of Canada, *Proceedings and Transactions*, 2d series, vol. 4, sec. 2, p. 133; Wrong, *New France*, 1:294. See also Jameson, *Narratives of New Netherland*, 175; Lalemant to Vimont, in the *Jesuit Relations*, 28:45.

[29] Vimont, *ibid.*, 25:37.

[30] *Ibid.*, 27:63. A famine also caused misery in Huronia, which was relieved by the providence of the priests. See also 22:249–267; 26:35–37, 63–67; 27:37; 28:45; and Charlevoix, *New France*, 2:176 ff.

[31] *Jesuit Relations*, 26:71; 27:89, 277.

[32] Lalemant to Vimont, *ibid.*, 26:69–71. This may be the circumstance referred to by Charlevoix as of 1636.

ing. The Hurons thought that their recent misfortunes might have been due to the eclipse of the moon three years before. Both the Hurons and the French were deeply worried and were in the proper frame of mind to receive proposals of peace, should they again be made, and the rumors of the spring of 1645 were auspicious of peace.[33]

The French, however, made the first move. In the spring seven Algonquins had routed a body of Iroquois on the river, killing eleven and bringing two captives to Quebec. The governor, ignoring the Hurons' pleas to be allowed to "caress the prisoners a little," released them with another captive Iroquois as messengers to their homeland, to carry word that the French would treat for peace with accredited representatives. They set out on May 18, and on July 5 returned with official deputies, including Kiotsaeton, the great Mohawk orator, and one Guillaume Couture, a Frenchman who had been captured with Jogues three years before and had since remained in Iroquoia. A week later Governor Montmagny arrived from Quebec, and French, Huron, Algonquin, Montagnais, Attikamegue, and Iroquois sat down to parley.[34]

The council blazed with Iroquoian rhetoric, and according to the accounts of the amazed spectators, Kiotsaeton made a great speech. He spoke for all the Iroquois, he said, but robbed his assertion of force by admitting that he had sent messengers to the upper nations only to stay their hatchets. He protested the love of the Iroquois for the French, especially their high regard for Father Jogues, a tribute that made Jogues smile, for he had barely survived the demonstrations of their affections. Especially did Kiotsaeton appeal to the Hurons. In the relentless fashion of Indian oratory, he proceeded to present twelve complimentary belts of porcelain as an introduction to the real business in hand, one to bind up wounds, another to dry tears, another to lift the canoes over rocky portages, still another to clear the brush from the way of travelers, and so on. With the thirteenth belt he ad-

[33] Ibid.; Journal des Jésuites, ibid., 22:295; 27:81.
[34] Ibid., 27:229–245, 247–253. The full account of the council is found in this volume, pp. 253–305, and also in the Lettres de la révérende Mère Marie de l'Incarnation (2 vols., 1876), 2:237–260, the "Lettre a son fils," September 14, 1645. Couture's capture is described in the Jesuit Relations, 24:281–285.

dressed himself directly to the Hurons. After reminding them of the failure of 1640, he said: "you had a pouch filled with porcelain beads and other presents, all ready to come and seek for peace. What made you change your minds? That pouch will upset, the presents will fall out and break, they will be dispersed; and you will lose courage."[35]

The fourteenth belt was "to urge the Hurons to make haste to speak, — not to be bashful, like women; and, after taking the resolution to go to the Iroquois country, *to pass by. that of the Alguonquins and the French.*" Another belt went to the Algonquins, with the closing words, "This present invites you to hunt, *we shall benefit by your skill.*" In such plain words were the principal terms of the treaty set forth. They were, indeed, the only terms of the treaty other than the vague promises of amicability which are included in all treaties and which mean so little. The French and their allies were to reply the next day.

On the surface the council had seemed serene, but the keen eyes of the Iroquois deputies had marked a certain diffidence on the part of the Algonquins. They had been hesitant to speak when addressed, and in extenuation had presented the plea that their chief, who alone might speak for them, was not present. They gave no excuse for his absence, however, and their lack of enthusiasm seemed more than suspicious to the Iroquois. That night, at a private conference with the governor, the Iroquois demanded that he make a peace ostensibly including the Algonquins but containing secret articles, known only to himself and the Iroquois, abandoning them. It was an idea worthy of a Charles II or a Metternich. When the governor refused, the Iroquois chieftain, evincing displeasure, made no further suggestion, and the conference ended.

The Jesuits Vimont and Le Jeune, however, perhaps recalling Ignatius' dictum on "average sanctity," thought that "the difficulty might be smoothed over," and at a second secret conference the governor and the Jesuits forsook the Algonquins. With thorough-

---

[35] The appeal to the Hurons is the story of 1634 as found in Jameson, *Narratives of New Netherland*, all over again. The author of the "Narrative of 1634–35" found the Iroquois always very anxious for trade with the French savages. See pages 139, 149, 150.

going duplicity they abandoned, not all the Algonquins, but only the non-Christians, dismissing these lost souls as masters of their own actions and not, like the others, united with the French. On the question of how an Iroquois warrior was to tell a Christian from a non-Christian Algonquin they were silent. The affair was kept secret between Montmagny, Vimont, and Le Jeune, and was written into the "Journal des Jésuites," when the fact finally became public, in Latin.[36]

The council was now perfectly serene, but all it could accomplish was preliminary work and terms, for the Iroquois insisted upon considering the terms in their own country, and promised to return with accredited representatives in September.

The Montagnais arrived for the September rendezvous in August, the unsuspecting Algonquins in early September, and on the tenth sixty Huron canoes loaded with fur and bearing Vimont's twenty soldiers laden with virtue and Christian truths. The French feared that the Iroquois might not come, but on the fifteenth and seventeenth the nine Iroquois ambassadors arrived. On the twentieth the council began. The Hurons gave twenty presents, the Algonquins, characteristically, gave five, and on the twenty-third the Iroquois departed, taking with them two Frenchmen, two Hurons, and two Algonquins. "The lynx, the panther, and the wolf," says Parkman, "had made a covenant of love."[37]

Father Lalemant "watched them at these assemblies with eyes

[36] The account is in the *Jesuit Relations*, 28:149-151. It first came to the attention of the other priests the following spring and was then put into the Journal. The Algonquins, of course, never knew of it.

[37] *Jesuits in North America*, 295. Parkman's comment on this peace is factually inadequate. Although the *Journal des Jésuites* was available to him, he mentions nothing of the secret articles involving the Algonquins, and even states directly (page 291) that it was understood "that the Indian allies of the French should be left unmolested." He comments (pages 203-204) on the cold treatment accorded the Algonquins on embassy in Iroquoia that autumn without understanding it. He says, further, that the belts of the Iroquois lied in claiming to represent the five cantons, but Kiotsaeton had already admitted the inaccuracy of this concept, and in February, 1646, before the peace was broken, he again explained the matter fully, saying that of course the peace was only binding upon the Mohawks, but that he had hoped and anticipated that it would become universal and that he would work toward that end. See the *Jesuit Relations*, 28:301. In the Mohawk confirmation councils no effort was made to deceive the French, who were told plainly to beware of the upper nations, the Mohawks promising to try to bring their brethren to time. *Ibid.*, 293. Kiotsaeton's claim was rhetorical and formulary, and was so understood by the French.

full of joy," being ignorant of the secret articles advocated by his colleagues. "If these Barbarians . . . do not disturb this peace," wrote Vimont, one of the advocates, " . . . it will be possible to go and suffer for Jesus Christ in a great many nations."

The round of negotiation was not yet finished. It was necessary for deputies from New France and her allies to go into the country of the Iroquois and confirm the peace there, and for another Iroquois deputation to return thence and confirm the confirmation of the confirmation. Accordingly an official embassy left Three Rivers, and three weeks later met in full council at the Mohawk towns, where the peace was confirmed in a most convincing manner. The Oneida, satellites of the Mohawks, were rebuked for insisting upon more presents, and a deputation from the Sokoqui of New England, asking for war against the French Indians, was so soundly rebuked that a French witness who understood the language remarked, "If there is deceit in this act, it is more than very subtle."[38] The embassy started upon its return journey before the freeze, only to find their canoes destroyed or stolen. They turned back and came later, in February, over the snow to Three Rivers, where Couture remained while the Iroquois escort hunted. The governor met them in May, and after warning him against the upper Iroquois, who were not yet parties to the peace, they departed.[39]

All seemed well, but Lalemant, recently made Father Superior, was unable to quell the apprehensions of the sagacious Le Borgne, chief of the Allumettes (who were Algonquins). Lalemant wondered at his distrust and tried honestly to reassure him, for he still knew nothing of the disgraceful "secret articles" of the peace. But Le Borgne's perceptions were acute, and there soon came evidence of their accuracy.

Early in January some Mohawks had told one Tandihetsi, a Huron chief, what they called "the secret of their country"—that the Algonquins had not been included in the peace and that the Iroquois were only awaiting an opportunity to exterminate them. Three hundred men, they boasted, would be up in February for

---

[38] *Jesuit Relations*, 23:287.
[39] The entire account is in the *Jesuit Relations*, 28:275-301.

that purpose. Now Tandihetsi was more exercised over the matter than another Huron chief might have been, for, unknown to the Mohawks, he had married an Algonquin woman and had many Algonquin relatives. So he posted off to Quebec and the supposedly sympathetic governor. A Mohawk, following him, assured the Fathers that all Tandihetsi had said was "false—at least in the main," but Lalemant now had knowledge of the duplicity of his fellow priests. "What was surprising therein," he remarked as he wrote the governor's confidential explanation into the Journal in Latin, "was that our Fathers sent us no word of all that."[40] Although a Father Superior, he was still learning that there was more in Jesuit policy than met even the Jesuit eye.

Meanwhile the arrogant Mohawks strutted before the unhappy Algonquins at Three Rivers and Montreal. A Mohawk would stand before a group of Algonquins and sing, "I wished to kill some Algonquins, but Onontio has arrested my anger, . . . he has saved the lives of many men." Nevertheless the peace held, and not even the Algonquins were actually attacked. True, Le Borgne was attacked and defeated above the Long Sault by a party of Indians, but they kept only a woman prisoner and excused themselves by saying that they had thought his to be a Huron party. Moreover, the identity of the aggressors was not certain; although it was rumored that there had been one or two Mohawks among them, there was no proof. Everything considered, the peace seemed to have been made in earnest by the Mohawks, and in May, 1646, Father Jogues was sent to them to establish a mission. He was also commissioned to persuade the Mohawks to discipline the upper Iroquois by denying them passage eastward to the Dutch trading center at Fort Orange until they should participate in the peace.[41] If this could be accomplished, the treaty would seem secure.

Thus, to summarize the Iroquois-Huron relationship up to this point in 1646, it appears that the contention between them was from the first over the matter of trade, and that the Iroquois tried repeatedly to establish accord through the negotiation of treaties with the French, the Hurons, and the Algonquins. In this they

---

[40] *Journal des Jésuites, ibid.,* 27:147–155. [41] *Jesuit Relations,* 29:151, 183.

were unsuccessful because of the machinations of the French and the indifference of the French Indians, some of whom were uncooperative as late as 1645. It further appears that until after 1641 the Iroquois were far from aggressive; the Hurons and Algonquins invaded their country at pleasure, and felt carelessly secure in their own lands. Between 1640 and 1645 the Iroquois, finding it necessary to their own maintenance to acquire furs, and discovering that the Huron fur brigades were vulnerable, became increasingly aggressive, and their ambuscades on the river became so numerous and so successful that the French hoped for relief through a peace. In the peace arranged in 1645 there appears to have been but one provision of importance, the one enunciated by Kiotsaeton to the Hurons and Algonquins, that both were to come to the Iroquois to trade. Otherwise the whole solemn negotiation is meaningless. Until the autumn of 1646 the peace was kept inviolate. The next chapter deals with the circumstances of its fracture. Should the renewal of the war also prove to have been concerned with the trade, it would seem to add post facto evidence of the nature of the treaty, if, indeed, any is needed.[42]

✳ ✳ ✳

Father Jogues arrived at the Mohawk towns on June 5, 1646, and was welcomed "with every mark of sincere friendship and endless courtesy."[43] Feasts and councils followed one another, and Jogues did not hesitate to broach the principal object of his mission. The Mohawks, he said, if they were sincere in their protestations of friendship, ought to further peace between the French and the upper nations, who used Mohawk territory as a war road to the St. Lawrence and Ottawa as well as to Fort Orange. Let the Mohawks forbid them the use of Mohawk land

[42] Historians have overlooked the significance of this treaty, while noticing, sometimes at considerable length, the fact of its existence. Parkman notices neither the secret articles not the trade stipulations, nor does Charlevoix. Ferland gives perfunctory notice to the secret articles, but none to the trade stipulations, and Rochemonteix notices neither. See Parkman, *Jesuits in North America*, 194–205; Charlevoix, *New France*, 2:190–195; Ferland, *Histoire du Canada*, 1:336–338; and Rochemonteix, *Jésuites et la Nouvelle-France*, 2:44–46. Considering the prominence they all give to the renewal of the war and the martyrdom of Jogues, their lack of curiosity and uncritical acceptance of traditional reasons for those phenomena prevent an understanding of the true situation.

[43] In the *Jesuit Relations*, 29:51–53, is a complete account of Jogues' journey.

as a highway, and all would be well. The council give him grave attention, and promised to do all in their power to mend the matter. Jogues, wishing to go to the French settlements before winter set in, left them on June 16 and arrived safely at Fort Richelieu on the twenty-seventh. So far, the peace seemed not only sincere but secure, and if its terms in the matter of trade were kept by the Hurons and Algonquins, it might endure indefinitely.

The French colonists were happy over another development. The year before the trade monopoly had been taken from the Company and trading privileges given to the habitans, who had enjoyed a good profit from the sixty or more boatloads of fur in 1645. The arrival of the fateful Huron fleet of 1646 was, then, an occasion for celebration, for more than eighty canoes, loaded with fur, beached at Montreal on September 12 and pulled away a fortnight later with a dozen bales of skins still unsold for want of merchandise. The greatest fur fleet in the history of New France left with the habitans skins to the value of 320,000 livres.[44] More than that, they had come the whole way without once being challenged by the Iroquois. The Company monopoly was broken, the Mohawks were at peace with New France, the river was open, and the fur was coming through; the habitans could hardly contain their joy. What would have been their feeling could they have looked three weeks ahead! For within that time the peace was to be blasted and another war begun, this time a war of disaster. On September 24 Jogues left Montreal for the country of the Mohawks. Less than a month later he was dead.

Before Jogues met the Mohawks they had sent deputies to rally the Seneca and Onondaga for war,[45] and the first party he met was a party of four hundred on their way north, accoutered and painted for battle. Seizing him, they returned to the villages with their prisoner, who had been so highly honored in June. Of the three Mohawk clans, two, the Wolf and the Turtle, did not favor putting him to death, but the Bear clan carried the decision and killed him with an axe as he was entering a lodge for a meal. For more than a year the French heard nothing of him, but finally

[44] Jogues to Castillion, September 12, 1646, in the *Jesuit Relations*, 28:141; *Journal des Jésuites*, *ibid.*, 28:231–235.
[45] Lalemant, *ibid.*, 30:227.

a letter for Montmagny arrived at Quebec from Kieft, governor of New Netherland, with an enclosure for the Sieur Bourdon, and the truth and the circumstances became known. Later in the year an Iroquois prisoner repeatedly testified, under the closest questioning, that the death of Jogues had not been planned, that it had been opposed by the Wolf and Turtle clans, and that it had been no part of Mohawk policy. The circumstances surrounding his impromptu execution seemed to confirm this statement.[46]

The letters from New Netherland offered only one explanation for the breaking of the peace: Jogues had left among the Iroquois a little black box containing ritual material, and they thought that a disease which had broken out later, and the worms that had infested their corn, were the result of magic worked by him with that little black box. Therefore, according to this explanation, the Mohawk tribe painted and conspired for war, not only upon Jogues because of his little black box, but upon Huron, Algonquin, and Frenchman. This explanation, considered in the light of the known facts, appears not only unlikely but practically impossible.

The pertinent facts in the order of their occurrence seem to be these. First, a protracted struggle, fundamentally commercial, ends in a treaty, the only definite terms of which are commercial. The treaty, confirmed many times, is honored and is popular in the Mohawk country, and in the next year a French priest is overwhelmingly popular there, being shown every mark of honor and respect. The conduct of the Mohawks convinces veteran observers that they are perfectly honest in the matter, and content with the treaty terms for which they have so long striven. Presently, however, the treaty is broken, and out of the greatest fur fleet ever to descend the Ottawa the Iroquois get not so much as one skin. The priest, returning a month after the fleet has beached in Montreal, finds a state of war and is killed. The reason given is that disease and corn-worms had made the Mohawks antagonistic. That reason is much less than convincing. In view of the fact that the explanation for the breaking of the peace comes from the chief competitors of the French, and that they in turn

<hr/>

[46] Kieft to Montmagny, *ibid.*, 31:117–119; also 32:25.

had it second-hand, the details of Jogues' death demand consideration.

Father Jogues left Montreal for the country of the Mohawks on September 24, 1646. On October 15, when two days' march from Osseronon, the Mohawk village, he was met by a Mohawk war party on its way to attack Fort Richelieu and was escorted back with blows and incidental torture. Of the three Mohawk clans, only one, the Bear clan, wanted to kill him; the Turtle and Wolf clans went so far as to offer their lives to save him, but to no avail. Jogues was stealthily killed, and the Wolf and Turtle clans were presented with *un fait accompli*.[47] The features of his experience particularly worthy of notice here are these: that two large war parties were already under way when he arrived, that before he arrived the Mohawks had sent deputies to the other tribes to raise them in war, and that among the tribe as a whole his assassination was strongly disapproved.

From this latter fact alone it seems evident that the Pandora's box which Jogues had left among them and the misfortune they were said to have attributed to it could hardly have been the reason for the war, for as the supposed author of so much misfortune his death would have been popular. Considering the other facts, the war parties and the deputies sent to the other tribes, it appears certain that there was a more general and more important cause of war. Other tribes would hardly have been interested, or provoked to a general war, by worms in the corn of the Mohawks; this reason was advanced only by the Dutch, who, never having sat in an Iroquois council, would not have been in a position to know anything of their policy, and would have been unlikely to disclose it if they had been.

In the terms and circumstances of the treaty of 1645 and the great Huron trading fleet of the next year lie what is almost cer-

---

[47] See J. Scott Martin, S. J., *Isaac Jogues, Missioner and Martyr* (New York, 1927); Felix Martin, S. J., *The Life of Father Isaac Jogues, Missionary Priest of the Society of Jesus*, 3d edition, translated from the French by John G. Shea (New York, 1885). Scott Martin is mistaken as to the day of Jogues' departure, naming September 27. He actually left on September 24. Felix Martin is mistaken as to the day of his arrival, naming October 19, whereas he was killed on the eighteenth. See the *Jesuit Relations*, 21:III, 117. See also Rochemonteix, *Jésuites et la Nouvelle-France*, 2:54; M. Dionne, "Figures oubliees de votre histoire," in the *Revue Canadienne*, June, 1888.

tainly the real cause of the war. The Iroquois had made a commercial treaty and had held to its terms, since its fulfillment was of vital importance to them. It had been broken by the French and the Hurons at the first opportunity, whereupon the Mohawks painted for war, a war in which the murder of Jogues must have been a minor incident, unsupported by public opinion. It is unlikely that absolute proof of the cause of the war can ever be presented, but every circumstance points away from the box of Father Jogues and toward the broken treaty made by Kiotsaeton in 1645.

VII. THE GREAT DISPERSION

To THE HURON NATION the peace of 1645 was no less important than to the settlements of lower Canada, and Ragueneau, writing in May of 1646, was optimistic. The general condition of Huronia was good, he said, the people were happy, and everything was improving. The trade of 1645 had been good, there was a good crop of corn, the plague had ceased, and the future looked bright.[1] The great trading fleet of 1646 brought an unprecedented amount of wealth up the Ottawa in the autumn, and the Hurons had a happy winter, disturbed only toward the end by the rumors of the new Iroquois war. No feature of that war perturbed them greatly except the possibility of a blockade of the Ottawa, and if that should happen the summer traders could simply stay at home, the trade goods of 1646 being ample for two years. Should there be rumors of an invasion the warriors could stay and defend the region, but the possibility of invasion seemed remote, for no Iroquois force worth notice had yet penetrated Huronia and there was no reason to suppose that one would. Thus the Hurons were far from supine and terrified when they heard of the resumption of the war.[2] Rather they were confident in the light of the past, and without appreciation of the new and insistent motive that drove their enemies on. An army of a thousand men with a single purpose invading from distant Iroquoia was entirely beyond their calculations, and certainly outside their experience.

News of the war arrived early in 1647 with two Susquehannah

[1] Huron Relation, May 1, 1646, in the *Jesuit Relations*, 29:247. Ragueneau was writing from Huronia.

[2] Charlevoix pictures the Hurons as being at first supine and then terrified and incapable of offering resistance. *New France*, 2:138.

deputies, who, "deputed by their captains," offered help to their allies if the Hurons felt in need of it. The Hurons were not indifferent to this opportunity, and in April an embassy left Huronia, which arrived at Andastoé, the capital of the Susquehannah, in June. There the Huron chief, Ondaaiondiont, sought aid, drawing a harrowing and quite false picture of Huron misery, and the Susquehannah dispatched embassies to the Iroquois, begging them to consent again to a peace "which would not hinder the trade of all these countries with one another."[3] Had the embassy but known it, trade was indeed a sorry argument to present to the Iroquois in pleading for peace. Trade had been their reason for making war in the first place; trade had been their reason for making peace, and any peace which allowed the trade to continue as it had in the past they would certainly oppose. So the Susquehannah embassies went to the Iroquois pleading for a continuance of a trade in which the Iroquois were to have no part.

The embassy was wisely directed, however, and approached only the Onondaga, where the greatest chance for success appeared to lie. As Le Jeune had early noticed, it was the Huron policy to encircle the Iroquois by alliances,[4] which policy they supplemented in 1647 by an attempt to divide the league. The Onondaga had less at stake in the trade than did the Mohawks and were further from the Hurons than the Seneca, and the Susquehannah embassy hoped, at the worst, to reduce their enemies to two of the three great cantons.[5] Ondaaiondiont waited in Andastoé until mid-August, and then, the embassy not yet having returned from Onondaga, he set out for home with presents of fourteen thousand beads, being anxious to bring news of success to Huronia before the winter. The Seneca, knowing of his mission, lay in wait for him, but he detoured, perhaps around the western end of Lake Erie, and eluded them, arriving in Huronia after seven weeks of travel. One Huron was left in Andastoé to bring news of the success of the embassy to Onondaga.[6]

[3] Ragueneau, in the *Jesuit Relations*, 33:129-133.   [4] Le Jeune, *ibid.*, 5:209.

[5] Ragueneau, *ibid.*, 32:173. The Onondaga, moreover, were beginning to fear and distrust the Mohawks, who had lately grown insolent and arrogant, and even Parkman, who insists upon the efficiency of the League, admits that here it was in danger of falling apart. *Ibid.*, 123; Parkman, *Jesuits in North America*, 344.

[6] *Jesuit Relations*, 33:133, 185.

Ondaaiondiont found his people confident and successful, on their own account, in a projected division of the Iroquois, direct negotiations with the Onondaga being already far advanced. In the half year which had elapsed since his departure the Huron elders had been busy with the reception and despatching of embassies, and seemed in a fair way to succeed without the intervention of the Susquehannah. They had not made the trip to Montreal, but had defeated a party of invading Onondaga, killing many and capturing an important Onondaga chief named Annenraes, whom they had spared and sent back on an independent mission of peace to his tribe. After crossing Lake Ontario, Annenraes had met a second Onondaga party of three hundred, who were planning to effect a junction with eight hundred Seneca and Cayuga in a great invasion of Huronia. He had persuaded them to return home, where they held a council and sent a return embassy, which arrived in Huronia on July 9. The Hurons were not united in a desire for peace, the frontier towns ardently wishing it and the powerful Bear clan hanging back, but after many councils a second embassy of five Hurons departed for Onondaga "in order to see more clearly into the matter." On their arrival they found the Susquehannah deputies already there, and after a solid month of councils the Onondaga despatched a small party to Huronia under chief Scandaouati, which arrived with fifteen Huron prisoners and the promise of one hundred more as soon as negotiations should be completed. Scandaouati remained in the Huron towns as a hostage.[7]

All this had come to pass while Ondaaiondiont had been away, and when Scandaouati and his party arrived in Huronia toward the close of October, the hoped-for division of the Iroquois seemed an accomplished fact. No one could have foreseen that that division would not suffice to save Huronia, and that the Huron nation had little more than a year to live. The French were optimistic, and Mère Marie de l'Incarnation reflected that if the Lord afflicted the church in one way he consoled it in another, and even had great hopes of converting the Susquehannah through the newly strengthened alliance. It was even thought that the Sus-

[7] *Ibid.*, 117–125.

quehannah would fall upon the Iroquois from the rear if need be.[8] No one anticipated the lightning speed and power of the single Iroquois stroke of 1649.

Meanwhile in Iroquoia, especially in the country of the Seneca and that of the Mohawks, there was less confidence than apprehension and a swiftly maturing resolution. There was no possibility of alliances, for the interests of all the other tribes lay elsewhere; the Iroquois position was peculiar to them alone. They did have an understanding with the Dutch, but the French and Hurons had sold them out after the treaty of 1645; the Susquehannah had no need of them, and neither had the Neutrals, upon whose growing trade with the Hurons and French the Iroquois had begun to look with deep distrust. Even the Onondaga were no longer compliant, and had failed to keep a rendezvous with the Seneca. The disgruntled Seneca had raided a Neutral town in a misdirected vengeance that was a mistake in policy, even though the Neutrals could never be their friends.[9] The news of the Susquehannah-Huron-Onondaga negotiations roused them almost to desperation, for it was clear that if this alliance were to be concluded, the Iroquois would be not only encircled but divided, and each of the great hostile tribes, the Seneca and the Mohawks, would be entirely surrounded with enemies. The Mohawks had with them, perhaps, the Oneida, but the Cayuga, heretofore the satellites of the Seneca, were themselves treating for peace with the Hurons. The Seneca and the Mohawks regarded themselves as lost men if they did not act swiftly and in some way smash the chain drawing about them.[10]

The Mohawks moved in January and fell upon a Huron embassy to Onondaga, cutting it to pieces and killing all but three. The chief Scandaouati, hostage in the Huron towns, killed himself on hearing the news. The Seneca concentrated a large force in the country of the Neutrals to break communications between

---

[8] Mère Marie de l'Incarnation, *Lettres*, 1:350; *Jesuit Relations*, 30:253.

[9] *Ibid.*, 33:81–83, 123.

[10] The Oneida had a special grudge against the Hurons, who had once nearly exterminated them. Vimont, in the *Jesuit Relations*, 27:297; Lalemant, *ibid.*, 28:281–283. See also Ragueneau, *ibid.*, 33:123, 125, and Rochemonteix, *Jésuites et la Nouvelle-France*, 2:69.

the allies by that route, and to assume a strategic position in relation to the Huron frontier. Communications between Hurons and Susquehannah and between Hurons and Onondaga were successfully broken off; in April, 1648, Ragueneau was still waiting for official confirmation from the Onondaga.[11] The embassy had dropped into a void.

But the enforced Mohawk-Seneca combination made little aggregate progress in 1648. A large Seneca war party fell upon St. Joseph II, a Huron frontier town, while most of the warriors were away, and the Huron loss was generously estimated at seven hundred, though Ragueneau thought that many more escaped than were taken.[12] This Seneca victory was partly offset by the heavy defeat suffered by a large Mohawk party that thought to waylay a Huron trading fleet within sight of Montreal. This defeat was so decisive that Lalemant, writing to the Father Provincial in October, thought that the Iroquois had lost more than they had gained.[13]

To the Mohawks and Seneca the situation became increasingly plain. They could continue independent and separate blockade and attack; they could capture Huron frontier towns and take women and children, as they had at St. Joseph II, but that policy would do neither of the two things that it was necessary to do. It would not break the encircling alliance nor would it divert the trade to them. It became evident that so long as the Hurons held the Georgian Bay–Lake Simcoe region they would control the northern fur trade. Repeated attempts to get the trade by treaty had failed, but there remained one way of obtaining it. If the Hurons were gone, nothing would stand in the path of Iroquois prosperity and ambition. The Hurons must go. That was the sure way, and the only way.

The trade of 1648 had been large at Montreal. Two hundred and fifty Hurons had come in fifty or sixty canoes, and the trade at Tadoussac had increased to two hundred and fifty thousand livres. The condition of Huronia had never been so good. Father

---

[11] Rochemonteix, *loc. cit.*; Ragueneau, *op. cit.*, 133.
[12] The Huron name for the town was Teanausteaye. *Jesuit Relations*, 34:87, 99.
[13] *Ibid.*, 127.

Ragueneau wrote to Caraffa in Rome that the faith was making such strides that the outlook for the church was better than ever before. The priests, he added, had provisions enough to last for three years, and were well supplied with pork, cattle, and dairy products. The white population had increased to sixty-four, including eight soldiers.[14]

Ragueneau's letter was written on March 1, 1649. Two weeks later, at dawn of March 16, a party of a thousand Iroquois of the Mohawk and Seneca nations, who had left their country the previous autumn and hunted throughout the winter in Ontario, fell upon the Huron town of St. Ignace while its inhabitants slept. Enjoying a false sense of security, the settlement was practically without guards, and only three Hurons escaped through the snow to St. Louis, three miles northwest, in the heart of Huronia. Moving with certainty and great speed, the Iroquois left a garrison in St. Ignace preparing refreshments and securing the rear, and before sunrise were assaulting St. Louis, which, despite a desperate defense, was stormed and fired by nine o'clock. Fathers Brébeuf and Gabriel Lalemant were taken and led back to St. Ignace to be tortured, while the Iroquois rested and reconnoitered Ste. Marie, the main Huron stronghold. In a night council they decided to attack it, but a Huron counter-attack the next day shifted the scene of battle to St. Louis, where a small Huron contingent of about a hundred and fifty warriors kept the whole Iroquois army engaged until far into the night, retiring only when all but a mere score had been killed. The eighteenth of March "passed in profound silence." The next day panic seized the Iroquois, and they retreated precipitately, carrying heavy spoil and such captives as could travel. The rest were tied in the cabins, which were fired. Seven hundred Petuns from St. Michel pursued them, but lack of provisions and "dread of combat without advantage" made them careful not to overtake the victors, who made good their escape.[15]

There seems to have been little reason, from a purely military

[14] Lalemant, in the *Journal des Jésuites*, *ibid.*, 32:97–99, 103, 185; Ragueneau to Caraffa, General of the Society of Jesus, March 1, 1649, *ibid.*, 33:253–255.

[15] Ragueneau, *ibid.*, 34:123–137; Kellogg, *French Régime*, 92; Jones, *8endake Ehen*, 380–402.

point of view, for the abject terror that now seized the entire
Huron nation. St. Ignace, having been abandoned by most of its
people before the attack, had had only about 400 souls within it,
of whom no more than 80 had been warriors; St. Louis had been
evacuated just before the assault by all except 80 men; and according to Ragueneau's figures no more than 150 or 175 of the
Huron warriors could have been killed in the second battle of St.
Louis. These figures total only a little more than 300 warriors,
whereas the Iroquois losses were in the neighborhood of 200.[16]
The Hurons, however, were capable of neither reason nor strategy. The unexpected, the virtually impossible, had occurred, and
the security of which they had been so confident had vanished;
the Iroquois had invaded their land successfully. Furthermore,
they had done so at a time of year when war had never before been
made; they had marched through deep snow, in numbers never
before seen, and with a singleness of purpose and minute organization that was daunting in itself. The Iroquois were devil men,
who needed nothing, and were hard to kill. The firm, familiar
world of Huronia seemed suddenly melting down and running
from under their feet, and with no thought beyond the immediate
future they incontinently fled in all directions.

Ragueneau, seeing no possibility of stopping the wild flight,
tried to give it intelligent direction by suggesting Manitoulin
Island, where a mission had been begun among the Ottawa the
previous autumn. He knew that there were plenty of fish on the
island, and that it was a fine trade location, but he knew also that
in the present condition of the tribe it would take a year or two to
make the passage, which would require careful preparation. The
panic-stricken Hurons, however, would hear of no delay, but
were insistent upon immediate flight, which meant flight to
Chaumonot's mission on near-by Christian Island. Ragueneau
yielded with many misgivings, for the island was barren and inhospitable, and there were few fish. By May 1 fifteen Huron villages had been abandoned and burned by the Hurons themselves,

[16] Ragueneau, in the *Jesuit Relations*, 34:123–137. This figure takes into account
10 killed at the taking of St. Ignace, 30 at St. Louis, 30 captured, and 100 killed at the
second battle of St. Louis. The Iroquois were apparently impressed by their own
losses, which left them without defenses and without resources in midwinter.

and between six and eight thousand terrified fugitives crowded upon the non-productive Christian Island.[17]

Ragueneau sent emissaries to the Algonquins and collected five or six hundred bushels of corn and a few fish, but the little corn planted on the island failed, and the Hurons, accustomed as they were to obtaining both corn and fish through trade, had no appreciable reserves. Even before winter set in they were starving. Many of their fellow tribesmen had gone beyond St. Joseph, but toward winter they again dispersed in various directions, a few returning to St. Joseph to swell the ranks of the starving.[18]

By spring the island was a place of horror, containing a few hundred Hurons who were little more than skeletons and who had for the most part survived only by practicing cannibalism. The remaining captains gravely estimated the losses at ten thousand, and it was resolved to leave the island. In June about five hundred Hurons began the final retreat to Quebec, where their descendants, the Hurons of Lorette, still dwell, the only survivors bearing the Huron name. A few left before the final decision was made and struck out for the country of the friendly Susquehannah, who had been unable, so swift and so secret had been the Iroquois attack, to raise a hatchet in their defense until it was over.[19]

Of the Hurons who did not seek St. Joseph Island, some went to the Petuns, where they suffered a second dispersion in December, 1649. Many fled to the Neutrals, who, no longer neutral now that the Hurons had been ruined, butchered and burned many of the bedraggled fugitives and carried the remainder into a harsh captivity.[20] A large number succeeded in reaching the country of the Erie, whom they reinforced against the Iroquois a few years later. The Iroquois blamed these Hurons for inciting the Erie to war against them in 1653 and 1654. One entire town of the Hurons, preferring slavery to starvation, delivered themselves to the Iroquois voluntarily, and received a few recruits from St.

---

[17] Ragueneau, *ibid.*, 34:203–207; 35:87. Manitoulin Island was known to the Hurons as Ekaentoton, and Christian Island was then called St. Joseph's Island by the Jesuits.

[18] *Ibid.*, 35:73–77, 85, 89.   [19] *Ibid.*, 193, 195–197.

[20] Ragueneau, *ibid.*, 34:197, 203; 35:79, 81; 36:119, 179; 45:243; Le Mercier, *ibid.*, 41:81–83.

Joseph Island in the spring of 1650.[21] All these fugitives lost forever their tribal identities, those fleeing to the Petuns, the Neutrals, and the Erie experiencing yet one more dispersion before five years had passed. Of the lately prosperous and flourishing Huronia there remained only skeletons and ashes.

The Petuns, who had supplied the war party that pursued the Iroquois on March 19, 1649, did not at first share the Huron terror, and remained unscathed, unperturbed, and unhelpful throughout the summer and throughout the Huron flight. Early in December they received news of an impending Iroquois attack and on December 5, not content with awaiting it, they went in search of the enemy. Two days later, at about three o'clock in the afternoon, the Iroquois party, having eluded the Petun warriors, fell upon the town of St. Jean in their absence. Father Garnier was killed in the battle, which was brief, the town being virtually undefended. The Petun warriors returned on December 9. As they viewed the shambles of St. Jean, they sat upon the ground in shame and mourning for half a day, without moving or uttering a sound.[22] Their dispersion had no Jesuit chronicler and its details are unknown; Chabanel, the only other Frenchman with the Petuns, was lost and died alone in the forest during the confusion of the Iroquois attack. It is thought likely that he was the victim of some straggling Petun or Iroquois, for possessions of his were later found in the hands of a Petun. It is certain, however, that the flight of the Petuns was less wild and disorderly than that of the Hurons proper. A few of them followed the Hurons to St. Joseph Island, but the larger portion of the tribe kept together, preserving their tribal identity, and with a few fugitive Hurons took refuge among the upper Algonquins, chiefly the Ottawa of Manitoulin Island.[23] With these Ottawa they fled westward before the Iroquois menace, and were next heard of near and among the Potawatomi of Washington Island, near the mouth of Green Bay. Their later peregrinations to the Mississippi River, Chequamegon Bay, back

---

[21] *Ibid.*, 35:193; 36:179.   [22] *Ibid.*, 35:109–119.

[23] G.W. Bruce, "The Petuns," in Ontario Historical Society, *Papers and Records*, 8:35–39; *Jesuit Relations*, 45:343. Bruce has an exaggerated opinion of Petun civilization, and is none too sure of the facts, as is revealed, for example, by his belief that they moved directly from Ontario to Detroit.

to Manitoulin Island, and eventually to Detroit will be sketched in succeeding chapters.

The Dispersion of the Neutrals

The Iroquois quarrel had not originally been with the Neutral nation, for the Neutrals were merely commercial satellites of the Hurons, selling them corn and a few furs, and permitting them to hunt beaver in Neutral territory. Their sole intertribal relation of consequence aside from this Huron connection was a perpetual state of war with the "Fire Nation" of Michigan, whose conquest had been completed in 1643. They are sometimes confused with the Erie, possibly because they were a consanguine tribe and were more or less merged with them in a double dispersion by the Iroquois within a very few years.[24]

Having no canoes and understanding neither their manufacture nor their management, the Neutrals had no commerce beyond their own territory. They could therefore be of no great service to the Iroquois in the all-important matter of obtaining furs. On the other hand, they might offer a haven to the French, who could then open direct trade with the nations beyond, using the Neutral nation as headquarters in the way that Huronia had been used. In fact, the French were already familiar with the Neutrals in spite of Huron efforts to keep them apart. More than that, they constituted a good part of a great threat to Iroquois hegemony as a tacit partner in the encircling alliances, and had been presumably willing hosts to the various Huron-Susquehannah embassies. A revival of an anti-Iroquois league was far from an impossibility, and it were better to defeat such a combination in detail than to be forced to face its combined strength.[25] That strategy had been successful with the Hurons. The Neutrals' enslavement of the fugitive Hurons was no proof of their friendship. At best the Neutrals were a block to Iroquois trade with the West, and at

[24] On the "Fire Nation" war see Ragueneau, in the *Jesuit Relations*, 27:25–27. An example of their confusion with the Erie occurs in Drake, *Indian Tribes of the United States*, 1:403, 406.

[25] The Neutrals did actually league with the Susquehannah in 1651 and defeat the Seneca. *Jesuit Relations*, 37:97. The defeat was so decisive that the Seneca moved their women to Cayuga.

worst were potential enemies and a nucleus for a hostile league already half formed. To trade with the West at all the Seneca were forced to pass the Neutral borders, and so long as they remained where they were, the task of clearing a path to the furs of the upper Lakes was only half accomplished.

To accomplish the dispersion of the Neutrals the Mohawks and Seneca once more leagued together, the Mohawks agreeing to help the Seneca against the Neutrals in return for Seneca aid against the French in the east.[26] A multitude of excuses for making war were available: the Neutrals had refused to surrender a Huron girl; the Neutrals had given up a Seneca to the Hurons. None of them is convincing, being the sort of thing that would have been easily forgotten had war not been desirable, like "border disputes" among modern nations. The Neutrals must have had some inkling of what was about to happen, for in the summer of 1650 Ragueneau heard at Quebec that a Neutral embassy was coming to the French for aid against the Iroquois. The embassy never arrived, and in the spring and summer of 1651 the news trickled in of a Neutral defeat.[27] Six hundred Iroquois had stormed a Neutral town of sixteen hundred, dispersing and incorporating, as was their wont, all the able-bodied, and wreaking carnage among the old men and small children. The Neutrals retaliated, taking a Seneca frontier town and scalping two hundred warriors, but their confidence had been destroyed, and the nation slowly disintegrated.

Part of them drifted south past the Erie, finally to penetrate Carolina and become a part of the Catawba.[28] Eight hundred of them wintered in 1652–53 at Sken-chio-é and when next heard of

[26] Ragueneau, in the *Jesuit Relations*, 38:63.

[27] *Ibid.*, 35:215. On the Neutral defeat see the *Journal des Jésuites*, ibid., 36:121, 141, 177–179; James H. Coyne, *The Country of the Neutrals* (St. Thomas, Ontario, 1895), 18, 19.

[28] An apparently authentic memoir of Catawba tradition states that they were once a northern tribe, driven south by the Connewango (Seneca) about 1650. After desperate rearguard fighting, they split into two bands, one of which became the Catawba. See Drake, *Indian Tribes of the United States*, 1:405–409. Frederick W. Hodge disagrees, classifying the Catawba as Siouan. See his *Handbook of American Indians*, 1:213–214. Linguistic evidence supports this latter view, and if there is anything in the tradition, it accounts for only a part of the Catawba.

were reduced to four cabins among the fugitive Hurons and
Ottawa on the islands around the mouth of Green Bay.[29] The
winter at Sken-chio-e is the last heard of the Neutrals under their
own name; like the Hurons, they lost their identity in dispersion.
It is probable that the small tribe of Negaouichirinouek, or Nega-
wichi, was a remnant of the Neutral nation.[30] A large number of
them were incorporated into the Iroquois, and in later years
priests found whole towns of them in Iroquoia.[31] As with the
Hurons, it is probable that not many of them were slain outright,
and it is likely that a considerable number of them remained in
Ontario. Nicolas Perrot's *Memoir* suggests that the Iroquois
merely incorporated the whole nation, which would have been in
line with their policy of incorporating large numbers of their captives rather than exterminating them.[32] Most of the Neutral country remained virtually uninhabited and served as a hunting ground
for the Iroquois and as winter quarters for many northern tribes.

The Iroquois seemed to have won their battle. The pestilent
Hurons had been dispersed, their monopoly of the northern and
western trade was ended, and the way cleared to the westward for

[29] *Journal des Jésuites*, in the *Jesuit Relations*, 38:181. Du Creux's map of 1660
locates Sken-chio-e on the peninsula between Saginaw Bay and Lake Huron, but
Thwaites thinks it should be located in the extreme west end of Neutral territory,
near Windsor, Ontario. See the *Jesuit Relations*, 8:302n; 38:294. He believes that the
Skenchiohronons mentioned by Le Jeune in 1640 were a Neutral subdivision. The
Neutrals wintering there in 1652–53 did not join the northwest confederacy, as had
been expected, but the Iroquois. See Nicolas Perrot, *Mémoire sur les mœurs, coustumes
et relligion des sauvages de l'Amérique Septentrionale*, edited by R. P. J. Tailhan
(Bibliotheca Americana, pt. 3, Leipzig and Paris, 1864), 80. At Green Bay they were
called "Awechi." See the *Jesuit Relations*, 38:181. By adding the prefix "Ont," which in
Indian tongues can be added or subtracted almost at will, and allowing a metathesis
because of the "a" in "awech," one would have "Nadawechi," which is identical with
"Nadouaich," the word used in the *Relations*. See Hjalmar R. Holand, "St. Michael,
the Gateway of the West," in the *Peninsula Historical Review*, 2:54n (Sturgeon Bay,
Wisconsin, 1928).

[30] The similarity between the words "Negawich" and "Nadawech" makes a connection seem likely. Thwaites is evidently confused about this tribe. In the *Jesuit
Relations*, 73:175, he describes them as an Ottawa band, whereas *ibid.*, 44:324, he
calls them Illinois. In his last assertion he is evidently following Tailhan, but there
is no evidence that there ever was such a band or clan among the Illinois, and for
Illinois they are far out of a likely location. See Holand, "St. Michael, the Gateway
of the West," in the *Peninsula Historical Review*, 2:54, and La Potherie, "Savage
Peoples," in Blair, *Indian Tribes*, 1:292.

[31] Fremin, in the *Jesuit Relations*, 54:81; 45:207.

[32] Blair, *Indian Tribes*, 1:150. Hodge, in his *Handbook of American Indians*, says
merely "political destruction."

such steps as it might be desirable to take. It would be wise to take care that the Hurons did not merely take root again among the Far Indians and reassume the monopoly, so occasional parties were sent into their old country, and even to the place where a remnant was gathered near the mouth of Green Bay. Perrot's *Mémoire* tells in considerable detail of a great defeat suffered there by the Iroquois. To this supposed defeat many authors have pinned a variety of consequences, but internal criticism and comparison of documents destroys the case.[33] Whatever the fate of the Iroquois parties, they were ranging far and wide and making contacts, usually hostile, with surrounding tribes, notably the Erie. In 1653 the Erie fired a Seneca town, and cut to pieces a rear guard of eighty men "returning from the great lake of the Hurons," capturing Annenraes, the ambassador of four years before.[34] It seemed that the Erie might also become a menace.

By the spring of 1653 the Seneca were ready for peace with New France, largely because there was no longer any reason for hostility. The real quarrel had been with the Hurons over their trade monopoly, and now the Hurons were gone. The French had never crossed the Seneca anyway, and they might be desirable allies in the event of a war with the Erie, which began to appear likely.[35] In the early summer the French learned that the Seneca would make peace and would bring the Cayuga with them. In June a great embassy arrived from Onondaga, and by August the Mohawks, seeing that they would be isolated if they continued their hostility, gave in with rather bad grace. There was no good·reason for continuing a war that could profit them nothing further, and their brothers in the League were even warning the French of their war parties, so effectively, moreover, that the French captured four of their important chiefs. The Onondaga, never bitterly hostile, had brought the Oneida into the peace with them, and the Mohawks bade fair to be completely isolated from the other Iroquois, among

[33] See Appendix C below.
[34] Le Mercier, in the *Jesuit Relations*, 41:81. Ondaaiondiont, the Huron ambassador of 1648, was killed at the storming of St. Louis in 1649.
[35] In 1654 a party of Erie penetrated to within a day's journey of Onondaga, the Iroquois capital, and killed three hunters. Le Mercier, writing from Le Moine's journal, in the *Jesuit Relations*, 41:107.

whom, as we have seen, they were already none too popular. By September the peace was signed, and during the winter and the following spring was ratified and re-ratified according to Iroquois custom. The Iroquois were again quite evidently sincere.[36]

This peace, like that of 1645, was destined not to last, but the reasons for its fracture were still beneath the horizon. No one could foresee the future, and both the French and the Iroquois were relieved and happy, except, possibly, the recalcitrant Mohawks, who feared that a French connection with the western Iroquois would rob them of the middleman status they had enjoyed while the Iroquois trade was limited to Fort Orange.[37] The old Mohawk-Onondaga rivalry was barely submerged and any sort of disturbance could easily bring it to the surface again. The attention of the Iroquois, however, was soon turned from intra-tribal affairs by the pressing problem of the Erie.

The Dispersion of the Erie Nation

The Erie were then, and remain now, the least known of all the Iroquoian tribes. Until the time of their dispersion no white man had ever visited their country. They were known to the French as the Cat Nation, and were supposed to have once inhabited the shores of Lake Erie, whence they had been driven inland by enemies from the west. There has been great division of opinion as to their true identity, but there seems to be no reason for trying to identify them as any other tribe than Erie. They lived south and west of the Seneca and south and east of Lake Erie, probably near the southeastern shore.[38]

---

[36] A full account of the making of the peace is given below in Appendix C. In connection with the question of the sincerity of the Iroquois may be mentioned the incident of the half-breed known as the Flemish Bastard, an Iroquois chief, who brought letters from the governor of Fort Orange and several Dutch tradesmen assuring the French that the Iroquois were undoubtedly sincere. See Le Mercier, in the *Jesuit Relations*, 41:85. There is no reason to doubt their sincerity.

[37] See the *Jesuit Relations*, especially 41:87, 199–201, 203, 219. Volume 43 is little more than a record of intra-Iroquois dissension. See also 42:51–53, and 44:149–151. Charlevoix has an excellent short essay on the situation. See his *New France*, 2:259–260, 264–266. He is wrong, however, in saying that "interest [was] a motive hitherto little known among these people." For a contradiction see Perrot, *Memoir*, in Blair, *Indian Tribes*, 1:144.

[38] See Gendron, *Quelques particularitez*, 8–9; Sagard, *Grand Voyage*, 217; *Jesuit Relations*, 33:63; 38:237. Parkman thought that they were the Carantouans mentioned by

They were said to have had no firearms, but to have used only bows and arrows. Dablon, however, ascribed their defeat in 1654 to a shortage of powder, thus admitting that they had firearms; and the Iroquois complained that they fought bravely, like Frenchmen, sustaining the first discharge of firearms and then closing quickly under a hail of poisoned arrows, giving eight or ten arrows for one musket shot. Their warriors were reckoned at two thousand. The refugee Hurons were charged with stirring up and sustaining the war. A traditional reason given is that the Erie were beaten by the Iroquois in intertribal athletic contests, but this is evidently a confusion with the Neutral tradition cited before.[39] The Erie were aggressive and obnoxious, and after the addition of the fugitive Hurons it seemed obvious that the Huron problem would not be solved until their hosts and comforters, the Erie, were decisively defeated.

By the summer of 1654 plans were well under way for raising the greatest army ever assembled in Iroquoia, a war party of eighteen hundred men, and the young commander came to Le Moine, the Jesuit resident in Onondaga, to ask his blessing. Later that summer the Iroquois stormed the principal Erie town with only seven hundred warriors; enduring the galling Erie fire with great courage, they erected a counter-palisade and scaled the walls, dispersing, destroying, and taking captive its inhabitants. As with the Hurons, the Petuns, and the Neutrals, the one heavy blow destroyed their tribal identity, though for several years the war continued as a series of forays. Dablon, who was in Iroquoia in 1656, mentioned straggling groups of Onondaga warriors arriving by two's and three's with captives and loot from the Erie country, and a year later Radisson witnessed the same thing. The

Champlain, but these are now known to have been the Susquehannah. See his *Jesuits in North America*, xlvi. Beauchamp thought that they were the Massawomecks mentioned by Smith, but these are now known to have been Mohawks, and could not possibly have been Erie. See his *New York Iroquois*, 194.

[39] On Erie firearms see the *Jesuit Relations*, 41:83; 42:181. On the use of poison see Le Mercier, *ibid.*, 41:81–83. Biard's Relation (*ibid.*, 3:101) tells of the trading of sublimate "and other poisons" to the Indians by the French, but since the Erie did not trade with the French, their arrow poison was probably a native compound. Its use was uncommon among American aborigines. See also Charlevoix, *New France*, 1:276; Le Mercier, in the *Jesuit Relations*, 41:81–83; and Beauchamp, *New York Iroquois*, 182, for opinions on the cause of the war.

number of captives must have been large, for Erie slaves were settled even at the mission near Montreal.[40]

There is no reason to suppose that they were utterly destroyed. On Herrman's map of 1670 appears a new tribe in the old land of the Erie on the upper Ohio River, the "Black Minquas." These Black Minquas, who later figured in the affairs of the Susquehannah, were undoubtedly the Erie. The name "Mingo," evidently a derivative of "Minqua," was indiscriminately applied to subtribes of the Iroquois at first, and later even to the Five Nations themselves. It is an Algonquin word meaning "rascal" or "bad man," and even the Susquehannah were known as "White Minquas." As late as 1755 the ruins of the Erie towns could still be seen, and there is little doubt that the Black Minquas of western Pennsylvania were the former Erie.[41]

For the moment, it appeared that the desires of the Iroquois were to be satisfied as a result of the peace of 1653 with the French. After more than fifteen years of ceaseless struggle to win the fur trade of the Northwest, by both peace and war, it seemed that they had at last overcome all obstacles, and that the cherished trade would soon be theirs. The Hurons were gone, or at least so far removed that they were no longer a menace, and the Iroquois knew nothing of the peculiar talents of the Ottawa.

But even while the peace was being ratified its destruction had begun. In the far Northwest was being assembled a fur brigade similar to that which had shattered the peace of 1645, manned by

[40] Le Moine's Journal, in the *Jesuit Relations*, 41:121. See also De Quen, *ibid.*, 42: 178–179; 45:209. There is, of course, great exaggeration in the Onondaga account of the victory, in which the visitors are pictured as "knee-deep in the blood of women and children." See also Radisson, *Voyages*, 113, and the *Jesuit Relations*, 42:191, 195, on the continuation of the Erie war.

[41] Augustine Herrman, a Bohemian adventurer, was commissioned by Lord Baltimore to map Maryland and Virginia to end the boundary dispute. The Maryland act naturalizing him spells his name "Herman." See the *Maryland Archives*, 2:144. The only known copy of the map is in the British Museum. See also the *Journal of Jasper Danckaerts, 1679–1680*, edited by Bartlett B. James and J. Franklin Jameson (New York, 1913), xix; Samuel Hazard, *Annals of Pennsylvania, from the Discovery of the Delaware, 1609–1682* (Philadelphia, 1850), 342 ff.; Amandus Johnson, *The Swedish Settlements on the Delaware* (2 vols., Philadelphia, 1911), 1:188–189, which contains a scholarly discussion of the Minqua problem; Lewis Evans, *An Analysis of a General Map of the Middle British Colonies in America and of the Country of the Confederate Indians* (*Geographical, Historical, Political, Philosophical, and Mechanical Essays*, [vol. 1], 2d ed., Philadelphia, 1755), 13.

a few fugitive Hurons of Green Bay and the ubiquitous Ottawa, upon whom had fallen the mantle of the Huron trade. In June of 1654 a great canoe fleet was sighted from Montreal, which was at first feared to be an enemy flotilla; but when it was recognized as Huron-Ottawa, "fear speedily turned to joy as the . . . friends of the French swept down the rapids, their canoes gay with decorations and loaded to the brim with precious beaver skins." The fact that the skins were later captured at sea by the English was unfortunate for the French, but it did not help the Iroquois. No fleet came in 1655, but in 1656 two traders, perhaps Radisson and Groseilliers, led fifty canoes out of the Northwest to the beach before Montreal, and the sullen Iroquois began gathering another army and plotting against the newly established French settlement at Onondaga.[42]

In December twelve hundred Iroquois took the war trail to "the country of the Outaouak"; another party followed them in January, and before March two hundred Mohawks had left for the St. Lawrence. Dissension was still rife among the Iroquois nations, and Stuyvesant, the Dutch governor, in presenting a keg of powder to the Seneca, found it necessary to warn them not to use it against the Mohawks, but against a common enemy for a common purpose. Fortified by a more or less informal agreement with the Dutch, they had little to fear from the rear, although the Susquehannah war was brewing and the Susquehannah were already moving up from the south and intercepting the Seneca traders on their way to Fort Orange.[43]

The Iroquois expedition against the "Outaouak" was in vain, for the Hurons and Ottawa of Washington Island, apprehensive of that very move, had kept scouting parties so constantly on the

[42] Kellogg, *French Régime*, 98–99; Le Mercier, in the *Jesuit Relations*, 41:77. This lot of skins was captured by the British in the English Channel. See Le Mercier, *ibid.*, 43. On the trading fleet of 1656 see De Quen, in the *Jesuit Relations*, 42:219, and his letter, *ibid.*, 33. Charlevoix says that the fleet was composed of only thirty Ottawa (*New France*, 2:270), but the Relation says *cicquante canots*. On the Iroquois preparation see Le Moine, in the *Jesuit Relations*, 44:205, 219; Radisson, *Voyages*, 123.

[43] Le Moine, *loc. cit.*; *New York Colonial Documents*, 13:186; Jan van Rensselaer to Jeremias van Rensselaer, in *The Correspondence of Jeremias van Rensselaer, 1651–1674*, edited by Arnold J. F. van Laer (Albany, 1932), 21. This treaty was evidently formal only with the Mohawks. See also *Early Records of Albany*, 1:237, and Lalemant, in the *Jesuit Relations*, 47:111.

watch that no such army could have escaped detection. They were nervous in their new home, and relations with the Potawatomi were none too pleasant. Presently they began a second migration westward, still together, the story of which is a veritable Anabasis. Upon striking the Mississippi they moved slowly upstream and up the Black River, finally arriving after several years at Chequamegon Bay, where Allouez and Marquette labored among them. After provoking a war with the Sioux, they fled once more, this time back to the old Ottawa home on Manitoulin Island, the Petuns remaining at Mackinac; about seventeen hundred removed to Detroit.[44]

The only alternative left to the Iroquois seemed to be the old technique of blockading the Ottawa, and they proceeded to put it into operation. They lurked all along the upper river, and the commerce of New France was paralyzed. The upper Indians, running out of powder and weapons, were also in an unenviable position, but the Ottawa was virtually closed. Radisson says that the mere sight of seven Iroquois stopped a brigade of three hundred and sixty canoes, and in August, 1660, only seven boats got through. Only the heroic death of Dollard and his seventeen men at the Long Sault gave New France the slightest relief, or the determined Iroquois the slightest setback.[45]

[44] Perrot describes this journey. See his *Memoir*, in Blair, *Indian Tribes*, 1:157–190. Father Ménard, the first Jesuit in Wisconsin, died in 1661 while trying to reach them.

[45] Radisson, *Voyages*, 175, 229–231; *Canadian Historical Review*, 13:121–138 (June, 1932), which contains an interesting debate on Dollard's exploit. E. R. Adair scouts the characterization of Dollard and his men as martyrs, and holds that his exploit redoubled the activity of the Iroquois. Gustave Lanctot, while admitting Dollard's motives to have been vainglorious, challenges Adair's interpretation of the results. See also Abbé Groulx, *Le Dossier de Dollard; la valeur des sources; la grandeur des résultats* (Montreal, 1932); William Kingsford, *History of Canada*, 1:261–262 (Toronto, 1887); and Parkman, *Old Régime in Canada*, 73–82

VIII. THE UPPER CANADA AND
MICHIGAN TRIBES

THE DISPERSION OF the Hurons was hardly more consequential to them than to the smaller tribes behind them who had been their customers and essential parts of their trading economy. With the Hurons gone, there was no longer a bulwark between these tribes and the Iroquois. Further, the Hurons had acted as a clearing house for all the trade of the small peoples of upper Canada, who were now without direction; few of them, probably, knew even the way to Montreal. Therefore they made no stand in their villages, but took well-known roads to the interior, roads already familiar to most of them, particularly the Nipissings. When Ragueneau led his unfortunate flock of starving Hurons down to Quebec in 1650 he noted, as he passed along the familiar French River–Lake Nipissing highway, that where the shores had once teemed with settlement they were now entirely deserted.[1]

It is interesting to note that, in dispersing, the various tribes moved toward regions already familiar to them: the Hurons and Ottawa toward Lake Superior, where they had been in the habit of doing business; the Neutrals and the Erie toward the south, to regions in which they preserved old contacts; and the Nipissings far to the north, where they had been wont to gather their furs for the Hurons. The Allumettes, having had no northern contacts, wandered miserably back and forth between their island and Quebec, unable to overcome the disadvantage of having been a strictly insular people.

These Allumettes, it may be recalled, had once made a peace with the Iroquois, but by 1636 had become nervous and had at-

---

[1] *Jesuit Relations*, 35:201.

tempted to ally themselves with the Nipissings and Hurons, only to be repulsed because of their former extortions from these tribes. In the years that followed they were joined by the Petite Nation. Although they suffered occasionally from the Iroquois raids on the Ottawa, they were never purposely invaded, for the reason that they did not, like the Hurons, hold the monopoly of the fur trade of "Le Haut Canada." They were present at the great council preceding the peace of 1645, and although greatly alarmed by the hostilities that broke out in 1646 and 1647, did not desert their island; they were there when Ragueneau came down the river with his Hurons in the summer of 1650. Le Borgne, the one-eyed chief, had the audacity to hang Ragueneau up by the armpits for asserting that the French were masters of the Allumettes. For this he was jailed and disciplined by the French the following year, and he and his band lived thereafter chiefly as hangers-on of the French settlements.[2]

After Ragueneau's descent of the Ottawa in the summer of 1650, nothing more was heard of the Nipissings until three years later, when three canoes stole into Three Rivers from the Petun-Ottawa retreat near Green Bay. To escape possible Iroquoian parties they had taken a circuitous route north of Lake Superior, by way of Nipigon and the northland portages across upper Canada to the headwaters of the St. Maurice River, known to them of old. At Lake Nipigon they had found the Nipissings, who had accommodated their talents to the possibilities of the region and had opened a profitable trade with the Cree, developing several routes into the latter's country and coming out with a considerable volume of furs.[3] The knowledge of the northern rivers which they had gained while serving as collectors for the Huron tradesmen had stood them in good stead in the dark hours of the Iroquois invasion.

Father Allouez, leaving Chequamegon Bay for Quebec in 1667, took in the Nipissing towns on his journey, going far out of his

[2] See Thwaites, in the *Jesuit Relations*, 22:17. They wintered with the Hurons in 1642–43. See Le Borgne's speech to the Hurons in the *Jesuit Relations*, 26:303, a speech that exaggerates the miseries of the Allumettes for a political purpose. See also *ibid.*, 19:147–149; 27:279; 28:147–157, 293, 301. The affair with Ragueneau is given in Perrot, *Memoir*, in Blair, *Indian Tribes*, 1:176–178. Perrot confuses Ragueneau with Lalemant. Ragueneau's Relation, perhaps naturally, does not mention the occurrence.

[3] See Kellogg, *French Régime*, 96; *Jesuit Relations*, 38:181; 44:243–249.

way to do so, for they had seen no priest for nearly twenty years. He found a score that still professed Christianity, but they had evidently had no contact with the French since coming to Nipigon. His visit re-established the connection, and by 1670 Nipissing canoes were visiting Montreal. Perrot found them on the south shore of Lake Superior at both Chequamegon Bay and Keweenaw, and in 1671 Father André visited them at their old home on Lake Nipissing, whither they had returned.[4] They had joined war parties against the Iroquois, along with the also fugitive Attikamegues, Montagnais, and Micmacs, but later consorted with the Iroquois, by whom, they said, they were kindly treated. It is entirely likely that the Iroquois did treat the Nipissings well, for that would have been quite in line with their policy if thereby they got Nipissing fur, and we know that in the 1680's the Iroquois were traveling to the Nipissing homeland to collect it.[5]

The Michigan Tribes

The Iroquois war ended rather than began the dispersion of the tribes of Michigan. The first knowledge the French had of the inhabitants of the great peninsula concerned a war waged by the Neutrals and Ottawa against a tribe in Michigan known as the "Nation of Fire," with whom the Hurons at times carried on commerce. The identity of this "Nation of Fire" has been the subject of much more or less fruitless speculation. The question is a particularly puzzling one in that there were two Michigan tribes known at one time or another as the "Fire Nation," the Potawatomi and the Mascouten. It is known that the Ottawa were hostile to the Potawatomi, although consanguine, and that the

[4] *Ibid.*, 51:63–71. Professor Burpee says that Nipigon was discovered by La Tourette in 1678 unless it had been seen by Radisson in 1662. See the *Journals and Letters of Pierre Gaultier de Varennes de la Vérendrye and His Sons*, edited by Lawrence J. Burpee (Toronto, 1927), 1:43. Radisson may be discounted, and it appears to the writer that Allouez is the true white discoverer of Lake Nipigon. See also Perrot, *Memoir*, in Blair, *Indian Tribes*, 1:179–181, 211–212; *Jesuit Relations*, 55:147–155.

[5] Perrot, *Memoir*, in Blair, *Indian Tribes*, 1:197. The Attikamegue, or "poisson blancs," also retired before the Iroquois menace from their headquarters on the upper St. Maurice. In 1659 they were met, far inland, by six canoes of Mississaga, who were coming from Lake Superior by the now frequently used St. Maurice route. See above, note 3. On this meeting see the *Jesuit Relations*, 45:105. On the Nipissing-Iroquois relations, see pp. 211–212, and Lamberville to Bruyas, November 4, 1686 (intercepted by the English), in *New York Colonial Documents*, 3:480.

Potawatomi were dispersed from Michigan some time before 1641. This circumstance, with the fact that the Potawatomi name means "keepers of the sacred fire," would seem to establish the identity of the Potawatomi and the "Fire Nation" were it not that the war continued after the known evacuation of the Potawatomi, the "Fire Nation" being defeated by the Neutrals in 1643. This particular "Fire Nation" seems certainly to have been the Mascouten, who, although their name properly means "prairie people," were, somewhat erroneously, called "Fire People" through a very slight twisting of the name.[6] The Mascouten were closely consanguine with the Potawatomi and are sometimes referred to as the "Prairie Potawatomi."[7] It seems reasonable to conclude that because of their close relationship and the similarity of the Huron words for "fire" and "prairie," no sufficient distinction was made between them, and the war was probably more or less continuously fought against both, the evacuation of the Potawatomi leaving the Mascouten heirs to the entire war. More than that, a statement that the "Fire Nation" was "more populous than the Neutral Nation, all the Hurons and all the Iroquois" combined would certainly indicate that it was larger than either Mascouten or Potawatomi alone. A statement made by Ragueneau in 1648 that the "Ouachaouanag [Shawnee] form a part of the nation of fire" indicates the folly of placing too strict an interpretation upon Indian terminology translated into several languages and repeated through several mediums.[8] A conclusion that would make all the references to the "Fire Nation" at least reasonable is that the phrase referred roughly, at times, to all the southern

---

[6] Champlain, Works, 3:43; 4:280–282; Sagard, Histoire du Canada, 1:192; Jesuit Relations, 27:25–27. The confusion concerning the name is between ich-koute or es-co-te and mas-koute or mas-co-te. See Lucien Carr, The Mascoutens (Worcester, Massachusetts, 1900), reprinted from American Antiquarian Society, Proceedings, new series, 13:448–462 (1899–1900); Jesuit Relations, 55:199; Radisson, Voyages, third voyage. Father André used the word as an adjective meaning "prairie" to describe the Iowa as "prairie Sioux," in the Jesuit Relations, 60:203.

[7] Alanson B. Skinner, The Mascoutens or Prairie Potawatomi Indians: Social Life and Ceremonies (Milwaukee Public Museum Bulletin, vol. 6, no. 1, Milwaukee, 1924), 15. Kellogg, French Régime, 57.

[8] The meaning of "Potawatomi" as "fire people" is confirmed by Kahquados, in Publius V. Lawson, "The Potawatomi," in the Wisconsin Archaeologist, vol. 19, no. 2, p. 42 (April, 1920), and by Edward D. Neill and William Warren, in Minnesota Historical Collections, 5:52. To say didactically that "Fire Nation" must mean Mascouten,

Michigan tribes, including the Sauk, Fox, Kickapoo, and their subtribes.

The Potawatomi were the first of the Michigan tribes to leave the peninsula. Forming the vanguard of the penetration of Michigan by the Chippewa-Ottawa-Potawatomi confederacy, they had advanced as far south as the St. Joseph River and had become more or less separated from their brethren the Ottawa, with whom their contacts shortly became unpleasant.[9] Gaining also the enmity of the near-by Iroquoian tribe of Neutrals, they retired northward to the vicinity of Mackinac and Sault Ste. Marie, and eventually moved west and south along the northwestern shore of Lake Michigan, finally making a settlement on the Wisconsin shore near the mouth of Green Bay.[10]

They were not permitted to remain there long in peace, for in 1640 and 1641 they were assaulted by the then populous and powerful Winnebago and driven back to Sault Ste. Marie, where they temporarily allied themselves with the Chippewa, a kindred tribe.[11] It is likely that the Potawatomi took a prominent part in the Huron-Ottawa commerce with Wisconsin before the dispersion of those tribes, and that their previous flight eastward had

as does Truman Michelson, is not only to deny expert testimony and the plain inference of history, but to ascribe a precision to aboriginal speech that is not found even in modern speech. The constant misuse of such terms as "Dutch" and "nigger" are modern illustrations.

[9] Blackbird, *Ottawa and Chippewa Indians of Michigan*, 94; Schoolcraft, *Indian Tribes*, 1:308. The writer suggests that Miss Kellogg may be mistaken in her conclusion that the Hurons were also hostile to the Potawatomi. The French sources make no mention of it, and according to Sagard the Hurons were almost ready on one occasion to ally themselves with the "Fire Nation" for war upon the Neutrals. There was a commercial connection. See Truman Michelson, "Preliminary Report on the Linguistic Classification of the Algonquian Tribes," in Bureau of American Ethnology, *Report*, 1906–07, pp. 225–290; Kellogg, *French Régime*, 57, 87.

[10] Le Jeune, in the *Jesuit Relations*, 18:231–233. Le Jeune got his information from Nicolet and a Huron map. Miss Kellogg thinks that the dispersion occurred in the 1620's while Nicolet was among the Nipissings (*French Régime*, 70, quoting *Early Narratives of the Northwest*, 23), but it appears that they had not yet moved to Washington Island when Nicolet was there.

[11] They were met in flight by Jogues and Raymbault. See the *Jesuit Relations*, 23:225. See also Lahontan, *New Voyages*, 1:149; *New York Colonial Documents*, 9:153. The old theory is that their foes were the Sioux, a theory born of the loose use of the word *nadoessioux* or "enemy." The Winnebago are a Siouan people and the error is pardonable, but the Sioux proper had not yet come nearly so far east. On the Sioux theory see Lawson, "The Potawatomi," in the *Wisconsin Archaeologist*, vol. 19, no. 2, p. 43; Morgan, *Ancient Society*, 108.

been a repercussion of the commercial war between the Ottawa and the Winnebago. The Potawatomi later showed themselves to be keen traders.

Returning to Wisconsin after the decline of the Winnebago power, they took up residence on Washington Island, and in 1650 became hosts to the fleeing Petuns and Ottawa. With them they built the famous old fortress at Méchingan (probably the original form of Michigan) and constituted the greater portion of its defenders, numbering at that time at least four hundred warriors.[12] They spread, in the following years, southward along the lake shore; La Salle's traders found one of their villages near the site of Milwaukee in 1679.[13] It is possible that Kahquados is right in his assertion that in their original retreat from Michigan a part of the tribe retreated southwest, following the Lake Michigan shore past the site of Chicago.[14] This would account for their seemingly swift spread over a great extent of territory. The later history of the Potawatomi belongs properly to Wisconsin, and will be resumed in the following chapter.

Their near relatives the Mascouten, or Mush-ko-dain-sug, the "people of the little prairie," were pushed into southern Michigan by the Ottawa and driven westward by the Neutrals about 1625. They are often confused in early writings with the Sauk and Foxes. Sulte believes them to have been identical. Governor Denonville of Canada places them in the country of the Sauk, or Sankinon (Saginaw), but he is obviously in error, for he quotes Champlain as having visited them and the Neutrals, when as a matter of fact Champlain never saw either nation. Le Jeune baptized a four-year-old boy of the "Fire Nation" who was a captive among the Algonquins of Quebec in 1632, and Butterfield tried to prove that a village of the "Fire Nation" was in Wisconsin in the days of

[12] There is little doubt that they were the On-ta-to-na-te-ni or O-to-na-ten-die mentioned in the *Jesuit Relations*, 38:181. A comparison of the syllabification with Radisson's Pon-ta-na-tem-ick (*Voyages*, 148) and with the rendering in the Potier MSS of the Huron name for the Potawatomi, On-da-tou-a-tan-dy, shows a close similarity if the fourth syllable of the Potier name is accented. See also Holand, "St. Michael," in the *Peninsula Historical Review*, vol. 2.

[13] La Salle, *Relation*, 49–55; Zénobe Membré, "Narrative of the Adventures of La Salle's Party at Fort Crevecoeur," in *Louisiana Historical Collections*, 4:150 (New York, 1852).

[14] Lawson, "The Potawatomi," in the *Wisconsin Archaeologist*, vol. 19, no. 2, p. 42.

Nicolet. Butterfield's theory fell to the ground, however, when research on Nicolet's voyage proved that he could not possibly have gone inland, as Butterfield asserted that he had.[15]

Out of all this maze of contradictory location and chronology a few valid conclusions begin to emerge. One is that the "Fire Nation" was a name loosely used by the Huron Iroquois and the Ottawa (and hence by the French) to denominate any of the tribes of southern Michigan with whom they were at odds. The kinship of all these tribes has added to the confusion.[16] Another possible conclusion, although it does not seem a very sound one to the writer, is that there were two divisions of the Mascouten, one in southern Michigan and the other in Wisconsin.[17] William Tooker wrote a whole book on a supposed empire of the Mascouten stretching over Iowa, Illinois, Indiana, and Ohio, but he gives no evidence. Carr thinks that they, or the confederacy to which they belonged, once held the region south of the lakes and north of the Ohio, including southern Michigan, a conclusion which is admissible only if all the southern Algonquin peoples are taken to be a confederacy. Sulte claims that the Mascouten migrated about 1656, and contemporary maps have them in southern Michigan as late as 1660.[18] The present writer, however, believes them

[15] See Skinner, *The Mascoutens;* Kellogg, *French Régime,* 57, 69–70; Schoolcraft' *Indian Tribes,* 1:307; Blackbird, *Ottawa and Chippewa Indians of Michigan,* 92, 94. The accusations of necromancy and "bad medicine" that have been brought against both Potawatomi and Mascouten also argue a near identity. The date of 1625 is at best approximate. Champlain located them within ten days' journey, and Sagard, a decade later, was told that they were two hundred leagues away. See Champlain, *Works,* 3:97, and Sagard, *Grand Voyage,* 53–54. Denonville's "Memoir" is in *New York Colonial Documents,* 9:378. See also the *Jesuit Relations,* 5:73, and Consul W. Butterfield, *History of the Discovery of the Northwest* (Cincinnati, 1881).

[16] Hodge, in his *Handbook of American Indians,* 2:472, supports this view. Tribes were often confounded with one another, not by the Indians but by the French traders and missionaries, although the missionaries in particular tried to be exact. Dreuillettes even distinguished between the Mascouten and the "Fire Nation." See the *Jesuit Relations,* 44:245–249.

[17] See Truman Michelson, "Identification of the Mascoutens," in the *American Anthropologist,* 36:226–233 (June, 1934). The Rasaoua-Koueton, located by Nicolet at Green Bay and believed by Thwaites to have been Mascouten, are now thought to have been the Nassauketons or "Nation of the Fork," an Ottawa tribe, from which the Langlade family traces its descent.

[18] William Tooker, *The Bocootawanaukes or the Fire Nation* (Algonquin Series, vol. 6, New York, 1901); Carr, *The Mascoutens,* 4. For contemporary maps see Justin Winsor, *Cartier to Frontenac* (New York, 1894), 179, 210, 216.

to have begun their emigration earlier than 1656, probably about 1643, inasmuch as there is no evidence that they delayed their dispersion for a decade and a half after their bloody defeat by the Neutrals. No Indian tribe is known to have delayed its dispersion after such a defeat. Whatever the date may have been, the history of the Mascouten after their dispersion belongs properly to Wisconsin.

Of the Sauk little is known until they arrived in Wisconsin. They were one of the tribes known to the French only as the "Fire People." The name was originally "O-saug-eeg" or "O-saw-gee," meaning "those who live by the entry," and they were later called by the French "Osauki" and "Saukies." The traditional account says that they were oppressed, like their southern brethren, by the Ottawa, and forced to join a loose confederacy. It is likely that this oppression followed the advent of the French, and that it was another aspect, like the Ottawa-Winnebago war, of the extension of Ottawa commerce. Their home is said to have been on the Saginaw River, and they told Dablon that they had recently lived on the mainland of Michigan. They did not use canoes, and therefore had little contact with distant tribes save those who came to them, such as the Ottawa. With the assault by the Neutrals, and the consequent exposure to the greater danger of the Iroquois, they moved southwest around the lake, probably before 1654.[19] Apparently they did not move in great haste, but paused from time to time on their journey, for years later Nouvel, writing from the Lake Erie country, spoke of it as the former home of the Sakis.[20] On coming around the lake they moved into what probably continued to be their main village at Red Banks,

[19] Blackbird, *Ottawa and Chippewa Indians of Michigan*, 94; William W. Warren, "History of the Ojibways," in *Minnesota Historical Collections*, 5:32 (St. Paul, 1885); Wilbert B. Hinsdale, *The First People of Michigan* (Ann Arbor, 1930), 15; Dablon, in the *Jesuit Relations*, 60:215; Bacqueville de la Potherie, *Histoire de l'Amérique Septentrionale* (Paris, 1722), reprinted in part in the *Wisconsin Historical Collections*, 16:8. Radisson's party, crossing from Lake Huron to Lake Michigan, found no tribes there then. Radisson, *Voyages*, 146.

[20] Dreuillettes locates them three days' journey inland by water from the mouth of Green Bay. See the *Jesuit Relations*, 44:245-249. Holand believes that they moved in after the Winnebago had been decimated, but this is too early. See his "St. Michael," in the *Peninsula Historical Review*, 2:50. Miss Kellogg thinks that they did not move to Red Banks until 1666, after the peace with the Iroquois.

near the head of Green Bay, and began an irregular and unsettled existence. Allouez reported that "they above all others can be called Savages" and that, like the Foxes, they were prone to kill Frenchmen without provocation. La Potherie characterized them as brutal and unruly, incapable of subordination to or cooperation with their friends.[21] The aggregate impression left upon the investigator is that their hunting economy and lack of commerce had simply resulted in a low standard of civilization, which was to improve only with time.

The nearest relatives and allies of the Sauk, called by the French "Renards" or "Foxes," present another curious problem in nomenclature and ethnology. Known as "O-daw-gaw-mee" or "Outagamie," meaning "dwellers on the other shore," they inhabited the southern part of Michigan until they dispersed, although their exact location on the peninsula is in doubt.[22] By some they are thought to have moved first to the western side of the peninsula, and there to have become embroiled with the Winnebago across Lake Michigan, who met disaster in an expedition against them.[23] But since, like their kinsmen, they were not canoemen, such a contact with the Winnebago is difficult to imagine. A more likely hypothesis regarding their name is that their first home in Wisconsin was at Red Banks (possibly with the Sauk or near them) on the east side of Green Bay, and that the appellation "dwellers on the other shore" was given them by the Indians on the western side of the bay.[24] This is supported by the fact that the Foxes did call themselves "Musquaki," or "red earth people." It has been suggested that the disaster in which five hundred Winnebago braves were said to have been lost in a storm on the water while attacking the Foxes really occurred during the Winnebago-Potawatomi war of 1640–41 in the rough

[21] *Jesuit Relations,* 51:45; La Potherie, in the *Wisconsin Historical Collections,* 16:8.

[22] Blackbird, *Ottawa and Chippewa Indians of Michigan,* 24. Blackbird locates them about the Detroit River, which is questionable. It is more likely that they lived originally in the vicinity of Saginaw and Thunder Bay, near the Sauk. Miss Kellogg supports this view in her paper on "The Fox Indians during the French Régime," in Wisconsin Historical Society, *Proceedings,* 1907, p. 144.

[23] Kellogg, *French Régime,* 87–88.

[24] Newton H. Winchell, "Were the Outagami of Iroquoian Origin?" in Mississippi Valley Historical Association, *Proceedings,* 4:184 (1910–11).

waters of Death's Door.[25] That cannot be proved, but the thesis that the name "Outagamie" was given from across Green Bay rather than from across Lake Michigan seems the the more likely one, inasmuch as the name is Menominee-Algonquin, and not Winnebago-Siouan—and the Menominee also lived on the opposite shore of Green Bay.[26]

Moving south from their second home on the Door County Peninsula, perhaps because of the hostility of the tribes already there, the Foxes took up residence on the Wolf River, where they were discovered by Allouez in 1667. It was not until 1680 that they moved their village down to the Fox River, giving the river the name of their tribe. Their residence was not a settled one, however. Being unhabituated to the region, they moved about a good deal, as did the other tribes recently come to Wisconsin. Occasionally they went up to Green Bay or far into the interior, where they eventually became embroiled with the Sioux. They were described as numerous, their main village having a thousand warriors, and as unskillful canoemen but successful agriculturists. They were polygamous, and considered to be choleric and quarrelsome, but they were by no means barbarous, for some of their speeches even attained elegance.[27]

The rest of the Michigan tribes are unimportant in themselves, being in the main only subtribes of the five great tribes, the

[25] Holand, "St. Michael," in the *Peninsula Historical Review*, 2:50, 55, and *Old Peninsula Days: Tales and Sketches of the Door County Peninsula* (Ephraim, Wisconsin, 1925), 14–19; *Jesuit Relations*, 23:222.

[26] The question whether the Foxes might not have been of Iroquoian origin was raised by J. W. Powell in a report of the Bureau of Ethnology, in which he objected to the classification of both Sauk and Foxes as Algonquin on a purely linguistic basis, pointing out that political or social affiliations might have changed the language of the Foxes. But his article is unconvincing. His argument, for instance, that the Foxes did not speak Algonquin, which is supported by a single statement from the *New York Colonial Documents*, falls before the fact that they did speak Algonquin. Moreover, there is no similarity between Fox and Iroquoian culture or social organization. Both Sauk and Foxes may be considered as merely the most backward of the Michigan tribes, their lack of commercial contacts having isolated them sufficiently to account for the development of a distinctive dialect.

[27] The Menominee, Potawatomi, Chippewa, and Ottawa drove them south. See La Potherie, in *Wisconsin Historical Collections*, 16:8, and 2:491. See also Kellogg, "Fox Indians," in Wisconsin Historical Society, *Proceedings*, 1907, p. 151, and the *Jesuit Relations*, 51:43–45; 54:205, 227; 55:219–221. The Relations agree as to their number, either "a thousand warriors" or two hundred cabins of five to ten families. The wives per warrior numbered from four to ten.

Potawatomi, the Sauk, the Foxes, the Mascouten, and the Ottawa. The Kickapoo, though a distinct people, were satellites of the Sauk and Foxes, and the Kiskakons were merely the "Short-tailed Bear" clan of the Ottawa. It is fair to conclude that by the middle of the sixth decade of the century the dispersion to Wisconsin had been completed.

✳   ✳   ✳

The question that now arises is what caused the dispersion of so many tribes from so great an expanse of territory, and what general conclusions can be drawn from it or about it. The causes lie mainly in the economic conditioning of the Michigan tribes. We know that none of them were canoe people, and that no canoes means no commerce, at least of any appreciable extent. We know further that they lived largely by hunting, quite unlike the sedentary and commercial tribes of Ontario, and that dispersion was unhindered by the problem of sustenance, which was simply a matter of finding game and preserving, perhaps, a little seed-corn, even that being unnecessary in the wild-rice country. The fact that they all led the same manner of life made internecine wars a logical development, for all the tribes were in direct competition; this accounts for the expulsion of the Potawatomi. The Neutrals, whom they all met in battle, had the same economy; they knew nothing of commerce, being merely hunters.

It may be taken practically as a principle of intertribal relations that hunter and trader never war with each other but do business on an amicable basis, each having a contribution to make to the welfare of the other. The clash between producer and distributor is a much more modern phenomenon. Aboriginal wars were fought, not between hunter and trader, but between hunter and hunter and between trader and trader; language, race, and customs played no very considerable part. The Iroquoian Hurons and the Algonquin Ottawa were never at war with each other, yet there was little affiliation between them other than an economic one, and no fundamental similarity between their societies. The Five Nations, on the other hand, when they found the commerce of the Hurons necessary to their economy, had a compelling incentive to make war. Theirs was the most hotly contested struggle in

Indian history, despite their consanguinity, with the possible exception of that between the Chippewa and Sioux for possession of the rice lakes of northern Wisconsin and Minnesota, which offers another example of the dominance of the economic motive in intertribal strife.

In southern Michigan hunter met hunter, and since dispersion was comparatively easy, the less firmly established tribes moved out, though with no such ghastly loss of life as accompanied the Huron dispersion, where a huge commercial community was thrown, virtually unprepared, upon the wilderness. With the first serious defeat the evacuation of Michigan was probably hastened, and the tribes swarmed into the hospitable valleys of Wisconsin, where a place had been almost providentially prepared for them by the decline and decimation of the once powerful Winnebago. They told no tales of extreme hardship or starvation, saying only that they feared the "Naudoway" and had gone.[28] The defeat of the Hurons increased their apprehension, and by 1654 Michigan had become a "borderland between nations . . . who did not enter it save by stealth." Charlevoix, visiting the St. Joseph River in 1721, said, "It has but few inhabitants on its banks; I do not know if ever any nation was fixed there."[29]

[28] This name, with several variants, ranging all the way to "Nadoessi," means, in the Algic tongues, "snake" and "enemy" and is a term of opprobrium that has been used to designate Iroquoian peoples ever since the sixteenth-century conflict. It does not necessarily refer to the Iroquois proper (the Five Nations), and in the Relations dealing with the Michigan tribes "Neutral" may be substituted for "Iroquois" where that term is used, for the Iroquois never fought those tribes in Michigan. J. N. B. Hewitt believes that the retreat from Michigan was north across Mackinac Strait and thence to Green Bay and the Fox River Valley. He reasons that the Indians, being masters of retreat, would naturally not expose flanks and rear. See Hodge, *Handbook of American Indians*, 2:474. Such an analysis reveals a lack of acquaintance with Indian methods of attack and of retreat, and with the specific retreat in question. It was not, as Hewitt seems to think, in the immediate presence of the enemy.

[29] La Salle, *Relation*, 159; Charlevoix, *Journal*, 1:269.

IX. THE WISCONSIN TRIBES

BEFORE JEAN NICOLET undertook his journey to Wisconsin in 1634, there had been many rumors in the French settlements about the unknown country and the strange people living beyond the Sault. Champlain, who sent Nicolet, had been the first to hear them, and though he was conservative enough to discount them greatly, it was probably at his behest that the hardy woodsman provided himself with the regalia of a mandarin before he went, on the bare possibility that he might find at least some of the outlying islands of Cathay. Champlain wrote that "several times they [*Algonquins and Ottawa*] told us that some prisoners from a hundred leagues off related to them that there were people there white like us and similar to us in other respects, and through their intermediary they had seen the scalp of these people which is very fair, and which they value highly because of their saying that they were like us. I can only think that those whom they say resemble us, are people more civilized than themselves."[1] The Nipissings and the Ottawa, who had extensive trade relations beyond the Sault, had also told tall tales, perhaps to Nicolet himself during his many years among them. Although Nicolet may not have expected to find people of another race, he probably was keenly disappointed to find himself among the squalid lodges of the Winnebago.

[1] Champlain, *Works*, 3:119–120. There is a possibility, though a remote one, that the reference was to the Mandan Indians, whom La Vérendrye described in 1738 as having among them individuals with light, even red, hair. See Burpee, *Journals and Letters of Vérendrye*, 107–108, 159, 340. Before Lewis and Clark and Catlin visited them they had been decimated by smallpox, and modern observers have been unable to discover these characteristics. The Mandan tradition of the Great Canoe of their origin, and the recent study of the Kensington Runestone in Minnesota, suggest fascinating, though fantastic, possibilities.

The Winnebago were Siouan, and if present-day opinion respecting the direction of the Siouan migrations is correct, they probably came up the Mississippi, up the Wisconsin or Rock, and down the Fox River, splitting Algonquin territory like a wedge and maintaining themselves on this interlocked water highway, possibly by a continued connection with their western brethren.[2] This theory is supported by linguistic evidence, whereas another, more recent, theory, that the Siouan tribes were formerly located north of Lake Superior, has nothing to recommend it except that the Winnebago tradition places their first home on Green Bay, and does not mention the Rock or the Wisconsin River. It may be remarked that neither does it mention the north country, which seems an inhospitable country of origin. Miss Kellogg's statement that the Iowa, Oto, and Missouri speak of the Winnebago as "elder brother," indicating a movement away from rather than toward Green Bay is significant, as is also the fact that the Winnebago refer to themselves as "people of the parent speech." On the other hand, the diffusion of the subtribes from Green Bay may have been only a resurgent movement westward, and the "parent speech" may be only relative to these subtribes, not to the Sioux as a whole. Of course the problem cannot be regarded as solved, but there is little or no reason to doubt that the Winnebago came into Wisconsin from the south.[3]

It is certain that when first known they had been in Wisconsin for a long time and that they were very numerous. The great number of their mounds, the huge trees growing on them, and the enormous number of implements found in Wisconsin seem to indicate either an inconceivable length of residence or an ancient population much greater than was ever seen by the white man. That the ancient population was much larger than has commonly

[2] James Owen Dorsey, "Migrations of Siouan Tribes," in the *American Naturalist,* 20:211–222 (March, 1886), and "Siouan Sociology," in Bureau of American Ethnology, *Report,* 1893–94, pp. 213–244; Reuben G. Thwaites, *Historic Waterways* (Chicago, 1888), 230–231; James M. Mooney, "Siouan Tribes of the East," in Bureau of American Ethnology Bulletin 22 (Washington, 1894), pp. 5–14; David I. Bushnell, Jr., *Native Villages and Village Sites East of the Mississippi* (Bureau of American Ethnology Bulletin 69, Washington, 1919), 15–16.

[3] Cyrus Thomas, "Some Suggestions in Regard to Primary Indian Migrations in North America," in the *Proceedings of the Fifteenth International Congress of Americanists,* 1906, 1:189–205; Kellogg, *French Régime,* 73–74.

been supposed is true, for the white man's pestilence preceded him as inevitably and as speedily as did his trade goods, and of the three thousand warriors who dealt with Nicolet it is doubtful whether five hundred could have been found a decade later. Not alone pestilence, but war and the elements, conspired to ruin the Winnebago nation before white men saw it again.[4]

The Winnebago, called by the French "Ouinipegouek," or "stinkards" (Puans), were early known as a fierce and intractable tribe, which held the little Menominee nation under its sway. "They believed themselves," wrote La Potherie, "to be the most powerful in the universe; they declared war on all nations whom they could discover." The Ottawa and their allies, he said, had forced the Winnebago to accept French trade goods by constant assaults after the Winnebago had eaten certain Ottawa deputies; but it is difficult to believe that the powerful tribe seen by Nicolet could have been beaten, while at the height of its power, by so unwarlike a tribe as the Ottawa, even with all the allies they could muster, and we know that they were taking French trade goods long before Nicolet saw them. More plausible is the thesis that European goods sold themselves to the Winnebago, after having been seen, perhaps, in war. At any rate, the Huron, Ottawa, and Nipissing tradesmen did a thriving business on Green Bay.[5]

The decline of the tribe was occasioned by a series of disasters, including the loss of several hundred warriors in a storm on the Bay, a visitation of the tribe by the plague (probably smallpox), and a virtually annihilating defeat by the Illinois. It is impossible to arrange these events authoritatively in chronological sequence, but it is probable that the defeat by the Illinois came last, for it dealt what must have been a final blow. First, while at odds with the Potawatomi across Green Bay, five hundred warriors are said to have been drowned in a storm while attempting a passage in canoes. Next a pestilence decimated the tribe, and finally the unhappy

[4] West, Copper, 67; De Quen, in the Jesuit Relations, 42:223. Nicolet is not named here, but it is evident that De Quen was referring to him.

[5] Bacqueville de la Potherie, "Savage Peoples," in Blair, Indian Tribes, 1:292–293; Sagard, Histoire du Canada, 1:194; Jesuit Relations, 15:247; 30:113. Blackbird declares that the Winnebago had even made an attempt to invade Manitoulin Island, but were repulsed by the Ottawa. See his Ottawa and Chippewa Indians of Michigan, 85–88.

Winnebago incurred the hostility of the Illinois.[6] The Illinois tradition says that during a hard winter the Illinois sent five hundred men under fifty chiefs to the Winnebago villages with loads of provisions as a present, though it is far more likely that the Illinois traders tried to drive a hard bargain with starving customers. While a dance was in progress, the Winnebago cut the Illinois bowstrings, massacred their philanthropic guests, and ate them, along with their corn. The Illinois towns now formed a coalition and crushed the Winnebago, killing or enslaving all except a few who had hidden among the erstwhile subservient Menominee. Allouez has them all captured except one, who, when a few hundred were released by the Illinois, was made king, because he alone had never been a slave.[7] This ended their attempts at intertribal dominance, for the survivors were so cowed that seldom if ever again did they take part in intertribal war during the seventeenth century. Occasionally they joined the Sioux war parties against the Chippewa when the latter came down the Wisconsin, but never openly, being surrounded by Algic tribes. They acknowledged their kinship with the Sioux, calling themselves the "fisheating Dakota" or the "Trout Nation," but despite this kinship and a turbulent past, they kept on remarkably good terms with all the neighboring tribes, even through the wars of the Sioux, Sauk, Chippewa, and Foxes that later disturbed the region.

The Chippewa, the first tribe known to have inhabited the south shore of Lake Superior, have a traditional history indicating former residence as far east as the St. Lawrence River, and pos-

[6] See La Potherie, "Savage Peoples," in Blair, *Indian Tribes*, 1:292–293. This would indicate the Fox tribe and the circumstance mentioned in the previous chapter. There is a tradition among the Peninsula Indians, however, of a Winnebago-Potawatomi war in which the Winnebago were victorious, only to lose hundreds of their warriors in a pursuit such as La Potherie describes. See Holand, "St. Michael," in the *Peninsula Historical Review*, 2:50–55. George Fox, in the *Wisconsin Archaeologist*, 13:169, describes an identical misfortune which the Noquet suffered while attacking the same Potawatomi. The tale is apparently based upon fact, and it was probably the Winnebago that suffered. This tradition fits in with the appearance of the Potawatomi in flight at the Sault in 1641, and the decline of the Winnebago may have occasioned their return.

[7] La Potherie, "Savage Peoples," in Blair, *Indian Tribes*, 1:295–300; *Jesuit Relations*, 54:237; 55:183. It is noteworthy that Allouez, writing in 1670, thought that the incident had occurred about thirty years earlier, which seems to indicate that the dates and sequence mentioned above are approximately accurate.

sibly an early home on the Atlantic Ocean. According to this tradition, they moved westward in successive migrations, each of which was occasioned, as nearly as can be told, by a tribal disaster, such as pestilence or famine. Stays were made on the St. Lawrence near Montreal and on Lake Huron near Mackinac, and a final settlement was made near La Pointe, on Chequamegon Bay, where they seem to have arrived toward the close of the fifteenth century.[8] At the outlet of Lake Superior a division seems to have taken place, the Ottawa remaining in the vicinity, the Potawatomi moving south into Michigan, and the residual Chippewa splitting on Lake Superior, one group taking the north shore and the other the south shore, and a few remaining at Bow-e-ting (Sault Ste. Marie), "the place of the falls." Until about 1660 these were the only members of their tribe known to the French, who called them "Sauteurs," or "dwellers by the Sault." They were the nucleus of the great concourse of tribes that gathered there every season for the fishing, the whitefish being numerous there and easy to catch.

The first settlement and subsequent abandonment of La Pointe was one of the periodically recurring tragedies that drove the Chippewa constantly west, and one that is perhaps common among peoples who live by hunting. The story is that the medicine men got some subtle poison and killed anyone who opposed them. Cannibalism then appeared, and the people fell entirely into the clutches of the priestcraft, finally deserting the island in horror. Some, it is said, wandered back to Keweenaw and Sault Ste. Marie. The tradition is confusing, but it seems likely that a protracted period of starvation had resulted in cannibalism, and that to the survivors the place seemed accursed.[9]

[8] See Warren, "Ojibways," in *Minnesota Historical Collections*, vol. 5; Reuben G. Thwaites, "The Story of Chequamegon Bay," in *Wisconsin Historical Collections*, 13: 399; Peter Jones, *History of the Ojebway Indians* (London [1867]), 32; George Copway, *The Traditional History and Characteristic Sketches of the Ojibway Nation* (Boston, 1851), 31; Drake, *Indian Tribes*, 1:289; Hinsdale, *First People of Michigan*, 13. It is probably significant that one of the two religious divisions among them has a seashell as a symbol. The Crane clan possessed in 1885 a hieroglyphic copper plate marking eight generations since the arrival at La Pointe. A hat on one figure showed the coming of the white man. See Warren, *op. cit.*, 89–90.

[9] For Radisson and Groseilliers, see Kellogg, *French Régime*, 109. Radisson's chronology is at best confusing, but Miss Kellogg's theory is the most satisfactory of any so far advanced. Perrot's *Memoir* (Blair, *Indian Tribes*, 1:157–190) describes

Whatever the cause, the Chippewa had deserted their island in Chequamegon Bay before Radisson and Groseilliers arrived there, probably in the late autumn of 1658. The two traders built a fort and proceeded inland to meet the Ottawa, who were then at Lac Court Oreilles. These Ottawa were those who, with the Petuns, had fled from the fort at Mèchingan, in the Green Bay region, at least a year and a half before and, ascending the Mississippi, had pushed up one of its tributaries, leaving the Petuns some distance behind. Radisson and Groseilliers did not immediately return to Chequamegon, but visited a rendezvous with the Cree at the west end of the lake and returned via the villages of the Sioux, with whom they had opened up a trade. By the time they returned to Chequamegon the Ottawa had already arrived and had begun what was to be a more or less permanent fishing and trading settlement, at which a mission was to be maintained intermittently for over a decade. By the autumn of 1661 the Hurons of Black River had joined them.

Seven traders came to Chequamegon in 1660, bringing Father Ménard, the first white missionary in Wisconsin, with them as far as Keweenaw, where he was accidentally detained and spent a miserable winter. He arrived at Chequamegon the following spring. In July he was lost while attempting to reach the Hurons of Black River, who must even then have been preparing for their journey to Chequamegon, where he would have met them had he delayed another two months.[10] The traders were unable to return until 1663, but when they did so it was to find that in their absence an extensive Indian settlement had grown up on the shores of the Bay. It flourished as a result of the Iroquoian dispersions, the Hurons and Ottawa coming up from the south and other fugitives

the Petun-Ottawa wandering. It does not seem possible that the Chequamegon region was entirely unknown to white men in 1658. Radisson and Groseilliers had preknowledge of the Ottawa on Lac Court Oreilles; they had a rendenzvous with the Cree, and the Cree came readily to Chequamegon to trade with them. It is true that there are no written records, but early traders often tried to conceal trading locations from competitors. Further, Warren's traditional account of the first white men in the region does not at all agree with the circumstances of the Radisson-Groseilliers expedition, notwithstanding Thwaites's acceptance of the two accounts as practically identical. See *Wisconsin Historical Collections*, 13:401, 403.

[10] Kellogg, *French Régime*, 146–152, has a detailed and authoritative account of Ménard's journey and death. See also pages 114–117.

crowding in pell-mell along the Lake Superior shore from the east. Here they found refuge, good fishing, and the white man's trade, and the population mushroomed. The inhabitants kept up a connection with the people around the Sault, and according to Perrot it was they who, with other expatriates at Keweenaw, were responsible for a bloody defeat inflicted upon an Iroquois raiding party at Point Iroquois.

Allouez, the first permanent priest, found there in 1665 a polyglot population of most of the eastern Algonquins in addition to the Petun Hurons. He counted eight hundred warriors of seven nations, and was rapturous over the beauty of the place. Here came also the northern Illinois, who had been kind to the fleeing Hurons and Ottawa and perhaps were attracted to Chequamegon by them. The Illinois traded slaves to the Ottawa, and by 1669 were coming in great numbers for trade goods. In 1665 Allouez was pleased to have the opportunity to preach to one band of eighty Illinois men, but within five years there were more than fifty villages at the Bay. The population was transient rather than permanent, but it was steady.[11]

By spring of 1666 Allouez had begun to comprehend the difficulties facing the mission at Chequamegon. He reported that during the winter season the tribes led a miserable existence, having only fish for meat and living for weeks on moss and pounded bark. Further, the peace made with the Iroquois in 1666 was beginning to have its effect on the settlement, and it seemed that the population might prove to be only temporary, each tribe returning to its old habitat after the Iroquois danger was removed. It was rumored that the Iroquois were preparing an embassy to the Sault, and were really anxious for peace with the northern tribes. If that should happen, the end of the Chequamegon mission was in sight. Not many conversions had been made anyway, and Allouez was frankly discouraged. In 1668 Father Nicolas was sent to the mission, only to be replaced the next autumn by Marquette, the last priest to visit Chequamegon for a hundred and fifty years.[12]

[11] See Thwaites, "Chequamegon Bay," in *Wisconsin Historical Collections*, 13:405–406; *Jesuit Relations*, 45:235; 50:273 ff.; 51:49, 71; letter of Marquette, in the *Jesuit Relations*, 54:165, 177, 191, 197.
[12] *Jesuit Relations*, 50:213; 51:71; 52:201.

Even while Allouez was spending his two short days of vacation at Quebec, events were shaping in the Northwest that were to make fruitless all further effort on behalf of the mission by completely dispersing the peoples of the settlement. The Hurons and Ottawa, while still on the Mississippi, had made the acquaintance of the Sioux, who, supposing them to be superior beings because of their equipment, and desiring trade goods above all else, had treated them well and even venerated them, thereby earning the contempt of the more sophisticated Hurons and Ottawa. These worthies, as was their wont, returned nothing but evil for all the good they had of the Sioux, and eventually provoked the anger of these formidable adversaries. It was the incursions of the Sioux that forced the Ottawa up the Black River and finally to Chequamegon, where they were later joined by the Hurons.[13] Five years later a friendly contact was made and trade was resumed, but in 1670 a new treachery, at the bottom of which were the Sinago Ottawa, filled the Chequamegon towns with apprehension. The people fled to Mackinac, arriving there shortly after St. Lusson had concluded a ceremony in which he formally took possession of all the country in the name of France. The peace made with the Iroquois and their moderate attitude toward the northern tribes who would trade with them undoubtedly made it much easier for them to leave Chequamegon, a move that had been prophesied by Allouez three years before. The exodus foreseen by him took place, and the ill-fated settlement was ended. Marquette, released from an unsuccessful mission, was enabled to begin his exploration of the Mississippi and the Illinois country.

The Sioux, who are here met for the first time, little deserve the name "the Iroquois of the west" given them by Burpee[14] unless praise of the Iroquois is intended, for they were the mildest mannered, the most thoroughly honorable, and the gentlest people of this period and region, and perhaps in the whole of North America. If one may believe Perrot, they were scurvily treated

---

[13] Perrot, *Memoir*, in Blair, *Indian Tribes*, 159–166.

[14] See Burpee, *Journals and Letters of Vérendrye*, 332n. Burpee got this name from the *Jesuit Relations*, but instead of qualifying it by explanation, he added "the Ishmaelites of the prairie," which is quite misleading. See the *Jesuit Relations*, 54:191; 55:169.

throughout by their enemies, and he had the advantage of knowing both them and their enemies very well. Not only were they friendly to strangers, but they never tortured their prisoners of war by fire until their enemies had treated them so, and they often released them, continually attempting negotiation. Marquette said of them that they never attacked until they were themselves attacked, and that they kept their word inviolate. But for all their gentleness, they were brave warriors. They found themselves constantly at odds with the comparatively fierce and bloodthirsty Lakes tribes, as well as with the Cree and Assiniboins of the West. Their last peace embassy to the Lakes peoples, one of ten deputies, was brutally massacred at the Sault in 1673. They never made war in the East, for by that time an age-long struggle for possession of the rice lakes had begun with the Chippewa, a war which was to last well into the nineteenth century. By 1675 they were embroiled with both the Foxes and the Illinois, and were not allowed to remain at peace until 1890, when the whites subdued their last uprising. With the beginning of the Sioux wars, intertribal relations in northern Wisconsin assumed what was to become a chronic condition, which none of the French traders, not even Perrot nor Duluth, could bring to an end, much as they desired it. The struggle remained Western, however, the Lakes peoples, except the Chippewa, being little concerned before the end of the century.[15]

Lower Wisconsin and the Great Migration

In occupying the place prepared for them by the fall of the Winnebago nation, the fugitives from Michigan came upon a veritable paradise, for it was above all others a region capable of receiving and supporting great numbers of people. Corn grew luxuriantly, and throughout the region the wild rice was abundant. There were deer at all times, and bear and beaver could be taken in the winter, to say nothing of the wild fowl, which were so numerous that they could be caught in nets. And should the game fail, there were sturgeon in the lake and great schools of herring in

[15] Perrot, *Memoir*, in Blair, *Indian Tribes*, 1:169; *Jesuit Relations*, 54:191, 193; 58: 257–263.

the falls; fishery alone, said La Potherie, was sufficient to maintain large villages. So the villages on Green Bay and along the Fox River grew apace, and there was little quarreling among the tribes. They were obliged to be peaceful, remarked Radisson, "considering the enemy of theirs that came like a thunderbolt upon them, so that they joyned with them (neighbors) to forget what was past for their own preservation."[16]

The great Fox River settlement grew by leaps and bounds as the expatriated and roving tribes gathered there more and more permanently for the trade. In 1670 Dablon estimated it at three thousand inhabitants, and by 1672 it held over six thousand Mascouten, Kickapoo, Miami, Illinois proper, and Wea (a Miami tribe). As early as 1672 starvation in the winter had begun to prove that the immediate region was overpopulated.[17]

The Foxes, already beginning to deserve the reputation they were to bear in the next century, were scattered through the region, sometimes in smaller villages, which gave observers the impression that they were not very numerous, and sometimes in great towns of as many as a thousand warriors. They were already hostile to the French, whom they killed, it was said, because they hated their beards. They tolerated the Sauk, and were intermittently friendly with the Miami, but seemingly had no other friends. They were at war even with the Sioux, whom they had met while they were allies of the Ottawa during an ill-fated expedition to the Chequamegon region in 1671. Their war with the Sioux was an inconsequential and indecisive dispute having no real motive, and defeats and victories were small affairs which practically balanced one another. A wandering band of Iroquois struck a Fox village in March, 1669, and nearly wiped it out, but the Foxes chose to offer no reprisals, not even joining the Illinois in their war against the Iroquois a decade later. They remained unruly and self-sufficient, asking no favors and receiving none, and taking no part in intertribal affairs.[18]

---

[16] *Wisconsin Historical Collections*, 16:9–10; Radisson, *Voyages*, 147.

[17] *Jesuit Relations*, 55:199–201; 58:23, 63, 293. The starvation was particularly severe among the Miami.

[18] *Ibid.*, 51:43, 45; 54:205–207, 219, 227; 55:219–221; 58:65–67. The Iroquois incursion is probably the one mentioned by Perrot in his *Memoir*. See Blair, *Indian*

The Mascouten lived with the Miami in a huge town on the upper Fox River, south of the present site of Berlin, Wisconsin; Allouez complained that "if the country of this Nation somewhat resembles an earthly Paradise in beauty, the way leading to it may also be said to bear some likeness to the one depicted by our Lord as leading to heaven." Dreuillettes numbered them at thirty villages, but his information probably came from Radisson and is none too accurate. This association of Miami and Mascouten continued, and about 1672 the near-by Kickapoo joined them.[19]

The Potawatomi, "scattered right and left along the Mecheygan" (the Lake Michigan shore), were the traders and purveyors of French goods for the region. According to contemporary accounts, they were intelligent, affable, and courteous. They were friendly with the lower Wisconsin tribes and acted as arbiters in intertribal disputes, being anxious, as were all traders, that no trouble should interfere with their commerce. Allouez, for some reason, described them as warlike, but if they were, they never demonstrated it in the region in which they lived, and no other contemporary observer ever heard of their going to war. They even traded with the Illinois far to the south, and continued to do so after they moved to the St. Joseph River in later years. Because of their wandering it is impossible to number them even approximately, their towns changing too swiftly in both size and location.[20] The largest single village appears to have remained for some time on Washington Island, but another permanent settlement on

Tribes, 1:227. The Seneca gave La Salle a curious bit of misinformation at this time, telling him (as La Salle understood it) that the Foxes and Mascouten were far down the Ohio River. See Rene de Bréhant Galinée, "Narrative of the Most Noteworthy Incidents in the Journey of Messieurs Dollier and Galinée, 1669–1670," in Kellogg, Early Narratives, 170–171. The Seneca probably did not intend to deceive, but were simply mistaken, having no contact with these tribes. The remark has been taken as authoritative by historians and has led to great confusion with respect to the location of the Foxes. La Salle found a Fox village as far away as the Illinois River a decade later, but even this was merely a small hunting camp. The Seneca were speaking of a probability, not factual knowledge.

[19] Jesuit Relations, 55:191. The passage of the lower Fox was very difficult because of rapids and sharp stones. See Radisson, Voyages, 148; Marquette, in the Jesuit Relations, 59:101.

[20] Perrot, Memoir, in Blair, Indian Tribes, 1:301–303; Jesuit Relations, 51:27; 59: 165, 173–179; 66:285. The same town was reduced from three thousand to half that number in nine years. Compare the Relations, 44:245, and 51:27. The first figure is, however, open to question.

the Milwaukee River was also of considerable importance. Holand locates five separate villages of Potawatomi in the Green Bay vicinity alone, but it is possible that there is a great amount of duplication.[21]

The Miami, whose advent greatly swelled the population of southern Wisconsin, may not have been entirely unfamiliar with the region before they came. Miss Kellogg thinks that they had lived near the southern end of Lake Michigan before, and had moved or been driven west across the Mississippi River, possibly by the Iroquois. La Salle said they had been so driven, but he did not quote the Miami as saying so, and was probably following the French account. The sources available, which are very complete for the Iroquois, do not mention a conflict between the Iroquois and any of the Illinois tribes that would have dispersed them. In fact, only one affray is mentioned, and that resulted in the overwhelming defeat of the Iroquois.[22] The earliest mention of them is by Dreuillettes, who located them about sixty leagues from his newly conceived Potawatomi mission at St. Michael. He did not mention in what direction it lay, and Thwaites for some reason measured the sixty leagues eastward across Lake Michigan, placing them in southwestern Michigan. Perrot supports Dreuillettes as to the distance, but places them sixty leagues *west* of Green Bay, which is at least believable. Marquette had heard of them at Chequamegon in 1670, and located them vaguely somewhere between Chequamegon and the Illinois towns west of the Mississippi. If we put these conclusions together, their location seems to have been in northeastern Iowa or southeastern Minnesota.[23]

[21] La Salle, *Relation*, 43, 49–55; Holand, "St. Michael," in the *Peninsula Historical Review*, 2:44.

[22] For Miss Kellogg's opinion see Charlevoix, *Journal*, 1:269n. An argument for this view, and perhaps the only one, is that the Miami, moving east after the Iroquois peace, seemed to be returning to a familiar country. They never said so, and the belief can be nothing but an assumption.

[23] La Salle, *Relation*, 191; Perrot, *Memoir*, in Blair, *Indian Tribes*, 1:154–157, 245; *Jesuit Relations*, 44:247, 324; 54:185. A Jesuit mission began with its conception, not its establishment. Dreuillettes, according to this curious custom, began the Potawatomi mission when he himself was on the Saguenay. A possible reason for Thwaites's notion as to their location may be that La Salle always knew the St. Joseph River in Michigan as "the river of the Myamis," for they were there when he came.

By the decade of the 1670's the Miami were moving east in great numbers, gathering on the Fox River and trading at Green Bay. One theory of this migration is that they were driven from their former home by wars with the Sioux, but there is no evidence to support it. Neither Sioux nor Miami, then or in later years, mentioned such a clash, and it seems clear that the trade of the Bay, plus the deliberate efforts of the priests to attract them to the mission, are the real reasons for their movement. Dreuillettes, following Radisson, gave them eight thousand warriors, "or more than 24,000 souls," and Perrot estimated that their settlement numbered from four to five thousand warriors. This great migration, added to the already considerable numbers gathered in southern Wisconsin, overtaxed the food supply, and in 1672–73 there was starvation in the Miami villages. Being the later comers and not yet stabilized, the Miami were the first to move out, traveling through northern Illinois and around the tip of Lake Michigan and settling on the St. Joseph River between 1674 and 1679. They took an active part in the Iroquois wars of the next decade, and by fortuitous circumstance and shrewd diplomacy barely escaped destruction at the hands of the Five Nations in that struggle in the west.[24]

The end of the third quarter of the seventeenth century is a convenient place at which to leave the Wisconsin tribes. It was an unsettled, though not a turbulent quarter century, which opened with the inrush of countless dispersed people from Michigan and closed with the beginning of a movement back toward the homeland, a movement which was never completed. Two factors probably contributed to the outward migration, the insufficient food supply and the temporary decline and diversion of the military power of the Iroquois. About 1662 defeat and disease began to stalk the hitherto fortunate Five Nations, and they were forced to a peace, following an invasion of the Mohawk country by the French in 1666. The plague, long delayed, began to take its toll of their strength, and they found themselves challenged in another

[24] *Jesuit Relations*, 44:247, 324; 55:199–201; 58:23ff., 41, 63; La Salle, *Relation*, 193; Perrot, *Memoir*, in Blair, *Indian Tribes*, 1:223. The starvation of the Miami was intensified by the fact that they had no snowshoes, and winter hunting was therefore difficult for them.

essentially commercial war by the powerful and aggressive Susquehannah nation to the south. The Iroquois had neither the resources nor the inclination for more than one war at a time, and until about 1680 were content to let the Western tribes go in peace wherever they would. So a hesitant outward movement began, the Miami marching east to the St. Joseph, and the other tribes edging south along the tributaries of the Illinois.

In the north the Lake Superior shore was virtually clear except for roving bands of various nations, and the ubiquitous Ottawa kept a monopoly of the trade. The small Menominee tribe remained on their river, and except for occasional forays of eastern parties against the Sioux the region was peaceful.

X. THE SUSQUEHANNAH WAR

As WE HAVE SEEN, the peace of 1653 proved to be of little value to the Iroquois. The Hurons were dispersed, but the trade of the far nations of the upper Lakes, which should have come to and through the Iroquois, was as remote as ever, for the Ottawa, admirably fitted for it by their long apprenticeship to the Hurons, merely licked up the trade where the Hurons dropped it, and despite the efforts of other Lakes peoples to break the monopoly, held it steadily. The Iroquois expeditions to the north and west fared none too well, and by the time they had finished with the Neutrals and the Erie, the great trading fleet of 1654 and another following it in 1656 showed them all too clearly what was to be the fate of the trade for which they had hoped.

Casting about for a means whereby to injure or influence their enemies, they found one ready to hand in the Jesuit settlement at Onondaga, which by 1656 was fairly well established. The original offer of the Iroquois to permit the mission and their later active desire for it seem to have been in perfectly good faith. At any rate, the Jesuits, who were far from ingenuous men, particularly when dealing with the Iroquois, whom they had every reason to distrust, believed that the Iroquois desire for peace and for a mission was genuine. And for this conclusion they had ample evidence. The competition beween Mohawks and Onondaga over the location of the mission was very keen, the Mohawks even uttering a scarcely veiled threat to the French in their plea. Styling the Mohawk tribe the eastern door of the Long House, a Mohawk spokesman said: "Will you not enter the cabin by the door . . . ? It is with us . . . that you should begin; whereas you, by beginning with the Onnontaehronnons, try to enter by the roof and through the chimney. Have you no fear that the smoke may blind you, our fire not being extinguished, and that you may fall from the top to the bottom?"[1]

The Mohawk and Onondaga tribesmen even came to battle over the matter; several men were killed, and the smouldering emnity between the Mohawks and the upper Iroquois was fanned anew. One of the Jesuits, viewing the whole situation, drew the very sound conclusion that:

> True though it be that the Iroquois are subtle, adroit, and arrant knaves, yet I cannot persuade myself that they possess so much intelligence and address, and are such great politicians, as to employ . . . the subterfuges and intrigues imputed to them. . . .
>   . . . The two sides [Mohawk and Onondaga] fought with each other until the ground was stained with blood and murder. Some believe that all this was a mere feint to mask their game the better; but, it seems to me, the game is hardly a pleasant one in which bloodshed and human lives are involved, and I greatly doubt whether Iroquois policy can go so far, and whether Barbarians, who have little dependence on one another, can so long conceal their intrigues.[2]

While Iroquois political skill can scarcely be overestimated, the priest was quite right in believing that aboriginal political policy was never so subtle as to include fatal conflict between tribes, particularly between Mohawks and Onondaga, as part of a deception.

In 1656 a body of intrepid priests and brothers entered Iroquoia. Chaumonot went to the Seneca, Ménard to the Cayuga, Le Moine to the Mohawks. Fremin undertook a roving mission among the upper Iroquois, and Dablon, Le Mercier, and Brothers Brouet and Bourier remained at the headquarters among the Onondaga. The next year Ragueneau joined the Onondaga group, and occasional recruits increased the French population there to about sixty men. Great hopes and greater memories were built into the insubstantial walls of the modest mission house and chapel. At last there was a mission among the Iroquois; should it win, the old horizons of a decade before might be visible, for both the church and New France. They were in the country where Jogues

---

[1] *Jesuit Relations*, 41:87.   [2] *Ibid.*, 44:149–151.

had suffered mutilation and death; they were among the slayers of Garreau, Garnier, Daniel, and the great-hearted Brébeuf and Gabriel Lalemant. Perhaps in memory of these men, and perhaps in hope for the future, they named the mission Ste. Marie for that other Ste. Marie on the Wye, from which Ragueneau had watched the dissolution of the mission in Huronia, and which he had fired with his own hand. They could not have suspected that even as they built it, its doom was being prepared among the Mohawks.

The Mohawks, always envious of the mission headquarters among the Onondaga, had a *casus belli* against the mission that appealed to more than them. That the peace was a failure could now be plainly seen, for they were getting none of the trade, and in this mission and its inhabitants was a means by which they could almost work their will upon New France. The Onondaga were let into the plot, though they did not originate it, and it was planned to seize the French as hostages and by threat of torture by fire to obtain such terms as they wanted at Quebec. A formal declaration of war had already been made by the intractable Oneida, and it seemed the part of wisdom to strike before the summer brought news to the small French garrison.[3]

The white men, however, having bribed a councilor, were as well informed as the Iroquois, and after building a boat secretly within the mission house, a work of almost indescribable difficulty, they escaped by an amazing subterfuge near midnight of March 20, and after extreme hardship won through to Montreal. So ended the mission to Iroquoia, and so ended, formally, the peace of 1653, which, considering what the Iroquois had expected from it, never had a chance to become permanent.[4] The war was on

[3] Radisson gives the "lower Iroquois" credit for the plot, and Ragueneau blames the Mohawks and Oneida. Radisson, *Voyages*, 123; *Jesuit Relations*, 43:155–157.

[4] The full story of the escape is found in Radisson, *Voyages*, 123–134; Ragueneau's briefer account is in the *Jesuit Relations*, 43:155–157. After the evacuation of the mission, critics pointed out again and again that it should never have been begun, and united in proclaiming the inveterate treachery and fundamental rascality of the Iroquois, without mentioning, and probably without realizing, that their position and their relation to the French was utterly different in 1658 from what it had been when the mission was planned. But the critics spoke long and loudly, and the Jesuits were hardly in a position, after the failure of the mission, to argue the matter. Thus the issues were too deeply buried to catch the attention of the casual investigator or annalist.

again. Fortified by a new treaty with the Dutch, the Iroquois closed the Ottawa with an almost impenetrable blockade and closely besieged Montreal. "They come like foxes," wrote a Jesuit chronicler. "They attack like lions . . . They take flight like birds."[5]

All was not well with the Five Nations, however, and by the end of 1662 they seem to have fallen upon evil days, and to have met all possible misfortunes. First, a large war party in the north country had been attacked and utterly destroyed by a coalition of the northern tribes, which had gathered from as far west as Chequamegon. Secondly, the plague, in a long-delayed visitation of their towns, struck them heavily in 1662, carrying off many hundreds. The number who died is not known, but an idea of the fatalities may be gained from the fact that some captive Frenchmen baptized three hundred dying infants. Lalemant, when he heard of it in Quebec, rejoiced at this "abundant harvest for Eternity." A third trouble to perplex the Iroquois was that the Susquehannah, a powerful Iroquoian tribe to the south of them and late allies of the Hurons, were moving up and assaulting Iroquois towns and trade. "We doubt not," Lalemant added, "it is a stroke of Heaven that has, very seasonably . . . roused up in our behalf the Andastogueronnons . . . ever held in dread by the upper Iroquois." Fourth, the Algonquin tribes of the northeast were invading and killing many, and the defense of the Long Sault by Dollard and seventeen heroic Frenchmen had shown them the quality of opposition they had to face when the French actually went out to battle.[6]

In thus weakened a condition the Iroquois could hardly hope to deal with so formidable a foe as the Susquehannah; ringed about by enemies as they were, it seemed the part of wisdom to divide them, at least temporarily, to get a breathing space. The Seneca then tried for a French peace in 1663 in order to make head-

[5] Van Laer, *Court Minutes*, 211–219; *New York Colonial Documents*, 13:108–114; *Jesuit Relations*, 45:185–197; Radisson, *Voyages*, 159–172, 175–187; Sulte, "Les Coureurs des bois," in Royal Society of Canada, *Proceedings and Transactions*, 3d series, vol. 5, sec. 1, p. 252.

[6] Perrot, *Memoir*, in Blair, *Indian Tribes*, 1:178; *Jesuit Relations*, 48:75–77, 83, 107; J. B. to Jeremias van Rensselaer, in *Van Rensselaer Correspondence*, 332, 332n.

way against the Susquehannah, whom they described as a "re-doubtable enemy." The French had had enough of partial peace treaties with the Iroquois and were, moreover, of no mind to help them in an extremity.[7] Instead they imported the famous regiment of Carignan-Salières to attempt what had never before been attempted, an organized and purposeful invasion of Iroquois territory by the military. Two expeditions by Tracy and Courcelles in 1666 brought the Iroquois in, and by 1667, after innumerable embassies, a general peace was concluded. The French were well aware that the Seneca and Cayuga, at least, desired peace only to allow them to devote their energies to the Susquehannah, and knew that any peace between them and the Iroquois would be of short duration. They therefore coolly prepared to fracture the peace themselves, should a favorable opportunity present itself.[8]

Talon, the great intendant, presented a plan to Tracy and Courcelles for making war upon the Iroquois despite the peace, which was to be broken at the first advantageous moment. He admitted that his plan if followed might prevent maintenance of any peace made in the future, but added, with that instinct for realities which made him so great an administrator, that "between us and them there is no more good faith than between the most ferocious animals."[9]

The plan had the approval of Colbert, but by the next year it appeared inexpedient to Talon, who forthwith abandoned it. The Iroquois, however, kept the peace much better than had been expected. They were of course short of furs, but they fraternized with the Nipissings on the lower Ottawa and sent an ambassador to the Algonquins to try to make a settlement. They made a formal and final peace with the long-harassed Mahicans, with whom

---

[7] *Jesuit Relations*, 49:141. "The Iroquois . . . will . . . never ask peace from us unless he has some great scheme in his head, or is driven to it by some very pressing reason." *Ibid.*, 137–139. See also pages 143–145.

[8] On the expeditions see Perrot, *Memoir*, in Blair, *Indian Tribes*, 1:199–203; and *New York Colonial Documents*, 3:118–119, 126; 9:46, 86; on the peace, *ibid.*, 3:67, 121, 125; 9:45–47; *Jesuit Relations*, 52:197; 53:39–55; and Perrot, in Blair, *Indian Tribes*, 1:219–220.

[9] *New York Colonial Documents*, 9:52–54, 66.

they had warred for forty years, and were at last ready for a decisive blow at the Susquehannah.[10]

In the brilliant and resourceful Talon the Iroquois had a formidable antagonist, and it was through no fault or scruple of his that the French policy was no more successful than it was. Perennially handicapped by lack of funds and the maddening division of authority characteristic of French colonial administration, he was perhaps the first administrative officer in New France to realize that the policy of the Iroquois represented more than savage passion; that in dealing with them he was dealing with shrewd and penetrating diplomats, who did not indulge in meaningless gestures and who did not make war without a purpose. He wrote to Colbert:

It is well known that the Iroquois nations, especially the four upper ones, do not hunt any Beaver or Elk. They absolutely exhausted the side of Ontario which they inhabit, that is, the South side, *a long time ago* [*italics mine*], so that they experience the greatest difficulty in finding a single beaver there . . . The Iroquois, however, trade scarcely any with us.[11]

As if in echo of Talon, Nouvel wrote from Sault Ste. Marie, after observing an Iroquois embassy:

These presents say that the iroquois obey Onnontio as their common father; and that thus they have only gifts of peace, and are to love each other as brothers. There is no doubt that they are only using this bait either for the sake of their commerce with the outaouacs, at the solicitation of the dutch, or to beguile them.[12]

With the French thoroughly awake at last to the economic consequence of a true peace with the Iroquois, they could hardly be expected to take great pains to maintain it, and they did not. While such men as Allouez and Jolliet were releasing Iroquois prisoners

[10] *Ibid.*, 9:60, 70; Perrot, *Memoir*, in Blair, *Indian Tribes*, 1:210–211; *Jesuit Relations*, 56:43; *Van Rensselaer Correspondence*, 413–419.

[11] *New York Colonial Documents*, 9:80. It will be recalled that the present writer set 1640 as the beginning of this shortage, and has contended throughout that trade was the dominant motive in the Huron dispersions. It is curious that historians have so consistently overlooked the words of even Talon, whose views deserved, then and later, a better hearing.

[12] *Jesuit Relations*, 57:24–25. The "dutch" he mentions are the traders, the English having occupied New Amsterdam.

in the north and west and striving to keep the peace intact, brutal murders by French soldiers and traders kept the Five Nations enraged, and the peace dragged to an indeterminate end between 1675 and 1680, with the looting of the canoes of La Salle and the assault upon the Illinois.[13]

The peace of 1666–67 had been received in New York with mixed feelings. The English administration was not yet expansionist, and had even encouraged the Mohawks to join the peace. The Dutch traders, however, saw blood on the moon, and painted a terrible picture of the consequences of a diversion of the fur trade. Both the Dutch trader and the English administrator were extremely anxious for the preservation of their own alliance with the Mohawks. Professor Doyle thinks that the Mohawk alliance was what the Afghan alliance was in later days to England and Russia, and his verdict does not seem an exaggeration.[14]

The Susquehannah War

The Susquehannah were an Iroquoian people who had apparently split off from the southern wing of the Iroquoian migration into New York, following the Susquehannah Valley southeast and locating their chief town, Andastoé or Andastogue, not far above the headwaters of Chesapeake Bay. They were known to the Hurons as "Andastoguehronnons," which the French shortened to "Andastes" or "Andastogues"; to the Dutch as "Minquas" or "White Minquas"; and to the English as "Conestogas" and as "Susquehannahs," the name most familiar to Americans. As previously related, the Iroquois-Susquehannah quarrel originated when the Iroquois, harried by the Algonquins in the sixteenth century, retreated southward upon the Susquehannah, perhaps even trying to occupy Pennsylvania. Like all intertribal

[13] Kellogg, *Early Narratives*, 191–192; Perrot, *Memoir*, in Blair, *Indian Tribes*, 1:204–210. French culprits were punished when caught, but the fear of peace, among the traders, was greater than the fear of war, and they were unruly. The verdict of De Belmont that it was *une paix profonde* is quite without justification. *Histoire du Canada*, 33.

[14] See Arthur Buffinton, "The Policy of Albany and English Westward Expansion," in the *Mississippi Valley Historical Review*, 8:327–366 (1922). The author shows conclusively that the expansionist policy began with Governor Dongan. See also the Commissioners of Albany to Tracy, in *New York Colonial Documents*, 3:134; Stuyvesant to the Duke of York, October, 1667, *ibid.;* 164; and Doyle, *Middle Colonies*, 122.

conflicts of the time, the war, if so it may be called, was not national in scope but was limited to individual and largely purposeless raids. The Susquehannah had once raised a considerable force at the instigation of a white man, Étienne Brulé, in aid of the Hurons with Champlain, but they never did so on their own initiative until a national motive made the quarrel a national war. They maintained a close alliance with the Hurons, and cooperated with them in involved negotiations in an attempt to stay their dispersion, but did not go so far as to raise a single hatchet in their defense. When Iroquois conquest came nearer home in the dispersion of the Neutral nation, the Susquehannah are said to to have leagued with the Neutrals to inflict one defeat upon the Seneca, but so far as is known this battle, if it occurred at all, represented their only anti-Iroquois adventure for nearly half a century.[15]

If it is true that in this period and in this region the fur trade was the most important feature of Indian economy, and if it is true that significant intertribal conflicts have an economic basis, we should expect to find the Susquehannah war connected with the fur trade. As the fur country of the Susquehannah became exhausted, they might be expected to have moved, as had the Iroquois, in order to divert or intercept the fur trade of other nations, more especially that of the Iroquois, through whose country led the most lucrative, as well as the most vulnerable, trade route open to their attack. If the thesis continues to be applicable, we should also find that there had been a shift of emphasis in the Susquehannah-Iroquois enmity from the eastern cantons of Iroquois to the western, for the Mohawk and Onondaga were too far east to offer to the Susquehannah an extended trade route vulnerable to attack and blockade, as the Ottawa River route of the Hurons had been vulnerable to the Iroquois. It will be remembered that the original Susquehannah-Iroquois quarrel had been confined to the Mohawks and the Onondaga, the "Massawomecks" being the "invaders" mentioned by Smith, and the Onondaga being the canton against which the force raised by Brulé was directed. The

[15] There was mention of this battle in the *Journal des Jésuites* for April, 1652 (*Jesuit Relations*, 38:97), and it was said that the Seneca had been forced to remove their women to the near-by country of the Cayuga, but no more was heard of it.

shift of emphasis that might reasonably be expected would have directed the Susquehannah efforts against the western cantons, the Seneca and the Cayuga. This shift of emphasis actually did occur, and it happens that the economic motive is recorded.

To at least one of the Jesuits, probably Lalemant, the motive for the war was no mystery in 1661:

The Sonnontouaeronnons [*Seneca*] who carry their beaver-skins to the Dutch with great inconvenience and by long and perilous routes—the Andastogueronnons [*Susquehannah*] laying ambuscades for them at every step, and forcing them at present to form caravans of six hundred men when they go to do their trading—these people I say will be glad to be spared all those difficulties and to avoid all those dangers . . . [16]

Lalemant was right in ascribing the motive for the Seneca's offer of peace to a commercial difficulty no longer supportable. The Iroquois blockade of the Ottawa had ceased to be unique in intertribal tactics; the same motive that had impelled the Iroquois for two decades now brought upon them in turn, and in the same manner, a blockade of their own commerce. One might expect that the Mohawks would not have been particularly interested in war upon the Susquehannah, for the commercial difficulties of the Susquehannah concerned them no more than their own commercial difficulties for many years had concerned the western cantons. Such indifference was actually the attitude of the Mohawks. Governor Andros wrote to the governor of Maryland that they not only were willing to make peace with the Susquehannah but had never actually warred upon them, "though I find still the Sinneques wholly adverse to it [*peace*]," he continued, "desiring their Extirpaçon."[17] The motive for the war and the setting for it now become clear; the Seneca found the Susquehannah blockade so effective that it required nearly the whole strength of their tribe to fight through to the trade; and the eastern tribes, particularly the Mohawks, cared not a whit for the fate of the Seneca so long as their own commerce was unmolested. The Mohawks would continue to operate on the Ottawa and the St. Lawrence, and the Seneca could find their own way out of their difficulties.

[16] *Jesuit Relations*, 47:III.
[17] *New York Colonial Documents*, 13:491.

It was for that reason that the expeditions of Courcelles and Tracy were sent solely against the Mohawk towns.[18]

It might be expected that the Cayuga, satellites of the Seneca, would be their allies in the coming war, and that the Susquehannah invasions would fall upon them, as the weaker of the two tribes. This at any rate was the Susquehannah strategy, and by 1667 many of the Cayuga were driven in retreat clear across Lake Ontario, a separate mission being established among them by the Sulpicians. The Susquehannah had allies in the Shawnee, who make their first appearance here, and in the "Black Minquas," who, as has been suggested, were probably the remnant of the old Erie nation.[19]

In this war, soon to begin in earnest, the colonies of Maryland and Delaware took an active interest. The Swedes supplied the Susquehannah with cannon and small arms and instructed them in their use, and the English of Maryland sent fifty men to help garrison the Susquehannah fort, which it was expected would be attacked. The smallpox had descended upon the Susquehannah for the first time, and they were none too confident, going as far as the colony of New York in search of aid. The expected invasion of 1662 did not materialize, but in April of 1663 eight hundred Seneca left their country, confident of putting an end to the Susquehannah peril. In late May the English agent at Altona wrote to Stuyvesant in fright to say that sixteen hundred Seneca were but two days march from the Susquenhannah fort, and that they were in almost hourly expectation of attack. The sixteen hundred turned out to be only the eight hundred recorded by Lalemant, and

[18] The Onondaga laughed at the Mohawks in their extremity and refused them aid or comfort when they were starving as a result of the destruction of their corn. Perrot, *Memoir,* in Blair, *Indian Tribes,* 1:203.

[19] On the Cayuga see the *Jesuit Relations,* 50:326; 51:257, 290; Le Clercq, *Establishment of the Faith,* 2:64; La Salle, *Relation,* II; Charles Hawley, *Early Chapters of Cayuga History* (Auburn, New York, 1879), 83–99. On the Shawnee see Charlevoix, *New France,* 3:174; Gallatin, "Indian Tribes of North America," in American Antiquarian Society, *Transactions and Collections,* 2:73. Gallatin should be taken with reservations, for he has the Miami allied with the Susquehannah, which is impossible. The Shawnee alliance is partially confirmed in the *Jesuit Relations,* 47:145–147. On the Minquas see *New York Colonial Documents,* 12:419. They were expecting eight hundred "Black Minquas" to aid them, of whom two hundred had arrived. Beeckman to Stuyvesant, December 23, 1662, *loc. cit.*

they attempted to take the fort by strategy, finding it apparently impregnable to assault, with bastions and cannon. Twenty-five Iroquois sent in as deputies were seized and burned by the Susquehannah within sight of the Iroquois army, upon scaffolds especially erected for that purpose, and the Seneca retreated, pursued for two days by the Susquehannah and their allies.[20]

During the next few years the Seneca confined themselves to small raids into Susquehannah territory while attempting continually to arrange the peace with the French. Meanwhile many of the hapless Cayuga were forced across Lake Ontario, and even the Onondaga felt constrained to take some part in the war. The continual raids of the Seneca prompted Colonel Coursey of Maryland to undertake an unsuccessful mission to Albany for the purpose of persuading them to desist. He found it difficult to make much of an impression upon the Iroquois, for his own colony of Maryland had been of considerable aid to the Susquehanna—of so much aid, in fact, that the Iroquois deputies were unimpressed by his protestations of good will and peace, and the raids continued as before. The Susquehannah were annoyed but not kept at home by these small expeditions, which the Seneca probably continued only to forestall invasion. The Susquehannah were ranging wide, being accounted as a great danger by the Iroquois on both the Ohio River and Lake Ontario. To make a living and defend themselves at the same time, the Seneca found it necessary to divide all the available men into two bands, one of which went to war while the other went to the beaver hunt.[21]

[20] See the end of Chapter II for detailed reference to the firearms in the Susquehannah fort; confirmed in the *Jesuit Relations*, 48:77. See also Hazard, *Annals of Pennsylvania*, 326, quoting the *Albany Records*, 17:118; Israel Acrelius, "New Sweden," in *New York Historical Collections*, 2d series, 1:424, 429; *New York Colonial Documents*, 12:419; letter from Altona, in Hazard, *op. cit.* 346–347. In Hazard, *op. cit.*, 347, and the *Jesuit Relations*, 47:77–79, are accounts of the short siege of the Susquehannah fort, of which the Jesuit account is the more detailed. Parkman contradicts one page in Hazard, saying, "The story in Hazard's *Annals of Pennsylvania* that a hundred of them beat off sixteen hundred Senecas is disproved by the fact that the Senecas in their best estate never had so many warriors." See his *Jesuits in North America*, 34n. Apparently Parkman overlooked the fact that the number sixteen hundred was only a report, which was corrected on the next page, and that the "one hundred" were not Susquehannah at all, but their allies.

[21] Acrelius, "New Sweden," in *New York Historical Collections*, 2d series, 1:424; Charlevoix, *New France*, 2:134; *Jesuit Relations*, 51:257; Colden, *Five Nations of*

By 1673 the war had taken a somewhat different turn, and a decisive result, one way or another, was imminent. The Iroquois had composed their differences with the eastern tribes, and their repeated embassies to the upper Lakes had met with such success that Nouvel wrote to Frontenac that the Iroquois no longer had any enemies save the Susquehannah. The Iroquois had sent many embassies to the upper Lakes with presents, "to confirm, they say, The Peace that Onnontio made,—but rather to get their peltries." Had the suspicious Nouvel only known it, the Iroquois were for once, perhaps, as anxious for peace as for furs: the time was approaching when they must meet and deal with the menace of the Susquehannah. The unfortunate Cayuga were again invaded, and a Seneca party going to their aid was cut to pieces by the Susquehannah. "God help them," wrote the Jesuit chronicler of the Susquehannah as memories of Brébeuf and Gabriel Lalemant guided his pen.[22]

It now became evident that whatever the solution of the problems of the Iroquois was to be, they must find it alone, for Frontenac, the governor of Canada, refused to help them, badly as he needed their alliance. The Seneca complained to him that alone they could not hope to defeat the Susquehannah, who were superior to them in men, canoes, and forts, but Frontenac was evasive, promising them only that he would not see them oppressed. Meanwhile the Maryland legislature levied "5,000 pounds of tobacco for the purpose of furnishing and providing for powder for the use of the Susquehannahs and for their defense." The vengeful Cayuga caught three Susquehannah and burned them joyfully, but up to 1675 the only Iroquois triumphs had been minor ones, and they found their only satisfaction in burning captives, for they had achieved no military success.[23]

In 1675 the Susquehannah nation was destroyed, a large part

Canada, 1:23–24. From this point on, Colden is reliable, having his sources at hand. See also *New York Colonial Documents*, 3:172; Galinée, "Narrative," in Kellogg, *Early Narratives*, 187, and in Ontario Historical Society, *Records and Papers*, 4:19, 37, 45; Fremin, in the *Jesuit Relations*, 54:117–119.

[22] Van Laer, *Van Rensselaer Correspondence*, 413, 449; *Jesuit Relations*, 56:57; 57:22, 25.

[23] *New York Colonial Documents*, 9:110–111; *Maryland Archives*, 2:339; Lamberville, in the *Jesuit Relations*, 58:227.

dispersed, and a large part incorporated into the Seneca tribe. The details of the defeat and the reasons for it are hard to extract from the mass of apparently contradictory evidence. The consensus of opinion is that they were first attacked by a joint force of white men raised in Maryland and Virginia. Eshleman, a historian of the Susquehannah, refuses to accept this explanation, on the ground that no mention is made of it in the archives. It would indeed seem curious that a colony which two years before had appropriated five thousand pounds of tobacco to help the Susquehannah should have raised a force to destroy them. It is well known, however, that many expeditions against the Indians were unrecognized or unrecorded by the civil authorities. Lewis Evans, writing in the next century, gave a circumstantial account of the affair, and Sebastian F. Streeter has collected a considerable amount of information.[24] The most plausible theory is that the Maryland and Virginia borderers, infuriated by Indian murders, raised an extra-legal force and attacked the Susquehannah with that lack of discrimination between Indian tribes which is characteristic of such men, notwithstanding the probably righteous Susquehannah plea that the murders had been committed by marauding Seneca. After this initial defeat the task was eagerly and conscientiously finished by the Iroquois. Governor Nicolls of New York reported that the Susquehannah had been attacked *while in retreat* "behind Virginia" by the Iroquois, and confirmatory evidence makes it virtually certain that it was the white men, long the friends of the Susquehannah, who had first turned upon them in unreasoning fury.[25]

A portion of them "put themselves under the protection of the Cinnigoes" (Seneca) and were incorporated, and a large number went south and were finally exterminated by the whites, after playing a significant part in Bacon's Rebellion in Virginia. The remnant in Virginia were captured and sent to Massachusetts to

[24] Henry F. Eshleman, *Lancaster County Indians: Annals of the Susquehannocks and Other Indian Tribes* (Lancaster, Pennsylvania, 1903), 73; Evans, *General Map of the Middle British Colonies*, 12–14; Sebastian F. Streeter, "The Fall of the Susquehannocks," in the *Historical Magazine*, 1:65–73 (March, 1857).

[25] Nicolls to the Magistrates, in *New York Colonial Documents*, 13:516. John G. Shea, in the *Historical Magazine*, 2:297, differs with this opinion.

be sold as slaves, but the venture was not profitable to the thrifty Virginians, since the price of Indian slaves was very low. The few remaining in Pennsylvania appeared as signatories to Penn's treaty of 1701, and were finally massacred near Lancaster, Pennsylvania, in 1763 by the Paxton boys, a band of frontier ruffians.[26]

The Jesuits, knowing nothing of the details of the dispersion, merely chronicled regretfully that "those Barbarians have at last succeeded in exterminating the Andastoguetz, who have held out against them for 20 years," and noticed that now, freed from their enemies, "their insolence knows no bounds."[27] True it was that the Iroquois might turn their attention once more to the French trade with the north and the west.

[26] *New York Colonial Documents*, 9:227n; Osgood, *American Colonies*, 2:422; Streeter, "The Fall of the Susquehannocks," in the *Historical Magazine*, 1:65–73; Peter S. Du Ponceau and Joshua F. Fisher, "Memoir on the Celebrated Treaty Made by William Penn in the Year 1682," in Pennsylvania Historical Society, *Memoirs*, vol. 3, pt. 2, pp. 141–203 (Philadelphia, 1834); Benjamin Franklin, *A Narrative of the Late Massacres in Lancaster County* (Philadelphia, 1764).

[27] *Jesuit Relations*, 59:251; 60:173.

XI. THE WAR IN THE ILLINOIS COUNTRY

THE NAME "ILLINOIS," like "Ottawa" or "Outaouac," was originally a generic term. The French used it to designate all nations that came from the south to trade at Point Sainte Esprit and Chequamegon Bay, and the Iroquois themselves were none too certain what was its exact limitation, for they applied it to the Miami, and sometimes even to the Potawatomi and the Sauk. The great Illinois-Miami group of peoples were, however, a quite distinct and closely consanguine group of Algonquin tribes, inhabiting, when the white man first knew them, the Mississippi Valley and its eastern tributaries in the region of the present state of Illinois. The Miami, a northern branch of the group, had separated some time before, and in the late 1660's and early 1670's had moved into the Fox River–Green Bay region.[1]

It is generally held that the Illinois had once inhabited much of the present state of Illinois, that they had been driven across the Mississippi by Iroquois incursions, and that their advance eastward in the eighth and ninth decades of the seventeenth centuries was a gradual return to their homeland following the peace of 1666–67. With this opinion the present writer is unable to agree.

What is admittedly the first contact of the Illinois with the Iroquois took place in 1655, when a band of Iroquois marauders invaded Wisconsin, attacked a small Illinois village, and was pursued and nearly wiped out. Tailhan, editor of Perrot, claims that a war ensued which lasted for eleven years and brought about the ruin and dispersion of the Illinois to a region somewhere beyond the Mississippi, but no reliable mention of such a con-

[1] Dablon, in the *Jesuit Relations*, 55:207; Lamberville to Frontenac, Onondaga, September 20, 1682, in *New York Colonial Documents*, 9:192.

flict is to be found. True, Du Chesneau, writing in 1682, quoted the Iroquois as saying that they had about twenty years before "forced them to abandon their country and to seek for refuge in very distant parts," from whence they had returned during the Iroquois-Andaste war, but it must be remembered that this is Iroquois testimony, and that the Iroquois were striving desperately to establish a claim to the country of the Illinois. Writers on the Illinois who had contact with them at about the time of the supposed dispersion, or who knew them very well, either fail to mention any conquest or dispersion by the Iroquois, or question it if they do mention it. There seems to be little reason to accept the legend, particularly when it is remembered that we have a fairly accurate picture of the enterprises of the Iroquois in those years, and that throughout all that period they were desperately engaged elsewhere. It is quite possible that another band of Iroquois may have defeated a small village of Illinois and then magnified the incident to Du Chesneau, but as for an offensive of sufficient proportions to have driven the numerous and powerful Illinois across the Mississippi River, it can hardly be seriously entertained. Nevertheless, in view of the great dispersions of peoples by the Iroquois, it is not strange that they should have been given credit for some that they did not accomplish.[2]

[2] Perrot, *Memoir*, in Blair, *Indian Tribes*, 1:154–157; "Du Chesneau's Memoir on the Western Indians," in *New York Colonial Documents*, 9:162. If the legend is true, it is curious that neither Dablon nor Marquette, both of whom knew the Illinois very well, ever mentioned it in their intimate sketches of the tribe. The Illinois discussed their enemies with Marquette, and those enemies were not the Iroquois. See Harrison, "Aborigines of the Ohio Valley," in *Fergus Historical Series*, vol. 5, no. 26, p. 27; and Marquette, in the *Jesuit Relations*, 59:127. Allouez mentions an Iroquois-Illinois conflict, but he adds that he understands their language only very slightly, and talked to only one tribe which he could not identify. See the *Jesuit Relations*, 51:47. Nowhere does La Salle make mention of an Iroquois-Illinois war, though he does say that the Illinois feared the Iroquois after the destruction of the Erie nation. See Margry, *Découvertes et éstablissements des Français*, 1:505. Charlevoix remarked pertinently that it was strange that a nation spoken of in 1667 as having been destroyed by the Iroquois should fifty years later have a population of forty thousand. See his *Journal*, 2:183–184.

Hiram Beckwith's study of "The Illinois and Indiana Indians," in the *Fergus Historical Series*, vol. 5, no. 27 (Chicago, 1884), speaks of no dispersion, and Edward Everett, who traced down the legend, found it scarcely credible. See the *North American Review*, 51:59–60. Shea, on the other hand, in editing Charlevoix's *History of New France* (3:181), apparently accepted Tailhan's statement at its face value, although no authority is cited by either Perrot or Tailhan. Colden also was under the

The white men first heard of the Illinois as western neighbors of the Winnebago. They numbered sixty villages and twenty thousand men, which the priests estimated to mean one hundred thousand people. The first white man personally to observe and report the Illinois was Allouez, who met a number of the northern group, perhaps Miami, at Chequamegon, whither they had been drawn by the irresistible magnet of the white man's trade goods. Only eighty of them came in 1667, but two years later Allouez reported that they were coming in great numbers, and Marquette mentioned that they traded slaves to the Lakes tribes.[3] With the dispersion of the Chequamegon Indians, the Illinois began coming to the post on Green Bay, and a number of them even moved into the Miami-Mascouten village on the Fox River, where members from the greater Illinois tribe came to trade and visit relatives. In 1672 Charlevoix says the Iroquois began to make incursions, and the Illinois desired allies, particularly the French, but if any Iroquois incursions annoyed them, they failed to mention the matter to Marquette, who was in the great Illinois town on the lower Illinois River in the year following, 1673. They discussed their enemies with Marquette, too, but those enemies were not the Iroquois. They were south and west of them. Marquette did

impression that the affair of 1655 had caused the supposed trans-Mississippi migration, at the same time that he admitted, paradoxically, that it was a bad defeat for the small band of Illinois concerned. See his *Five Nations of Canada*, 1:14-15. Beauchamp, in his *New York Iroquois*, 226, even gives details of a conquest which, so far as can be discovered, never occurred. Thwaites says that the Ottawa, when they were discovered, were on Manitoulin Island, "whither they had sought an asylum from the Iroquois," although elsewhere he admits that it was their original home. See Lahontan, *New Voyages*, 1:153,340n. They were found there by Champlain, while the Iroquois were hiding in the woods in fear of Algonquins and Hurons. The tendency to ascribe everything to the Iroquois is noticeable in many contemporary and some later writers.

[3] For estimates of their number see De Quen, in the *Jesuit Relations*, 42:221; Dreuillettes, *ibid.*, 44:247; and Lalemant, *ibid.*, 45:235. All this information probably came from Radisson and Groseilliers and is not reliable. For their contact with Chequamegon see the *Jesuit Relations*, 51:49; 54:167, 177. The slaves they traded were probably Pawnee. The Pawnee supplied them with so many slaves that *pani* was synonymous with "slave." Perrot says that the calumet ceremonial came from the Pawnee and was spread by them throughout the North country. See his *Memoir*, in Blair, *Indian Tribes*, 1:186, 190, 190n. A Pawnee was the famous "Turk" of Coronado, who led the expedition to Quivira and was garrotted for his pains. See Winship, "The Coronado Expedition," in Bureau of American Ethnology, *Report*, 1892-93, pt. 1, p. 534. For more on Illinois slave trade and slavery, see Carr, *Mounds of the Mississippi Valley*, 30.

not live to identify them, but La Salle not only identified them but sketched their relations with the Illinois. They were jealous, he wrote, of the trade the Illinois had with the French, and they consisted, so far as he could name them, of the Osage, the Chickasaw, and the Arkansas. Tribes came to the Illinois from eighty or one hundred leagues west of the Great River, bearing horse-hoofs to trade, and telling of lance-bearing cavalry. The Shawnee had some contact with the Illinois, and the Chickasaw were long their enemies. La Salle added significantly that the wars of the Illinois were all fought in the south, and it seems certain that if there had been any war with the Iroqouis at all, to say nothing of a great dispersion, either La Salle or Marquette would have been told all about it, for they were among the Illinois, on friendly terms with them, and spoke the Illinois tongue.[4] The distances given by La Salle may not be accurate, and such tales as the one concerning cavalry who used lances may be discounted, but the fact is clear that all the intertribal contacts of the Illinois, both of commerce and of war, were in the south. This being true, it is fairly certain that the Illinois were met by the whites during the course of their first migration in a very long time toward the east and north. There appears to be no reason for an opposite contention except a desire to account for the population of a wide strip of territory, and to have all the Algonquin tribes closely contiguous. The barbarous Algonquin spoken by the Illinois argues that their separation from other Algonquin-speaking peoples had been a wide and a fairly long one.[5]

This movement up from the south and west is illustrated by the speed and direction of growth of the great village on the Illinois River. The Kaskaskia were the first inhabitants, having 74 cabins when Marquette found them in 1673. By the time of his second visit, in 1675, there were between 100 and 150 cabins ("five or six hundred fires") and in 1677 Allouez, using Marquette's old cabin in the same town, counted 351 cabins. La Salle found it to have 460 cabins two years later, which estimate is confirmed by Mem-

[4] Dablon, in the *Jesuit Relations*, 55:209, 215; Charlevoix, *New France*, 3:181; Marquette, in the *Jesuit Relations*, 59:117–127, 185–193; La Salle, *Relation*, 93, 105, 137, 141, 143; St. Cosme, in Shea, *Early Voyages*, 60, 66.
[5] Allouez, in the *Jesuit Relations*, 51:47.

bré. The Kaskaskia were at the eastern end of the town, and the other tribes joined on as they arrived.[6] This was certainly no migration back to a homeland from which they had been routed twenty years before, but the slow and natural drift by which tribes normally moved.

The trade of the Illinois with the French was considerable, and had become more important as Michigan and the shores of Lake Michigan had been exhausted of beaver. That trade appeared particularly important to the Iroquois because it could be more easily intercepted or diverted than that farther north along the Ottawa, and the alternatives to the Ottawa route, such as that along the St. Maurice, were well-nigh impossible to blockade. Therefore the Iroquois made war upon the Illinois as early as 1677, as soon as the Susquehannah menace was removed.[7]

The expeditions of La Salle opened their eyes in short order to what they might expect: that it was not only the Illinois that they must subdue, but the French also, for in La Salle's expedition, and particularly in the construction of his boat the *Griffin*, they saw the first serious move of the French into a new phase of the traffic, the actual transportation of furs on a great scale. No longer, as before, would the tribesmen carry their furs to the French—the French would come and get them. It was like shutting a door on the ambitions of the Iroquois. Indian transportation they might intercept; Indian trade they might divert, though they had been only half successful in that; but white transportation was a different and infinitely more difficult matter, for the whites were devil men, who thought of everything and were notoriously hard to kill.

La Salle was one of those rare men who seem to have been especially equipped by nature to deal with savage people. He comprehended their motives with a speed and clarity that was either disconcerting or reassuring, depending upon their interests. Although he failed in dealing with his own race, the savages were

[6] *Ibid.*, 59:159–161; La Salle, *Relation*, 85; Marion Habig, "The Site of the Great Illinois Village," in *Mid-America*, new series, 5:12 (July, 1933).

[7] Perrot, *Memoir*, in Blair, *Indian Tribes*, 1–110; Wentworth Greenhalgh, "Journal of a Tour to the Indians of Western New-York," in *New York Colonial Documents*, 3:252.

never a problem to him. Thus he understood the position and difficulty of the Iroquois perhaps more quickly and clearly than they themselves. He remarked that it was necessary for them to go to the western country for fur, and he also observed that they disapproved of his fort at Niagara, that they had taken offense at the building of his *Griffin*, and that they were by no means satisfied with his declaration that it would benefit them by bringing them more and cheaper goods. They furnished him no provisions, and plotted, somewhat belatedly, to burn his ship. They knew only too well that the *Griffin* had never been built for their benefit, but that it meant an extended trade with the Illinois, who were their own prospective supply depot of fur. Du Chesneau, writing to Seignelay, understood the Iroquois position and motive perfectly. "Their true motive, however," he wrote, " . . . was to force the Illinois to bring their beaver to them, . . . also, to intimidate the other nations and constrain them to do the same thing." He added that La Salle's attempted deception of the Iroquois was futile, as La Salle himself knew. He had pretended that discovery was his only motive, and yet he had traded with the Illinois directly, and for guns. To the Iroquois, La Salle was an imposing liar and an enemy trader.[8]

There was little choice for the Iroquois, if they hoped to stop the French-Illinois commerce, between attacking the French and attacking the Illinois. The French they had fought for years, with little profit and no satisfaction. To gain anything in that direction it would be necessary to drive the French from the continent, and the Iroquois had no stomach for a task such as that. It might be futile to attack the Illinois, but that plan had at least the possibility of success, and they did not delay long after La Salle and his *Griffin* had shown them what the future held.

In mid-September,[9] 1680, five hundred Iroquois burst into the quiet valley of the Illinois, to find that most of the Illinois warriors

[8] La Salle, *Relation*, 21–25; "Du Chesneau's Memoir," in *New York Colonial Documents*, 9:163.

[9] Membré says September 10; La Salle, September 18. Tonty does not give a date. Membré, "La Salle's Party at Fort Crevecoeur," in *Louisiana Historical Collections*, pt. 4, p. 154; La Salle, *Relation*, 193; Tonty, "Memoir," in *Illinois Historical Collections*, 1:132.

had gone hunting and that they had taken with them most of the guns. There were a few hundred warriors in the camp, armed for the most part with bows and arrows. The cautious Iroquois did not attack the town but remained on the opposite (south) side of the river and parleyed, while the undaunted Illinois sent their women and children down-river by night. Finally they crossed the river and attacked the Iroquois, who retreated more than a mile, the eleven tribes of the Illinois moving slowly away downstream. The Iroquois occupied their town, destroying huts and defiling the cemeteries, but they eventually recrossed the river and, remaining discreetly on the south side, kept pace with the slowly retreating Illinois. The Illinois were not greatly frightened, and eight of the eleven tribes moved leisurely out of the neighborhood, the Tamaroa and two fragmentary tribes remaining near by to hunt. Upon these overconfident fragments of the Illinois the Iroquois warriors fell in a brief battle; most of the warriors escaped, but the Iroquois killed a few and took prisoners several hundred women and children. Tonty, who had been wounded during the first battle a month before, had gone north to winter among the Potawatomi; La Salle, who saw the battlefield twelve days after the battle, greatly overestimated the damage done to the Illinois, only a fraction of whom had been engaged. This invasion was the last successful advance of the Iroquois into the Illinois country,[10] and a poor enough triumph it was.

La Salle, having missed Tonty and being somewhat discouraged, trailed back over the Kankakee portage to spend the winter among the Miami at the mouth of the St. Joseph River, for winter was already setting in. Among the Miami were a small band of New England Indians who, having been driven from home by

[10] For the number killed and captured, see La Salle, *Relation*, 195–237; Frontenac to the King, in *New York Colonical Documents*, 9:147. Tonty's long and heroic retreat is described by Louise Kellogg in "A Wisconsin Anabasis," in the *Wisconsin Magazine of History*, 7:322–339 (March, 1924). There are two theories of the motivation of the Iroquois onset of 1680. Charles A. Hanna thinks that they pursued the Shawnee hither. See *The Wilderness Trail* (New York, 1911), 1:158. Clarence Alvord, in *The Illinois Country* (Springfield, 1920), 85–86, suggests that they were egged on by the English. Buffinton's article on "The Policy of Albany," in the *Mississippi Valley Historical Review*, 8:327–366, disposes of Alvord's theory. It is the belief of this writer that a study of the sources reveals that the Iroquois were on their own mission and for their own purposes.

Iroquois oppression during King Philip's war, had been hunting in the West, and who intended eventually to ally themselves with the Iroquois, for there seemed to be little else left for them to do. One of them, a subchief named Nanagoucy, who knew La Salle, had in mind a most ambitious plan, a plan so far-reaching that he knew it required a La Salle to carry it out. Nanagoucy prevailed upon his compatriots to await La Salle's coming, and when he arrived proposed to him a confederation of all the Western tribes against the Iroquois, promising more recruits from New England and offering to help in the organization of such a league if La Salle would support him for the chieftainship of his own band. This was a plan to fire the enthusiasm of the discouraged La Salle, and immediately he began to lay the groundwork for the confederacy by gaining the confidence of his hosts, the Miami. The Miami were at first skeptical and hesitant, and they might well have let La Salle take his plan elsewhere had it not been for the arrival of news that practically drove them into his arms and at one stroke converted the whole band into organizers and backers of the project.

The Iroquois, retreating from their victory on the Illinois in the previous fall, had in a fit of wanton ferocity butchered two lodges of Miami, and after accepting three thousand beaver from a Miami embassy for the return of Miami prisoners, had at the last refused to return either the prisoners or the beaver. It was the sort of treatment the Miami might well have expected from the Iroquois, for they were already known as French Indians and traded with the French, but they had not expected it. They were amazed and terrified, for they had not got on well with the Illinois for several years because of trade rivalry, and now, with the baleful eye of the Five Nations turned upon them, they might well be lost men. So while, unknown to La Salle, they made surreptitious overtures to the Iroquois, they joined eagerly in his proposed confederation, deeming it wise to have an alternative in any case. La Salle dispatched the New England savages with fifty beaver for each of the surrounding tribes, and left for Quebec to interview Frontenac. The next year, 1682, he was back and hard at work building a fort around which to group his confederation.

He called it Fort St. Louis of the Illinois, and almost at once a considerable Indian encampment began growing up around it.[11] During the winter of 1682–83, while the fort was being completed, Tonty, La Salle's faithful lieutenant, worked ceaselessly to build up the confederation, notifying all the surrounding Indian nations and urging them to come in. By the summer of 1683 there were three hundred cabins of Illinois, Miami, and Shawnee clustered around the rock upon which the fort stood.[12]

Meanwhile, however, the enemies of La Salle, both Indian and white, had not been idle. Frontenac, his best friend and supporter, had been recalled in 1682 and replaced by Lefebvre la Barre, who seemed to regard the destruction of La Salle and all his works as a patriotic duty and sacred obligation. The Jesuits hated La Salle, whose imperial schemes could not be reconciled with the Jesuit dream of a pastoral and unexploited Indian interior, ruled over by the church, and La Salle repaid their hatred with interest, and was loud in his accusations regarding the venality of the priesthood. In this quarrel La Barre took the Jesuit side, intrigued with La Salle's enemies both in New France and in Paris, and even informed the Iroquois that they might plunder and kill him without fear of retribution.[13]

The Iroquois, on their own account, had almost succeeded in

[11] Most of the narrative may be found in La Salle's *Relation*, 249–255. On Miami diplomacy see Du Chesneau to Seignelay, in his "Memoir," in *New York Colonial Documents*, 9:162. Membré says that La Salle's enemies persuaded the Miami to seek the Iroquois alliance, the business being carried on by *coureurs du bois*. See "La Salle's Party at Fort Crevecoeur," in *Louisiana Historical Collections*, pt. 4, p. 154. On the relations between the Miami and Illinois, see Blair, *Indian Tribes*, 1:259n. La Salle's fort was so named to distinguish it from the other Fort St. Louis built in Texas.

[12] Tonty, "Memoir," in *Illinois Historical Collections*, 1:147. Franquelin's map of 1684 gives 1,200 Illinois, 1,300 Miami, 500 Wea (Ouiatonon), 300 Kilatica, 200 Shawnee, 160 Pepikokia, 150 Piankeshaw, and 70 Ouabona. Miss Kellogg, in her *French Régime*, 219, says that the confederation denuded central Wisconsin of its inhabitants. See the map in the *Jesuit Relations*, vol. 63, frontispiece; and Parkman, *La Salle*, 298.

[13] La Salle's charge of venality was an old one and practically groundless. Frontenac, an old opponent of the Jesuits, wrote in 1672: "to speak frankly to you, they think as much of the conversion of the beaver as of souls." See *New York Colonial Documents*, 9:93. Le Jeune's defense, in the *Jesuit Relations*, 9:171–183, is the best reply available. Parkman gives a very fair estimate of the merits of the charge. See his *Jesuits in North America*, 365n. La Barre's instructions to the Iroquois were denied neither by La Barre nor by Parkman and are probably true. *New York Colonial Documents*, 9:215; Parkman, *Count Frontenac*, 304.

dividing La Salle's confederacy before it was well begun by de-
taching the Miami. It seemed the part of wisdom to divide it if
an attack was to be made upon it, for the Illinois counted eighteen
hundred warriors and the Miami twelve or fifteen hundred, and
the combined number, especially under white leadership, would
have been far too many for the Iroquois. The division was made
easier by the fact that the Miami, notwithstanding a linguistic
affiliation with the Illinois, feared them and often disputed with
them, having been mildly hostile to them since about 1673.[14] By
masterly diplomacy the Iroquois had almost persuaded the Miami to
join them in their assault upon the Illinois in 1680, but the thought-
less destruction of the hapless Miami village by the retreating
Iroquois practically destroyed all hope for a permanent and effective Miami alliance. Up to the time their village was destroyed
the Miami had been active in the Iroquois behalf. They had even
tried to discourage the Illinois from allying themselves with La
Salle by telling them that La Salle only schemed for their destruction, that he was already allied with the Iroquois, as was proved by
his erection of a fort in Iroquoia. But an Iroquois embassy to the
Miami in the spring of 1681 had little success, for two reasons.
First, the wanton attack of the fall before had shaken their confidence, and, second, La Salle himself was present when the Iroquois deputies arrived, and his matchless skill in handling natives
completed the rout of the embassy.[15] So the Miami never joined
the Iroquois, and it was well for them that they did not, for, as it
developed later, the Iroquois were playing a deep game indeed
with the Miami; if the projected alliance had beaten the Illinois,
the Iroquois planned to turn upon the Miami and disperse them.

   This Iroquois-Miami-French-Illinois quadrangle alone would
go far to show, even were other proof lacking, the inherent logic

[14] For the numbers of the tribes see La Salle, *Relation*, 191, 193. On Miami-Illinois
relations see *Memoir sur l'etat present du Canada*, quoted by Tailhan in Blair, *Indian
Tribes*, 1:258n. This Miami-Illinois jealousy was over a trade rivalry, the Miami
lying between the French and the Illinois. The discord, as might be expected, began
when the Miami moved into that region, the tribes having been very friendly before.
[15] Parkman, *La Salle*, 205; La Salle, *Relation*, 97–99, 267–269. La Salle thought that
the Miami ambassador to the Illinois was a Jesuit emissary rather than the agent of
a purely Miami scheme. La Salle, a master hand in getting and keeping the devotion
of savages, could keep the loyalty of but few white men.

of Iroquois policy. They wished to eliminate all the tribes of the Illinois country as commercial factors, and to help them they found a commercial rivalry between the two strongest, which rivalry was easy to exploit. The Miami were to be used against the Illinois, and then, when they had served their purpose, were to be in turn dispersed. A permanent loyalty to the Miami was out of the question for the Iroquois, since that would have been only to substitute one rival for another, and the trade would still have gone to the French. They had learned in a hard school during the past several decades that a commercial agreement with other tribes was sure to be broken as soon as it was profitable to either party to break it, and that if the breaking was not profitable, neither was the treaty. The Iroquois had had far more experience than the Miami, and it is not strange that the Miami were puzzled and continually uncertain as to where their interest lay. The Iroquois weakness was not in diplomacy, but in control of their own people, and the wanton assault upon the Miami village in the fall of 1680 had given enemy diplomats a tremendous advantage in dealing with the Miami, for it could not be satisfactorily explained in terms of Iroquois friendship and alliance. It was an advantage they never failed to use to the utmost. There have been a number of great men among the American tribes who, had they been clothed with the authority necessary to work their will, could have done great things. Such men were Pontiac, Tecumseh, and Red Cloud, who failed not because of personal shortcomings but because of the inadequacy of the political institutions of their people, as did also the sagacious chieftains of the Iroquois.

In the north the Iroquois were unable to gain ground, although they pursued their ancient policy of sending alternately belts and hatchets toward Mackinac. The alliance of 1670 had not brought them the coveted northern trade any more than had the treaties of 1645 and 1653, for the Ottawa monopoly, though no longer complete, was shared only by northern tribes such as the Potawatomi, and the Ottawa alone supplied New France with two-thirds of the fur it received.

With the apparent failure of negotiation, the Iroquois resolved upon another invasion of the north country in 1683, which La Barre reported to Seignelay:

. . . as you are not informed of the cause which urges the Iroquois to declare war against us, it is necessary that I should, first of all, explain it to you according to the truth . . .

. . . as they perceived that they could not succeed better . . . than by destroying the Outaouax . . . who alone supply us with two-thirds of the Beaver that is sent to France, they made a great outcry, among themselves, about the death of a Seneca Captain, who had been killed four years ago by an Illinois at Missilimakinack, in the fort of the Outaouax called Kiskakons.

La Barre had been warned by Nipissing scouts about the contemplated assault upon Mackinac, and he forestalled the Iroquois by sending warning, reinforcements, and ammunition to Mackinac, where Duluth assumed command; the Iroquois, when they arrived, dared not attack and retired after the capture of five Petun scouts.[16]

Of course the Iroquois in the following year skillfully switched to peace offerings, and this time the Ottawa, attracted by the cheaper English goods, wavered so far in their alliance that it taxed the ingenuity of the French to keep them from going over entirely to the Iroquois. "I do not believe the next year will pass away without the whole trade being absolutely lost," wrote Denonville to Seignelay; "our friendly Indians revolting against us, and placing themselves at the mercy of the Iroquois . . . the whole of the Hurons [Petuns] are waiting only for the moment to do so." In spite of the gloomy forebodings of the French, the calamity they feared never occurred, for they had underestimated the shrewdness of their savage allies. They saw that, though the English goods were cheaper, an agreement with the Iroquois would mean the intervention of a middleman between themselves and the white men, which would surely mean a worse deal for them than they now had by dealing directly with the French. Being middlemen and Indians themselves, they knew the ways of

[16] The alliance of 1670 is merely the peace of 1666–67 confirmed by the upper tribes. See La Barre to Seignelay, November 4, 1683, in *New York Colonial Documents*, 9:201–202. Du Chesneau, a year before, had said that the French got all the peltries that came into the country from the Ottawa. Report of conference, in *New York Colonial Documents*, 9:171.

Indian middlemen, and the traffic which so far they had had through the Iroquois had been unsatisfactory. Moreover, the Iroquois had not yet shown themselves dangerous as far north as Mackinac, and the proffered alliance was rejected.[17]

In the Illinois country the Iroquois tried one more expedition against the Illinois in late March, 1684. They besieged Fort St. Louis on the Illinois for six days, but they were repulsed with considerable loss and, being far from their base, were forced to retreat with their few captives, most of whom escaped and returned.[18] This last expedition marks the end of the Iroquois attempt to gain the monopoly of the northern and western trade by military means, and marks the end of that shadowy "empire" over which the Iroquois have been said to hold sway. The end was not in any sense a dramatic one, but a sober rearrangement of Iroquois policy by the Iroquois themselves.

Throughout it all, the Iroquois had been wedded to the Albany alliance, and because of their fundamental enmity with the French, had never had the advantage of playing one competitor against another. The one market at Albany had satisfied them in the early years, but as their knowledge of values increased, they saw more and more clearly the disadvantage of being the monopolized party. They learned that any monopolist drives a very hard bargain indeed, and it began to appear the wiser policy, if possible, to observe something like neutrality toward both the French and English, and so be able to take their wares to the better market. The Mohawk who, when offered a handful of gun powder for a bearskin, remarked explosively that it took two handfuls to kill a bear was in his reaction fairly representative of the changing philosophy of his leaders. The better thing would have been to monopolize the trade of the far regions, but since that solution began to appear remote, if not impossible, it was necessary to get the best possible prices in whatever trade they were able to do. That, of course, could not be done if they were irrevocably

[17] For examples of Ottawa-Iroquois dickering see Colden, *Five Nations of Canada*, 1:246; and La Potherie, *Histoire de l'Amérique Septentrionale*, 2:298. See also Denonville to Seignelay, in *New York Colonial Documents*, 9:301.

[18] Tonty, "Memoir," in *Illinois Historical Collections*, 1:148. Tonty was in command at the fort.

committed to an English market, and a realignment of their trade connections seemed inescapable. The first enunciation of this new course was made by La Grande Gueule, an Iroquois orator, when, speaking to La Barre at La Famine in 1684, he said: "We neither depend upon Onnondio or Corlaer. We may go where we please, and carry with us whom we please, and buy and sell what we please. If your allies be your slaves, use them as such."

After the Denonville defeat of the Seneca in 1687, the Onondaga, Oneida, and Cayuga signed a declaration in Montreal in June, 1688, guaranteeing their "intention to observe a perfect neutrality," and though it was broken thereafter, neutrality between French and British, so far as it was possible, became a cornerstone of Iroquois policy.[19] With this change, the policy of the Iroquois could no longer be an independent policy, but must always be dependent in great measure upon French and British policy. The war in the Illinois country was their last independent venture; their subsequent campaigns through the next century were phases of the intercolonial wars and coterminous with them. With the siege of Fort St. Louis on the Illinois, were ended the wars that may properly be called "The Wars of the Iroquois."

At the end of our account of this phase of the history of the Iroquois, and the abandonment of their design for conquering the tribes of the north and west, it seems pertinent to suggest answers to two questions. First, how may one reasonably account for the apparently fierce spirit of nationality that held the Iroquois together, held them to a consistent policy and drove them through nearly fifty years of war when, by reason of war losses and the adoption of captives, there seemed to be little of the original Iroquois strain remaining in the Long House? Second, with what success had the long effort of the Five Nations been rewarded?

To the first of these questions two general answers have been given by other authors: first, the marvelous political and military

---

[19] For the speech of Le Grande Gueule see Lahontan, *Voyages*, 1:82. This is the only full report of the speech, but it may be taken as trustworthy. For the "neutrality treaty" see *New York Colonial Documents*, 9:384-385. The breaking of the treaty refers to King William's War and not to the La Chine massacre, in which the writer does not believe the Iroquois to have been guilty of bad faith, but tricked by the conniving French themselves and the astute Adario. *New York Colonial Documents*, 9:393n; Lahontan, *Voyages*, 1:149, 165, 220-223.

efficiency of the League of the Iroquois and, second, an inherent fierceness and lust for blood. The first of these arguments has already been considered. As for the second, it was Lalemant's contention that by 1660 it would have been difficult to find twelve hundred Iroquois of pure blood, and Lalemant was a shrewd and experienced observer. There were said to have been seven different nations among the Onondaga and eleven among the Seneca, and the small number of true Iroquois remaining was remarked upon many times.[20] If this study has come anywhere near the truth, the true answer seems inescapable. If Indians of other nations or institutions had lived in the country in which the Iroquois lived, they would have been subject to the same pressure of circumstance; the trade of other nations would have been desirable and even necessary to them; and they would, presumably, have taken about the same steps to obtain it as did the Iroquois. Had the position of the Hurons and Ottawa been exchanged for that of the Iroquois, it is scarcely a mere conjecture that the Iroquois would then have used the Ottawa River highway and that the tribes living in New York would have blockaded it and attempted to destroy them.We have seen an example, in the Susquehannah war, of how another nation found a blockade of the Iroquois commerce necessary to its own well-being, even though it passed along no river highway and was therefore much more difficult to accomplish. Lalemant, not fully understanding the Iroquois position, as, indeed, few men, if any, in his day did, marveled at the Iroquois. "It is a marvel," he wrote, "that so few people work such great havoc and render themselves so redoubtable to so great a number of tribes," and Parkman, in modern times, was scarcely less impressed.[21] If the answer suggested by this investigation is reasonable, it need no longer seem a marvel, for any nation with so great an economic need and so strong a military position could hardly have failed to be redoubtable unless it was or became degenerate. Of great assistance to the Iroquois purpose was the fact that by far the greater number of the incorporated captives were of Huron-Iroquois stock and spoke the Iroquois tongue with little difficulty. This, with the safety of the Iroquois position, made in-

[20] *Jesuit Relations*, 43:265; 45:207.
[21] *Ibid.*, 45:207; Parkman, *Jesuits in North America*, 444-445.

corporation relatively simple, and many members of enemy tribes deliberately chose to go to Iroquoia without direct compulsion. Lord Bacon might well have been thinking of the Iroquois when he wrote that the nation which could the most successfully incorporate other peoples was "the fittest for empire."

The supposed unity of the League, or the unity of action that has been ascribed to it, may be dismissed, for such unity never existed. In no war down to 1684 were all the tribes engaged, and intra-League war threatened again and again, actually coming to pass several times between the Mohawks and the upper Iroquois. Each tribe made war solely in its own interest, and the conspicuous feature of their League is its lack, not its possession, of political unity. It is true that because of the almost identical position of the five Iroquois cantons with reference to the northern and western trade, they were never sufficiently at odds to provoke an intra-tribal war. Never did one canton help another in a quarrel that was purely its own, and never did a canton make war unless its own interest was directly involved. The Onondaga were amused and even joyful over the invasion of Mohawk country by Courcelles; the Mohawks called the Susquehannah their children and wished them well when they were at death grips with the Seneca and Cayuga, and no canton aided the Seneca when Denonville struck them in 1687. The Mohawks regularly exploited and even fought the Seneca and Onondaga, and only the fact that the trade was more important to all of them than their differences with one another kept them at peace. Moreover, if unity of action be thought a criterion of the significance of the League, it must be pointed out that the unity of action of the Hurons and Algonquins, who were utterly dissimilar in institutions and had no organization between or among them, was more remarkable than that of the League of the Iroquois. It was not, then, the political magic of the League or any portion of venom in the Iroquois makeup that made them redoubtable. Neither was it that they were well armed while their victims were defenseless,[22] but a position and a set of circumstances in which they, through no particular fault or virtue of their own, found themselves.

[22] See Appendices A and B.

In answer to the second question, it may be said that the Iroquois failed completely in their primary objective, a monopoly of the northern and western trade. The "empire" claimed for them by some historians is purely imaginary and probably originated in claims made by the Iroquois when they had a land sale in prospect. They did control most of the present state of New York, at least threatened western Pennsylvania, and held a loose dominion over southwestern Ontario and eastern Ohio, but beyond that they were never more than a distant menace. They never won a battle north of Georgian Bay or in Wisconsin, and their sole victory over the Illinois was won over a single tribe, the Tamaroa, and was not damaging to the body of the Illinois. Although they were feared, and rightly so, in the whole region, the "empire" extending from Hudson Bay to the Mississippi and Carolina is an Iroquoian fiction which has received more credence than it deserves.

In maintaining themselves they were successful. By dispersing the peoples inhabiting a great stretch of territory they acquired that territory as a hunting ground and, with what fur they were able to gather themselves and in incidental trade, they achieved a competence sufficient to maintain themselves as the dominant power in their region until the battle of Oriskany. There have been many random speculations as to what the Iroquois might have been and what they might have done had circumstances been other than they were. Perhaps the most curious of these is that of Parkman, who says that the Iroquois, "but for the presence of Europeans would probably have subjected, absorbed, or exterminated every other Indian community east of the Mississippi and north of the Ohio."[23] Considering that when the Europeans came the Iroquois were a small and unobtrusive people who had been driven from their territory by Huron and Algonquin and who were on the defensive deep in their own forests, rising to power only after and because of the European trade, this conclusion seems at best a fantastic one. The European trade was the major circumstance of all intertribal relations in the Great Lakes area, and the Iroquois and all their works were phenomena of that contact.

[23] *Jesuits in North America*, xix–xx.

APPENDICES

A. THE DUTCH TRADE IN FIREARMS
WITH THE IROQUOIS

So IMPORTANT were the achievements of the Five Nations in the seventeenth century that historians have sought industriously for some key to their success and their almost constant belligerence. Some of their conclusions have already been mentioned, notably the supposedly plentiful supply of firearms, to which have been ascribed not only the successes of the Iroquois but their very motivation.

Indians simply like to fight, runs this line of reasoning; they like war for its own sake, and the possession of guns whets their savage ardor to the point where they can no longer resist temptation and hence set out on journeys of a thousand miles and more "seeking new nations to devour."[1] It is not strange that this conception of the Iroquois has become popular. Probably nine-tenths of the material written about them in the seventeenth century was written by Jesuit priests, who, while competent and careful reporters of fact, were often mistaken in their interpretation of cause and result. After all, the truly clerical mind did not concern itself overmuch with cause and result, for there was one cause to which could be ascribed all things difficult to understand, mysterious Providence and the hand of God. Thus Ragueneau explained the Huron disaster of 1649; thus Le Mercier explained the peace of 1653; thus all the priests explained the numberless devils clearly seen and even conversed with during the time of the earthquake and the comet. The Jesuits were keen men, but comparatively simple in the humanities, and they hated and feared the Iroquois above all things. "They are not men, they are wolves," sobbed an Algonquin woman to Buteux, and the priests heartily echoed her sentiment.

But the administrators of New France were hardly so simple. "It was politic to exaggerate more than ever the cruelties of the Iroquois," wrote Governor Dubois d'Avaugour in 1663, "in order the better to conceal

[1] Parkman, *La Salle*, 203–204.

the designs that might be adopted in this country; fearing lest English ignorance and Dutch weakness might be alarmed and have their jealousy excited." To all of New France it seemed evident that the Iroquois had guns, and that without guns they could not succeed. The Dutch were competitors, they were also heretics, and moreover their prices were much lower. Here was a scapegoat for their blame, and it is likely that the priests were entirely honest in their accusation. Parkman, writing almost altogether from French sources, reflected the French point of view, and his writings have had a tremendous circulation. Further, the Iroquois villain made a much more attractive figure than did the Iroquois tradesman, and furnished Parkman with a lurid background and a convincing explanation, which he needed even more than did Father Lalemant.[2] "Insensate blood-lust," "homicidal frenzy," "savage blindness and fury," "the tigers of America," have a sensual appeal to any reader.

Jesuitical and Parkmanesque interpretation cast the Iroquois and the Dutch together as complementary parts of a military machine that ruined New France; Iroquois ferocity eagerly armed with Dutch muskets, as a result of the greedy and unchristian policy of the Dutch. Complete statistics are not available on this trade because of the loss, by sale, of the records of the Dutch West India Company, but enough general information is available to justify a brief study of its extent, chronological and quantitative, and its probable motivation.

The Trade in Firearms to 1640

It seems always to have been contrary to the policy of the Dutch West India Company to trade guns to any Indians whatever. Fifteen years after the voyage of Hudson and ten years after the establishment of Fort Nassau, Wassenaer wrote that the natives not only had no firearms but even feared them excessively. Two years later, the circumstances of the death of Krieckebeeck and several of his men indicate that the Mohawks had, as yet, no firearms, and that their fighting was done entirely with bows and arrows, though this was a formally declared and important war.[3]

In the meantime the French were acquiring an unsavory reputation in New England, where it was said that the guns with which the savages

---

[2] D'Avaugour to the Minister, August 4, 1663, in *New York Colonial Documents*, 9:13. See also Lalemant, in the *Jesuit Relations*, 45:207, 211. "If the Iroquois possess any power, it is only because they are knavish and cruel."

[3] Wassenaer, *Historisch Verhael*, and *Historie van Europa*, in Jameson, *Narratives of New Netherland*, 73, 84, and O'Callaghan, *Documentary History of New Netherland*, 3:33, 43.

were armed came almost altogether from them. William Bradford, while regretting the use of wampum in the trade because it "fills them [*the Indians*] with peeces, powder and shote . . . by reason of yᵉ bassnes of sundry unworthy persons, both English, Dutch and French which may turne to yᵉ ruine of many," blamed especially the French, for "those Indeans . . . which had comerce with yᵉ French, got peces of them, and they in yᵉ end made a commone trade of it." He made a further protest against the French, which was echoed by William Wood, in his apprehension of the result of Indian ownership of "guns which they dayly trade for with the French, who will sell his eyes, as they say, for beaver." There were, of course, English renegades and free traders who were in the business, and one Richard Hopkins was "whipt & branded with a hott iron on one of his cheekes" for "selling peeces & powder & shott to the Indenes,[4] but the French were the most generally blamed. It was as safe and popular to blame "papists" in New England and New Netherland as it was to blame heretics in New France, the only difference between the two situations being that the protests of the French have in succeeding years received a wider circulation and advertisement.

In New Netherland, up to 1639, the trade in firearms had not yet become a pressing problem. De Vries, writing in 1632, testifies that "the weapons in war were bows and arrows, stone axes and claphammers" and the anonymous Traveler into the Iroquois country in 1634–35 found them interested in firearms only as a great wonder, and they asked him repeatedly to fire his pistols that they might observe it. Beyond that constant request, they apparently had no word for him of guns, but had much to say concerning prices. The Frenchmen who had recently been there, they said, were fine, generous fellows, while the Dutch were scoundrels who gave poor presents and low prices. The French gave six hands of seawan for a beaver; would the Dutch give four? The Traveler, looking about, saw evidences of the French visit in "very good axes to cut the underwood . . . and French shirts and coats and razors," but he made no mention of guns.[5]

Something had happened by 1639, however, for on March 31 of that

---

[4] William Bradford, *Plimouth Plantation* (1899 ed.), 283, 286, where he writes of the year 1628; *Wood's New England's Prospect, 1634;* John Noble, "Trial and Punishment of Crimes," in Colonial Society of Massachusetts, *Transactions*, 1895–97 (Publications, vol. 3, Boston, 1900), 3:56.

[5] David Pietersz de Vries, "Notes, Voyage from Holland to America," in *New York Historical Collections*, 2d series, vol. 3, pt. 2, p. 95. See also De Vries' "Notes" in Jameson, *Narratives of New Netherland*, where it is stated that in their hunting no guns were used. See also pages 146–147, 149, 151, 154.

year the director and council of New Netherland passed an ordinance
designed to stop an illicit trade which had seemingly grown up overnight:

Whereas . . . many persons . . . contrary to the orders and com-
mands of . . . the States General and the Chartered West India Company, have presumed to sell to the Indians in these parts, muskets, powder
and lead, which has already caused much evil . . . therefore every inhabitant of New Netherland . . . is most expressly forbidden to sell any
muskets, powder or lead to the Indians, on pain of being punished by
death, and if anyone shall inform against any person who shall violate
this law, he shall receive a reward of 50 guilders.[6]

There is some doubt whether the council had in mind the Iroquois or
the lower Indians, but the ordinance does not seem to have been enforced, perhaps because of the extreme penalty. Two years later the
colony of Rensselaerwyck took up the problem in an ordinance of their
own:

As the council . . . notice that many persons . . . make bold against
the . . . ordinance of the Chartered West India Company to sell to the
Indians . . . firearms, powder and lead . . . Therefore, every inhabitant
of the said colony . . . is expressly prohibited from selling, repairing or
lending any firearms, powder or lead on forfeiture of 100 guilders and on
pain of being sent home under such sentence as the case shall warrant,
and any one who shall inform . . . shall receive 50 guilders as a reward.[7]

Only one man appears to have been convicted and sentenced under this
ordinance, one Michiel Jansz, who was held to have forfeited his life under the general New Netherland ordinance of 1639, but he was let off
with a fine of fifty guilders, and all his property confiscated on other
convenient counts.[8] The evident fact that neither ordinance was strictly
enforced destroys the theory of R. J. Parker that the sudden cessation of
the Iroquois trade around 1640 was due to their effect. A report to the
Board of Accounts in 1644 laid the ruin of the trade to the fact that free
traders *had* sold guns to the Mohawks.[9] The ruin of the trade was due,
as has been shown, to the fact that the Mohawks had no more fur. If
given guns as "capital goods," they would bring in fur, as their later
history shows.

[6] Van Laer, *Van Rensselaer Bowier Manuscripts*, 426; Hubbard, *Indian Wars in New
England*, 2:250. Virginia had also passed the death penalty by ordinance.
[7] Van Laer, *Van Rensselaer Bowier Manuscripts*, 565.
[8] Van Laer, *Court Records*, 34-39.
[9] R. J. Parker, "The Iroquois and the Dutch Fur Trade," doctoral dissertation,
University of California, 1932, p. 25; *New York Colonial Documents*, 1:150.

It is impossible to make any accurate estimate of how many guns were possessed by the Iroquois when their sustained assault upon the Huron trade began, but the estimates available from the sources may be recorded and some idea may be gleaned from them. A Dutch estimate of 1644 said that four hundred guns had been sold. Another estimate of 1646, as of the year 1641, said "four hundred armed men," which probably meant men armed with guns. We have two French estimates of those years. In 1641 a body of five hundred Mohawks came to Three Rivers to attempt an agreement of some sort with New France. A Frenchman, Marguerie, who was their captive, came in as a spokesman, and informed the whites that they had thirty-six arquebusiers, whom he said to be very skillful. Two years later Vimont estimated the Mohawk forces to be seven or eight hundred warriors (a probably excessive estimate) and thought they had three hundred arquebuses.[10] This number, in view of the estimates in New Netherland, seems reasonable, but it should be remembered that four hundred guns sold by no means indicates four hundred in use, for they were put out of commission rapidly by the rough and ignorant handling of the savages. One of the constant demands of the Iroquois in later years was for smiths to repair guns, as a trifling defect rendered them unserviceable. It should be remembered, too, that the testimony of Marguerie is worth far more than that of Vimont. Marguerie was a soldier, knew what he was reporting, and reported vital information, whereas Vimont at best made a guess, and was reporting to the head of the Order in France.

It may be argued that there were five cantons of Iroquois, and that four hundred (the maximum possible number) multiplied by five gives two thousand muskets, the number assigned to the Iroquois by Miss Louise Kellogg in her *French Régime*. But two of the cantons were very small, and only one, the Mohawk, had direct trade with the Dutch. Even Vimont, in 1643, knew the four upper cantons only as "Santweronnons" and stated specifically that the Mohawks were the only ones who made trouble for the French, the others being neutral and apparently not as yet interested. The best and most revealing testimony is that of Marguerie, to the effect that five hundred "heavily armed" Mohawks had thirty-six arquebuses in the year 1641.

The Trade in Firearms, 1640–1650

The bedeviled merchants of New Netherland were in a quandary. They thought the prohibition of the trade in guns to be good in itself,

[10] For Dutch estimates see *New York Colonial Documents*, 1:150; "Journal of New Netherland," in O'Callaghan, *Documentary History of New York*, 4:8; Jameson,

but there were two phases of the situation which the Council and the director did not seem to appreciate. First, there were plenty of other places where Indians could buy guns, and the Indian trade was most apt to go where the guns were, which spoiled the business of the New Netherland merchants. Second, while the prohibition prevented a legitimate merchant from doing business of that sort, it was no bar at all for the illicit trader. A gun brought twenty beavers to the English of New England and Hartford, and powder ten or twelve guilders a pound; free traders all around them were making money.[11] Would not the Council relent?

In 1649 the Company relented and permitted the director to supply the Indians "sparingly" with munitions, but at the conservative rates of six guilders per gun, four guilders per pistol, and six guilders per pound of powder. But wilder yet was the cry that arose from the merchants when the permission was made public. Six and four guilders indeed! Indians would pay 120 guilders in beaver for a gun, and twenty times the price asked for powder. Was the Council crazy or deliberately trying to ruin the merchants? Stuyvesant knew and appreciated their troubles, and that they were losing trade, not only to the English but also to the Swedes, who were reaching far north for the Albany trade and getting a considerable portion of it. The Swedes had no scruples whatever about selling guns to the Indians, and even trained them in the use of cannon. Stuyvesant tried faithfully, however, to stop the illicit trade, but he was unsuccessful, so unsuccessful that dealing in "stamped" guns (illicit in trade and used only for defense) was one of the charges leveled at him.[12] Of course he was innocent, but the merchants were like aroused hornets, ready to sting indiscriminately anyone who had, or seemed to have, authority.

The director and Council, trying vainly for a compromise acceptable

Narratives of New Netherland, 274. For French estimates see the *Jesuit Relations*, 21: 35–37; 34:271.

[11] Jameson, *Narratives of New Netherland*, 274. In the *New York Colonial Documents* see "The Eight Men to the Assembly," 5:190; "Observation on the Duties," *ibid.*, 373–374; "Journal of New Netherland," 1:322.

[12] *New York Colonial Documents*, 5:373–374; "Excuses and Highly Injurious Neglect," *ibid.*, 337, 392; Stuyvesant to Andreas Hudde, *ibid.*, 12:372–373. The Swedes, said Stuyvesant, were not only crossing the Schuylkill, but were coming as far north as the Mohawk River and stealing much of the trade from Fort Orange. See also a pamphlet published in 1648 and reprinted in Proud, *History of Pennsylvania*, 1:111; Bozman, *Maryland*, 2:273; and Shea, "Identity of the Andastes," in the *Historical Magazine*, 2:294–297. On Stuyvesant's efforts in Rensselaerwyck, see Van Tienhoven to the States General, in *New York Colonial Documents*, 1:427–428, and "Excuses and Highly Injurious Neglect," *ibid.*, 1:335, 337, 345.

to both the merchants and the Company, decided to barter "sparingly" in guns through the commissary at Orange, but they found that an inch given meant an ell taken, and in 1652, pursuant to recommendations of the Committee of the States General, the trade in guns through any agency whatsoever was again prohibited to freemen or private traders and reserved to the Company commissaries at the store. Within two years the futility of this policy was in turn apparent, and the Council of New Netherland passed a resolution in February to provide the Mohawks with munitions "but as sparingly and secretly as possible, for reasons and motives, which in time shall be communicated."[13]

Only most unwillingly had New Netherland partially capitulated to the trade in firearms, and they could hardly have done otherwise. Their own illicit traders they might, with great difficulty and expense, have controlled, but had they been more than men they could hardly have controlled the illicit traders of every other colony on the coast, who forced their policy upon the Dutch. Probably every colony firmly believed that its neighbors helped the Indians hostile to it for either trade or conquest. Maryland blamed the Swedes and the Dutch, New England blamed the French and the Dutch, the French blamed the English and the Dutch, and the Swedes traded firearms freely and participated happily in all charges and counter charges.[14] It seems that the position of the Iroquois in regard to munitions of war was as fortunate as their geographic position, for they were at the center of a lively competition where there was no practical solution of the problem open to the white colonists. If they had a superiority in weapons it was certainly not so great as has been imagined, and was traceable to their position rather than to the trading policy of the Dutch, for the Dutch did everything in their power to stop the trade, and their policy was much less generous to the trade than was that of the French, who were their most uncompromising critics.[15]

What might the Council of New Netherland have thought could they have read Father Vimont's letter of 1643: "We have had letters from France that the design of the Dutch is to have the French harassed by the Iroquois, to such an extent that they may constrain them to . . . aban-

[13] Van Tienhoven to the States General, *ibid.*, 427–428; also *ibid.*, 501, and 13: 35–36.
[14] Hubbard, *Indian Wars of New England*, 2:265–267; "Lord Baltimore's Printed Case Uncased and Answered," in Hall, *Narratives of Early Maryland*, 190; *ante*, note 4; Johnson, *Swedish Settlements on the Delaware*, 1:377–378, quoting the *Plymouth Colonial Record*, Report, 1647, Document XII, p. 67.
[15] See below, Appendix B, for a discussion of French policy and trade.

don everything . . . they ought to apply to it a remedy . . . *That is very easy for them*" (italics mine). Knowing by bitter experience how "easy for them" it was, the Dutch would probably have considered Vimont's letter a sorry return for their ransom of many French prisoners, to which both the Company and settlers had contributed, and which was never paid to them by the French. In the French trade policy lies the second reason for such advantage in armament as the Iroquois had; it consists not in the repression of the trade in firearms, but in prices, which, as a result of the monopolistic French policy, were very high in New France. Small credit has New Netherland ever received for its truly moderate and always humane attitude toward its French competitors. True expansion at Albany did not begin under the Dutch at all, but under the energetic Dongan, in 1684.[16]

[16] Vimont, in the *Jesuit Relations*, 24:273; Directors to Stuyvesant, in *New York Colonial Documents*, 13:28; Munsell, *Albany Records*, 4:49, and *Annals of Albany*, 4:70. The fact that French high prices were responsible for the comparatively poor armament of their Indians was unwarily admitted even by the French governor. See *New York Colonial Documents*, 9:196. See also Jogues, "Novum Belgium," in the *Jesuit Relations*, 28:113; Jameson, *Narratives of New Netherland*, 262; Lahontan, *New Voyages*, 1:58–59. On English expansion see Buffinton, "The Policy of Albany," in the *Mississippi Valley Historical Review*, 8:327–366.

B. THE FRENCH TRADE IN FIREARMS

THAT THE FRENCH policy was against trading firearms to Indians is a statement often given credence but actually far from the truth. Authority for the statement that they did, during their first occupation, trade them indiscriminately to the savages of New England, has already been cited in note 4 of Appendix A. During the second occupation the policy was more restrained but never prohibitive, many of the parties of French savages being well, even heavily, armed.

The permanent French policy, established by Montmagny, was to refuse the sale of firearms to infidels, and to sell only to Christian neophytes, although even that regulation was not strictly observed. So closely related were the missions and the trade, and so greatly did one depend upon the other, that the regulation served a double purpose to the benefit of both. There was no objection at all to the possession of arquebuses by neophytes. Governor Montmagny is found presenting a gun with his own hands to a convert, and Vimont wrote that "it seems that our Lord intends to use this means in order to render Christianity acceptable in these regions."[1]

Throughout the early 1640's the Iroquois do not seem to have had superiority in firearms, nor, for that matter, were they often victorious in the field, save when assaulting trading bands on the rivers, when the advantage of ambush and the lack of baggage tipped the scales heavily in their favor. Invading parties of French Indians seemed to have no lack of arms; for example, one party of seven Algonquins possessed at least six arquebuses, and in another party five French Indians had three arquebuses each, all loaded with chain-shot. The descriptions of these encounters by the Jesuits are invariably favorable to the French Indians, and in the effort to show that the Iroquois were better armed they are often misleading, as in the account of a dozen Algonquins meeting more than two score Iroquois, who had "twice as many arquebuses." It oc-

[1] *Jesuit Relations*, 25:9, II, 27, 219–223.

curs even to the casual reader that the Iroquois had also practically twice as many men, and that the disparity in proportional armament is purely dialectic.[2]

There is little doubt, however, that at the time of the Huron downfall in 1649, the French Indians were, as compared with the Iroquois, inadequately armed. From the account of the death of Father Daniel it would seem that the Iroquois were armed mostly with bows and arrows, but they probably had a better supply of guns than did the French Indians. Yet it may be clearly seen and even proved that French policy was not responsible for that defect in armament. After calculating the number of conversions in Huronia, and the number eligible for firearms if they could have afforded them, one is forced to the conclusion that French prices, held up by monopoly and exploitative lust, must bear the responsibility.[3]

Brébeuf alone saw seven thousand Hurons baptized, and the letters of Ragueneau reveal that almost three thousand were baptized in the three years before 1649, exclusive of a huge number baptized *in extremis* by Father Daniel in the Petun villages. The two hundred and fifty Hurons who came down to Montreal in 1648 seem to have been well supplied with arquebuses, and the savages at Three Rivers in the same year welcomed the Attikamegue with "a neat salute of many arquebus shots." Dablon, describing the reception accorded him far up the Saguenay and toward the Great Bay, speaks of a great fusillade of muskets like "miniature thunder" from savages that had seldom if ever seen a white man. The Erie of 1654 were supposed to have had no guns, using bows and arrows alone, but Dablon, in an unguarded moment, ascribed their defeat to a shortage of *powder*. The defeat of the Tamaroa Illinois is usually ascribed to lack of weapons, but La Salle's *Relation* indicates that they suffered no shortage in weapons, had the warriors bearing them only been at home. If, notwithstanding all the evidence, it be asserted that the French Indians and very numerous converts were inadequately armed, one is moved to inquire why; no French regulation prohibited it, nor did French usage, and by 1649 great numbers were eligible. The opinions of representative Frenchmen as to the difference in prices are as revealing as an examination of price tables, which are found throughout the *New York Colonial Documents* and the *Manuscrits inedits*.[4]

[2] *Ibid.*, 24:291; 27:229–231; Beauchamp, *New York Iroquois*, 191; Colden, *Five Nations of Canada*, 1:7–9.

[3] On Daniel's death see Ragueneau to Caraffa, in the *Jesuit Relations*, 33:263; 34:91.

[4] *Ibid.*, 24:159; 32:177, 188 ff., 283; 33:69, 257; 34:83, 103, 159, 227; 41:83; 42:181; 46:275–277; La Salle, *Relation*, 67. The representative opinions referred to above

Notwithstanding these indications that French Indians were well armed, it seems fair to conclude that the Iroquois were better armed, as indeed they needed to be. It is hardly fair to contrast La Salle's report on the Illinois trade—"hatchets, knives, needles and awls, which are the merchandise held by them in best esteem"—with the Iroquois insistence upon firearms at Three Rivers in 1641. By that year guns had already become the "capital goods" of the Iroquois, their only means of acquiring the furs that were now indispensable to them. Hampered somewhat, though but temporarily, by the Dutch prohibition of the trade in guns on penalty of death, they were going into the only market they knew in which guns were sold. It is significant that never again did they insist upon guns from the French.[5]

are to be found in Jogues' account, in the *Jesuit Relations*, 27:113; Jameson, *Narratives of New Netherland*, 262; Lahontan, *New Voyages*, 1:58–59; abstract of letters from the governor of Canada, in *New York Colonial Documents*, 9:196.

[5] La Salle, *Relation*, 143; Le Jeune, in the *Jesuit Relations*, 21:53–61. On the Dutch prohibition see the case of Michiel Jansz, discussed above, Appendix A, and Van Laer, *Van Rensselaer Bowier Manuscripts*, 426, 565. The colony of Rensselaerwyck imposed a penalty of only one hundred guilders, but the death penalty imposed by New Netherland was general.

C. THE PEACE OF 1653

In 1653 the Iroquois made peace with New France, and it seemed to the inhabitants of that frightened and war-weary little colony to be providential, for of all dark years since its establishment 1653 was without doubt the darkest. The missions among the far tribes had been ruined, and, what was more to the point, the trade also. Not for five years had one of the great trading fleets traveled the Ottawa, and the whole white population of New France was scarcely half the number of the Iroquois warriors. Early in the spring of 1653 three canoes had stolen in from the far country beyond the Sault to tell the French that the flotsam of their former allies had found lodgment in the land where only Nicolet, of all the whites, had thus far penetrated, two decades before. Here a settlement and a center of resistance was still being planned, but that was cold comfort for New France, for meanwhile the Mohawk storm howled about Montreal and Three Rivers. Such was the picture in May, and by November the five Iroquois cantons had come in separately and made peace!

The French were dumfounded, almost alarmed, at this sudden turn of good fortune. Plans for evacuation, already far advanced, were postponed, and when six score of their old allies came down the Ottawa in the following June, "Plenty and prosperity once more visted the colony. Canada reawoke to life and hope."[1]

There was a great deal of speculation in the colony as to the motives impelling the Iroquois to this peace. They had come independently of one another, and apparently were genuinely desirous of establishing and maintaining a peaceful relationship. "The Iroquois have made peace," wrote Father Le Mercier. "Or, rather, let us say that it is God." News reached him that the Seneca were impelled by fear of the Erie, or Cat Nation, who had burned a town and cut to pieces a Seneca rear guard of eighty picked men, but that did not account for the other four cantons,

[1] Kellogg, *French Régime*, 99; *Jesuit Relations*, 41:78.

and Le Mercier continued to wonder as weeks passed and no news came of disaster to Mohawk, Oneida, Cayuga, or Onondaga.[2]

Subsequent historians, up to 1925, did little to solve the puzzle. Charlevoix, the great Jesuit historian, adopted Le Mercier's conclusion, that "He apparently wished but to suspend for a brief period the enemies of His name." Belmont, almost a contemporary of the peace, was incurious, and Beauchamp, in modern times, was satisfied with the Seneca reference to the Erie menace. It is curious that the *Jesuit Relations* of the following years offer no explanation, for the peace, although subsequently broken, was an important one, and possibly prevented the destruction of New France.[3]

Since 1925 the peace has been accounted for in a manner apparently satisfactory to historians. The belief is that an Iroquois war party, eight hundred or more strong, had besieged the Hurons (Petuns) and Ottawa in their fort at Méchingan, somewhere on or near the Door County Peninsula in Wisconsin, and had been unsuccessful. Dividing into two bands, they retreated by both northern and southern routes, but being fallen upon by enemies, all but a very few were killed. The Iroquois, it was thought, humbled and terrified by this great defeat, had begged peace from the French, who knew nothing of their plight. Unquestionably such a defeat and loss, had it happened before the negotiations for peace, would have so resulted, for the Iroquois cantons never boasted many more than two thousand warriors, and the loss of eight hundred or more would have sunk them into despair.[4]

To the writer, however, this explanation of the peace is not satisfactory. The sole source cited is Perrot's *Memoir*, and a careful reading of the circumstances of the peace negotiations on the St. Lawrence, compared with the *Memoir*, leaves a conviction that the connection drawn between them is not only unlikely but impossible. Further, it leaves the conviction that the affair mentioned by Perrot occurred in 1655 if it occurred at all, and that it is most probable that it never occurred at all, in just the manner in which he told it; that for all these reasons the defeat mentioned by Perrot was not and could not have been the reason for

[2] Le Mercier, in the *Jesuit Relations*, 157 ff., 163; Charlevoix, *New France*, 2:256; "Copie de deux lettres," in the *Jesuit Relations*, 41:81, 217.

[3] Charlevoix, *New France*, 2:256; Belmont, *Histoire du Canada*, 29; Beauchamp, *New York Iroquois*, 204.

[4] Perrot, *Memoir*, in Blair, *Indian Tribes*, 1:151–157; Kellogg, *French Régime*, 98; Hjalmar R. Holand, "Radisson's Two Western Journeys," in *Minnesota History*, 15:158 (1934), and in the *Peninsula Historical Review*, 2:58. The figure of about two thousand warriors is the result of more than thirty different estimates, most of which agree closely.

this important peace. To justify this conclusion it will be necessary to review the circumstances of the peace, with a certain emphasis upon chronology, and to present the *Memoir* for examination.

The peace, although astonishing, was not precipitate. The priests had had word from the Seneca in the spring that they wished to make peace, and that they were planning to bring in the Cayuga with them. On the twenty-sixth of June, sixty Onondaga appeared at Montreal, "sent on behalf of their whole nation to learn whether the hearts of the French would be inclined to peace." They were sent on to the governor at Quebec, where they held a council and concluded a formal peace. It is not likely that all sixty of the Onondaga went to Quebec, for a part of them, returning, visited the Oneida, and "declared they were really going to contract a close alliance with them [the French]." They urged the Oneida to join in the peace, and the Oneida, wishing to be parties to it if it pleased the powerful Onondaga, promptly sent an embassy of their own to Montreal. To prove their sincerity, they warned the French of a party of six hundred Mohawks who were stalking Three Rivers, and the French, forewarned, were able to capture the Mohawk chief and four of his followers, which helped considerably in the negotiations of September.[5]

Meanwhile the Onondaga at Quebec had concluded their business, and prepared to return to their own country. Late in August the lurking Mohawks before mentioned had captured some Hurons who held Iroquois prisoners, and the returning Onondagas, meeting the party near Montreal, stood between the Mohawks and their Huron victims, declaring that "they would risk their own lives for them." The Hurons were released, their baggage returned, and even their loss of a gun made good by the proffer of a hundred guns. The Mohawks, impressed, then and there decided upon peace; sending a chief back to bring Father Poncet, a captive in their towns, they went themselves to the governor. A council was held, and peace decided upon. Father Poncet left Iroquoia on October 3 and reached Quebec on November 5. He had been told of the peace on September 18 or 19, while the Mohawks were still parleying at Quebec.[6]

Perrot in his *Memoir*, after sketching the fall of the Hurons in 1649 and that of their Algonquin allies in the next years, accounts for the apparently mysterious peace as follows:

[5] Le Mercier, in the *Jesuit Relations*, 40:89, 163; *Journal des Jésuites, ibid.*, 38:179, 165–169; 40:91, 95.

[6] *Ibid.*, 40:115, 141, 175–183, 191.

The early relations of these events describe them quite fully; accordingly I do not expatiate upon them here, but limit myself to an account only of such things as they have ommitted and which I have learned from the lips of the old men among the Outaouas tribes.

The following year (1653) the Irroquois sent out another expedition which counted eight hundred men, to attack the Outaouas; but those tribes, feeling sure that the enemy had ascertained the place where they had established themselves, and would certainly make another attack against them, had taken the precaution to send out one of their scouting parties, who went as far as the former country of the Hurons, from which they had been driven. These men descried the Irroquois party who were marching against them and hastened back to carry the news of this incursion to their own people at that (Huron) island. They immediately abandoned that place and retreated to Mechingan, where they constructed a fort, resolving to await there the enemy. The Irroquois (came to that place but) were unable to accomplish anything during the first two years. They made further efforts to succeed and put in the field a little army, as it were, intending to destroy the villages of that new settlement, at which a considerable extent of land had already been cleared. But the Outaouas had time enough to harvest their grain before the arrival of the enemy . . . The Irroquois finally appeared one morning before the fort. . . . In the following year (1656) the Outaouas descended in a body to Three Rivers. Missionaries were allotted to them: the Hurons had Father Garot, and the Outaouas had Father Mesnard with five Frenchmen who accompanied them. Father Garot was slain by the war-party of the Flemish Bastard.[7]

The line "But the Outaouas had time enough to harvest their grain before the arrival of the enemy" is a most significant one, for it places the Iroquois arrival after the ripening season of the grain, which was certainly corn. The reference to the cleared land and the huge supply of corn within the fort establish the fact. The fact that the peaceful intentions of all the five cantons were accounted for by August 30, and the peace signed before the middle of September, makes it impossible that the defeat of which Perrot tells could have been the reason for the peace, whose circumstances we know, even if the defeat occurred in the year 1653.

As to the dates, it is perfectly evident that such phrases as "were unable to accomplish anything during the first two years" and "They made further efforts to succeed," coming as they do after "The following

[7] Perrot, *Memoir*, in Blair, *Indian Tribes*, 1:151–152, 157. Between these two passages is an account of the siege and retreat, accompanied by disaster in the Iroquois army. It is indicated by the marks of elision in the quotation.

year (1653)" would place the defeat in 1655. But the dates in parentheses are not those of Perrot, but those of his editor, Tailhan, and Tailhan is sometimes in error. It has been suggested to the writer by Mr. Hjalmar R. Holand that the date in the first parentheses, the year subsequent to the destruction of the Hurons and their allies, should be 1651. Then, counting forward two years, the defeat would be placed (and ought to be, Mr. Holand thinks) in the year 1653, and the parenthetical date in the line "In the following year (1656)" should be changed to 1654.

It can be shown, however, that this change cannot be made, and that Mr. Holand is dating from the wrong direction, for the date 1656 is the very date of which we can be certain. The descent of the Ottawa, the assignment of the missionaries, and the death of Father Garreau at the hands of an Iroquois war party are told in the *Relations*, and the date is certified as 1656. There is one error in Perrot in the substitution of Ménard for Dreuillettes, who accompanied Garreau, but the other circumstances are identical, even as told by Mr. Holand in his own article.[8] This is undoubtedly the method used by Tailhan in arriving at his dates, which seems to be perfectly correct. This places the defeat, if it occurred at all, in 1655.

There is still the doubt that any such number of Iroquois were exterminated in any year. Miss Kellogg thinks that the besieging army was larger than the original force of eight hundred men sent out. Mr. Holand has it the same army, although a close reading of the *Memoir* shows it certainly to have been another one. Granting such a large number, it would have been impossible to make it up from any one canton, and it would have represented between a third and a half of the whole Iroquois fighting force. Besides, the proponents of the "1653" theory must note that in the summer of that year there were six hundred Mohawks about Montreal. In any case, the destruction of so large a number would have produced a condition in Iroquoia impossible to conceal from the keen-eyed priests who followed the peace into the cantons. Poncet was a captive in Iroquoia and he never heard of this defeat. Le Moine was there the following summer and many more followed, yet they saw nothing to indicate a severe loss. In 1654, for example, the Iroquois were raising an army of eighteen hundred men against the Erie.[9]

[8] On the events of 1656 see De Quen, in the *Jesuit Relations*, 42:33, 225, 228–231. Holand's article is in the *Peninsula Historical Review*, 2:41–62.

[9] Kellogg, *French Régime*, 97; Holand, in the *Peninsula Historical Review*, 52–56. Mr. Holand says that eight hundred men represented one-fourth of the Iroquois fighting force, but this is an estimate of Iroquois numbers. On the preparation for the Erie war see the *Jesuit Relations*, 41:83, 121.

Such a defeat would have had repercussions all through the Lakes region. The Ottawa coming down their river in the next June would have been full of it, and the pride of the northern tribes would have made it impossible as well as undesirable to conceal such a triumph. Yet never a whisper was heard in the land about this great victory; the ruin of a huge fraction of the Iroquois warriors, if it occurred, had dropped into a void. If, as Mr. Holand thinks, the Ottawa brigade came down the river "joyous in a victory of the year before over the terrible Iroquois," they were singularly silent about it. They were joyous enough over the capture of thirteen Seneca on the way, not yet having heard of the peace, but they seem to have forgotten the "victory of the year before" if it had occurred.[10]

Radisson and Groseilliers were probably in the West that year (1654) and, Mr. Holand thinks, at the very fort of Méchingan, yet they never heard of it, though they helped to capture and burn a few lurking Iroquois.[11] The complete absence of any sort of confirmation of so important an event assumes the proportions of positive rather than negative evidence, particularly when the source is a most doubtful one. Were the testimony that of Nicolas Perrot, it would be less doubtful, but, as he says, it is only what the old men among the Ottawa told him, and it was written in 1718, in his old age.

To sum up, it seems impossible so to read the source as to account for the peace of 1653. Unless the Ottawa harvest of their grain is ignored, it is necessary to put the supposed defeat back in 1652, which is the more difficult in that the Seneca fought and were defeated in that year by a Neutral-Susquehannah combination, and the distance from the assuredly reliable date of 1656 is the greater. Reading the source as it is, the date of 1655 for whatever did happen is inescapable, and the weight of evidence against an Iroquois loss of eight hundred or more men at any time is too formidable even to deny.

[10] Holand, "Radisson's Two Western Journeys," in *Minnesota History*, 15:158; *Jesuit Relations*, 41:79.
[11] Radisson, *Voyages*, 147; Holand, "Radisson's Two Western Journeys," in *Minnesota History*, 15:158. As Mr. Holand says, the chronology of Radisson is probably hopeless.

BIBLIOGRAPHY AND INDEX

BIBLIOGRAPHY

DESPITE the importance of this remarkable people, there is no satisfactory history of them, and only two have been attempted. The first of these was Cadwallader Colden's *History of the Five Nations*, which was written in 1727 with a special object in view, to stop the trade of New York with Canada in Indian goods. As the only history available for 178 years, it had a wide circulation, though literary form and style were its sole virtues. Having a special object, Colden omitted most of the material not relevant to that object. He practically confined himself to the New York Indian Records of 1678-98, dismissing Iroquois history up to 1650 in ten short pages, most of which he lifted almost bodily from Lahontan and Lafitau. His errors upon easily ascertainable and even generally known facts are ridiculous,[1] and the book can be relied upon only in its literal, though incomplete, transcriptions from the Records. Since the Records to which he had access began in 1678, the only part of his work which has any merit at all begins at a period in which the most important phase of Iroquois history was practically over.

The first volume of Charlevoix's *Histoire* was long considered authoritative in its brief references to the Iroquois wars and was used freely by American historians after Shea's translation of 1866-72. Partially, perhaps, because Charlevoix was himself a cleric and surrounded by clerical influences, and partially because the sources were not readily available to him, his view of the Iroquois is as astigmatic as that of his brothers of the previous century, or that of Francis Parkman of the century following him. The *Jesuit Relations* had not been printed when he wrote,

[1] Colden locates the Nipissings on the St. Lawrence River, when all contemporary maps gave the name of Lake Nipissing, and has the Huron nation destroyed in "a dreadful battle fought within two leagues of Quebec . . . in sight of the French Settlements" (vol. I, p. II). The battle was fought approximately five hundred miles from Quebec, and the French did not learn of it for many months. He has over a thousand French killed by a few hundred Iroquois warriors in the La Chine massacre of July, 1688 (p. 96), when one hundred is probably an excessive estimate. These misstatements are, unfortunately, representative.

and although he consulted them, he seems to have had difficulty with his chronology. His mistake of four years in the date of the first Iroquois invasion of Huronia (see above, page 72) is a peculiarly vital one, since an invasion in the year 1636 has a meaning entirely different from one in 1640. None of the Holland Documents were available to him, and any comment or opinion on the Iroquois, unsupported by the documents of the colony with which the Iroquois were most closely associated in both commerce and war, would necessarily have little weight. Charlevoix was certainly competent, and usually cautious, but he was scarcely in a position to write upon the Iroquois.

William M. Beauchamp's *History of the New York Iroquois* (New York, 1905) is superior to Colden's, although it depends too much upon Colden and Charlevoix to be of real historical value. The introductory pages dealing with the prehistoric period are authoritative (for 1905), falling within the author's field of archeology. The bibliography is not impressive, and all periodical and unedited material is ignored. The use of the *Jesuit Relations* and the abundant material in the *New York Colonial Documents* is fragmentary, and the author is both uncritical of sources and incurious concerning motives. He accepts at face value Tailhan's notes on Perrot's *Mémoire*, notwithstanding their insufficiency and very common error; following Morgan blindly, he insists upon treating the League of the Iroquois in its assumed perfections, apparently thinking that the League of 1850 must have been the same in 1650. Although much of Iroquois history was made north and west of Lake Ontario and the St. Lawrence River, all intertribal relations outside the territory of the state of New York are little more than hinted at, when not omitted entirely.[2] Since Beauchamp wrote, much material has become available in the English language, notably the Van Laer translations and editions of the *Van Rensselaer Bowier Manuscripts*, and the Fort Orange and Beverwyck papers. Jameson's *Early Narratives of New Netherland* would probably have been of great assistance to Beauchamp, although he passed

---

[2] Beauchamp makes an unfortunately characteristic error in his identification of the "Massawomecks" met by Smith in Virginia. He asserts confidently that they were Erie (p. 194) for no ascertainable reason other than that they "inhabit upon a great water beyond the mountains." (Smith, *Generall Historie of Virginia*, 1:127.) Upon the same page is found the statement that they went to the French "to have their hatchets and commodities by trade," though the French never saw an Erie until, after their destruction in 1655, they were met as prisoners in the Iroquois towns. A glance at Smith's map shows them *north* of the Susquehannah, destroying any possibility of their having been Erie. Schoolcraft in his *Notes on the Iroquois* has the astounding conclusion that "by this term [Massawomecks] the Iroquois denominated the confederacy of Powhatanic tribes in Virginia" (p. 155), when the word was a Powhatanic term for someone else, probably an Iroquois.

over many of them which could have been found in the *New York Historical Collections* had he chosen to make use of them. Beauchamp says that he wrote the book because he was directed to do so, which may account for his somewhat pedestrian use of materials.

Francis Parkman's pronouncements on the Iroquois, though his treatment of them is incidental to his main themes, are not trustworthy. Despite the brilliance of his work on New France, his fundamental misconception of the entire interracial and intertribal problem, with his predilection for French sources and attitudes, invalidates his opinions concerning the Iroquois. It may at first seem strange that Parkman, who could be so impartially and keenly critical of the Jesuit institution and clerical views on worldly matters, should have adopted uncritically and quite without reservation the clerical explanation of the phenomenon of the Iroquois. Yet it may not be strange. As depicted by Parkman, the Five Nations furnish a lurid background of fire, blood, and villainy against which to draw in bold lines the failure of New France. As has been remarked elsewhere, the Iroquois tradesman is not an especially romantic figure, and it may be that the artist in Parkman responded more readily to the Iroquois warrior. But neither the Iroquois institution nor their achievements can be thus neatly explained by innate treachery, unqualified cruelty, and insensate blood-lust. The shortcomings of a people can hardly be the reasons for their greatness.

Lewis Morgan's *League of the Iroquois* is a monumental and definitive work on the Iroquois political structure, but it makes small pretense of being a history. Morgan concerned himself solely with the organizational and traditional origin of the League and used Colden liberally as a background, which means Lahontan and Lafitau, neither of whom possessed any appreciable information concerning the Iroquois of the seventeenth century. Morgan was quite innocent of any knowledge of sources for that century, and probably did not know that any existed. Notwithstanding Morgan's stature in his own field, his work is valueless as history, for he consulted few or no sources save the Iroquois themselves. As George Hyde has said (see above, page 9, note 14), there is no worse source than unsupported memory or tradition.

The best historical writing yet done on the Iroquois is, curiously, an "Introduction," by Charles H. McIlwain, to Wraxall's *Abridgement of the Indian Affairs Transacted in New York* (Cambridge, 1915), the same records mulled over by Colden nearly two centuries before. Though necessarily brief, it is based upon a comprehensive study of most of the source material available at the time, with the notable exception of the *Jesuit Relations*. There is need for a complete history of the Iroquois, as well as for a rewriting, from sources, of the frontier conflict of the seventeenth century.

In the field of aboriginal history west of Lake Ontario there is only one work to be cited. That is Louise Phelps Kellogg's scholarly *French Régime in Wisconsin and the Northwest* (Madison, 1925). Because of the scope of the book, intertribal relations are incidental, being largely confined to one chapter, into which is packed a great store of information. Throughout the book is found a broad outline of tribal histories, though any detailed examination of motives is necessarily lacking. One may differ with the author in interpretation, but the errors of fact, if any, are few and insignificant.

Of source material there are two tremendous collections, the Thwaites edition of *The Jesuit Relations and Allied Documents* and O'Callaghan's *Documents Relative to the Colonial History of the State of New York*, the one comprising seventy-three volumes and the other fifteen. Each contains such various materials that it has been difficult to follow any rule concerning citation. In many cases a simple citation is plainly insufficient, for the nature of the document to which reference is made, the author or authors, and the date and place of writing are often of great importance in determining the weight of evidence. There may be a vital distinction between a personal letter from the Superior of the Huron mission to a friend, the Huron Relation of the same individual to the Father Superior at Quebec, and the report of the Father Superior to France or Rome, even when all three documents discuss the same matter.[3] Yet to give full particulars in each case would make citation itself a monumental task. Therefore information concerning the writer, the particular document, and the conditions of writing has been given whenever the author has thought that such information seemed relevant or desirable. The same plan has been followed with some secondary material. In only a few cases, for example, has the author gone back of the name of Justin Winsor

---

[3] For example, Lalemant's letter to Richelieu in March, 1640, tells an altogether different story from his letter to Vitelleschi at Rome, written four days later but on the same subject. Writing to Richelieu, he ascribes the diminution in the number of the Hurons to losses inflicted by the Iroquois, putting upon them the sole responsibility. Writing to Vitelleschi four days later, he attributes the losses solely to the plague. The latter statement is the truth, for in 1640 the Hurons had lost practically no warriors to the Iroquois. Lalemant wanted money from Richelieu, and Iroquois war parties made a much better background for a plea than did disease, for defense required funds for forts and armaments, whereas disease required only fortitude. For these letters see the *Jesuit Relations*, 17: 223, 229. Richelieu did contribute a year later, when Le Jeune, on a trip to France, contrived to approach him through the Duchesse d'Eguillon. See above, page 75, note 27.

in citing his *Narrative and Critical History*. Winsor probably wrote the unsigned essays himself, and for those he did not write his name is a better guarantee of authority than are the names of any of his collaborators.

Where several good translations and editions of well-known sources are available, such as the memoir of Tonty and the narrative of Galinée, there is a temptation to adopt a rule, and use exclusively either the latest edition or the best edition. The author has chosen to cite, in each case, the edition which, because of editorial policy or annotation seemed most suitable to the matter in hand. For example, when discussing the use of elm bark for canoes, the Coyne edition of Galinée seemed slightly the more suitable, despite the fact that the Kellogg edition is in general a much better piece of work and much more readily available to most readers.

Only twice has it been found necessary to cite material in a foreign language when an English translation was available. One of these instances involves Tailhan's edition of the *Mémoire* of Perrot, when the writer differed with Tailhan's editorial comment. The other instance is that of the early edition (French) of the *Jesuit Relations*, to point out an obvious mistranslation which had been made before the Thwaites edition.

The following bibliographical list includes only those materials actually cited, and is in no sense a comprehensive bibliography of the subject, which would be many times longer.

ADAIR, E. R. "Dollard des Ormeaux and the Fight at the Long Sault: A Re-interpretation of Dollard's Exploit." *Canadian Historical Review*, new series, 13:121–138. June, 1932.

ADAIR, JAMES. *History of the American Indians*, edited by Samuel C. Williams. Johnson City, Tennessee, 1930.

ADAMS, ARTHUR T. "The Radisson Problem." *Minnesota History*, 15:317–327. 1934.

ALSOP, GEO. E. "A Character of the Province of Maryland." Clayton L. Hall, ed., *Narratives of Early Maryland, 1633–1684*. New York, 1910.

ALVORD, CLARENCE W. *The Illinois Country, 1673–1818* (*Centennial History of Illinois*, vol. 1). Springfield, 1920.

————— and LEE BIDGOOD, eds. *The First Explorations of the Trans-Allegheny Region by the Virginians, 1650–1674*. Cleveland, 1912.

AUDET, FRANCIS J. "Le Regiment de Carignan." *Proceedings and Transactions of the Royal Society of Canada*, 1921 (3d series, vol. 16), sec. 1, pp. 129–141. Toronto, 1922.

BAILEY, JOHN R. *Mackinac, Formerly Michilimackinac*. 2d edition. Lansing, Michigan, 1896.

BAKER, VIRGINIA, and CROTHERS, HAYES. *The French and Indian War*. Chicago, 1928.

BALDWIN, C. C. "Early Indian Migrations in Ohio." *American Antiquarian*, 1:227–239. 1878.

BANCROFT, GEORGE. *History of the United States of America from the Discovery of the Continent*, vol. 1. New York, 1891.

BATEMAN, NEWTON, and PAUL SELBY. *Historical Encyclopedia of Illinois and Peoria County.* 2 vols. Chicago, 1905.

BEACH, WILLIAM W., ed. *The Indian Miscellany, Containing Papers on the History Antiquities, Arts, Languages, Religions, Traditions, and Superstitions of the American Aborigines.* Albany, 1877.

BEAUCHAMP, WILLIAM M. "Earthenware of the New York Aborigines." New York State Museum Bulletin, vol. 5, no. 22, pp. 71–146. October, 1898.

———— *A History of the New York Iroquois, Now Commonly Called the Six Nations.* New York State Museum Bulletin no. 78. New York, 1905.

———— "Origins of the Iroquois." *American Antiquarian*, new series, 16:61–69. March, 1894.

BECKWITH, HIRAM. "The Illinois and Indiana Indians." *Fergus Historical Series*, vol. 5, no. 27, pp. 99–183. Chicago, 1884.

BIGGAR, HENRY P. *The Early Trading Companies of New France: A Contribution to the History of Commerce and Discovery in North America.* University of Toronto Studies in History, edited by George M. Wrong. Toronto, 1901.

BLACKBIRD, ANDREW J. *History of the Ottawa and Chippewa Indians of Michigan.* Ypsilanti, Michigan, 1887.

BLAIR, EMMA HELEN, ed. *The Indian Tribes of the Upper Mississippi Valley and Region of the Great Lakes.* 2 vols. Cleveland, 1911–12.

BLAKE, FREEMAN N. *History of the Indians in British North America, Showing Their Condition and Management.* 41 Congress, 2 session, House Miscellaneous Document no. 35. Washington, 1870.

BOYLE, DAVID. "The Iroquois." *Archaeological Report of the Provincial Museum of Ontario*, 1905. Toronto, 1906. Also in *Report of the Minister of Education for Ontario*, 1905, appendix; and in *Sessional Papers*, 11th Legislature of the Province of Ontario, 2d session.

———— *Notes on Primitive Man in Ontario.* Appendix to the *Report of the Minister of Education for Ontario*, 1894. Toronto, 1895.

BOZMAN, JOHN L. *The History of Maryland from Its First Settlement in 1633 to the Restoration in 1660.* Baltimore, 1837.

BRADFORD, WILLIAM. *Bradford's History "Of Plimoth Plantation," from the Original Manuscript, with a Report of the Proceedings Incident to the Return of the Manuscript to Massachusetts.* Boston, 1899.

BREBNER, JOHN B. *The Explorers of North America, 1492–1806.* One of the *Pioneer Histories* series, edited by V. T. Harlow and J. A. Williamson. New York, 1933.

BRESSANI, FRANCESCO GIUSEPPE. *Les Jésuites, martyrs du Canada: Relation Abrégée de quelques missions des pères de la Compagnie de Jèsus dans la Nouvelle France*, edited by Felix Martin. Montreal, 1877.

BRINTON, DANIEL G. *The Lenâpé and Their Legends.* Philadelphia, 1885.

———— "The Shawnees and Their Migrations." *Historical Magazine*, 10:1–4. January, 1866.

BRODHEAD, JOHN R. *History of the State of New York, 1609–1691.* 2 vols. New York, 1853, 1871.

———— "Memoir of the Early Colonization of New Netherland." *New York Historical Collections*, 2d series, 2:355–366. New York, 1849.

BRUCE, G. W. "The Petuns." *Papers and Records of the Ontario Historical Society*, 8:34–39. Toronto, 1915.

BUFFINTON, ARTHUR. "The Policy of Albany and English Westward Expansion."
Mississippi Valley Historical Review, 8:327–366. 1922.

BURRAGE, HENRY S., ed. *Early English and French Voyages.* J. Franklin Jameson,
ed., *Original Narratives of Early American History.* New York, 1906.

BUSHNELL, DAVID I., Jr. *Native Villages and Village Sites East of the Mississippi.*
Bureau of American Ethnology Bulletin 69. Washington, 1919.

———— *Tribal Migrations East of the Mississippi River.* Smithsonian Miscellaneous
Collections, vol. 89, no. 12. Washington, 1934.

CADILLAC, LA MOTHE. "Relation." *Wisconsin Historical Collections*, 16:360–363.
Madison, 1902.

CARR, LUCIEN. "The Food of Certain American Indians and Their Methods of
Preparing It." *Proceedings of the American Antiquarian Society*, new series, 10:
155–190 (1895).

———— *The Mascoutens.* Reprinted from the *Proceedings of the American Antiquarian
Society*, new series, 13:448–462 (1899–1900). Worcester, Massachusetts, 1900.

———— *Mounds of the Mississippi Valley, Historically Considered.* Frankfort, 1882.

CARTIER, JACQUES. *Brief recit, & succincte narration, de la nauigation faicte en ysles de
Canada, Hochelage & Saguenay & Autres.* Paris, 1545. Photostatic copy in the
Wisconsin State Historical Library.

CELESTE, SISTER MARY. "The Miami Indians Prior to 1700." *Mid-America*, new
series. 5:225–234. July, 1934.

CHALMERS, GEORGE. *History of the Revolt of the American Colonies.* Boston, 1845.

———— *Political Annals.* New York State Historical Society Publication Fund,
5th series, book 2. New York, 1868.

CHAMBERLAIN, A. F. "Notes on the History, Customs, and Beliefs of the Mis-
sissagua Indians." *Journal of American Folk-Lore*, 1:150–160. 1888.

CHAMPLAIN, SAMUEL DE. *The Works of Samuel de Champlain*, translated and an-
notated under the general editorship of Henry P. Biggar. 6 vols. Toronto,
1922–36.

CHANNING, EDWARD. *A History of the United States.* 6 vols. New York, 1905–25.

CHARLEVOIX, PIERRE F. X. DE. *History and General Description of New France*,
translated from the French by John G. Shea. 6 vols. New York, 1866–72.

CLARK, DAN ELBERT. "Early Forts on the Upper Mississippi." *Proceedings of
the Mississippi Valley Historical Association*, 4:91–101 (1910–11). Cedar Rapids,
Iowa, 1912.

CLARKE, PETER D. *Origin and Traditional History of the Wyandotts and Sketches of
Other Indian Tribes of North America.* Toronto, 1870.

COBB, WILLIAM H., ANDREW PRICE, and H. MAXWELL. *History of the Mingo
Indians.* Cumberland, Maryland, 1921.

COLDEN, CADWALLADER. *The History of the Five Nations of Canada.* 2 vols. New
York, 1904.

*Collection de manuscrits contenant lettres, mémoires et autres documents historiques relatifs
à la Nouvelle-France.* 4 vols. Quebec, 1883–85.

*Collection de mémoires et de relations sur l'histoire ancienne du Canada, d'après des manu-
scrits récevement obtenus des archives et bureaux publics en France.* Quebec, 1840.

CONNELLEY, WILLIAM E. "The Habitat of the Hurons." *Archaeological Report of
the Ontario Provincial Museum*, 1899, pp. 92–109. Toronto, 1899.

COOK, SAMUEL F. *Mackinaw in History.* Lansing, 1895.

COPWAY, GEORGE. *The Traditional History and Characteristic Sketches of the Ojibway
Nation.* Boston, 1851.

COWIE, ISAAC. *The Company of Adventurers: A Narrative of Seven Years in the
Service of the Hudson's Bay Company during 1867–1874 on the Great Buffalo Plains.*
Toronto, 1913.

COYNE, JAMES H. *The Country of the Neutrals.* St. Thomas, Ontario, 1895. Pamphlet.

———— "The Dollier-Galinée Expedition, 1669–70." *Papers and Records of the Ontario Historical Society,* 20:75–81. Toronto, 1923.

———— "The Identification of the Site near Port Dover of the Wintering Place of Dollier de Casson and Bréhant de Galinée, 1669–70." *Proceedings and Transactions of the Royal Society of Canada,* 1925 (3d series, vol. 19), sec. 2, pp. 67–75.

CUSICK DAVID. *David Cusick's Sketches of Ancient History of the Six Nations.* Lockport, New York, 1848.

DANCKAERTS, JASPER. *Journal of Jasper Danckaerts, 1679–1680,* edited by Bartlett B. James and J. Franklin Jameson. New York, 1913.

DARTAIGUIETTE, DIRON. "Journal." Newton D. Mereness, ed., *Travels in the North American Colonies,* 17–96. New York, 1916.

DE BELMONT, F. V. *Histoire du Canada.* Transactions of the Quebec Literary and Historical Society, 1918. De Belmont was a contemporary, lived in Canada, and witnessed much of what he wrote about.

DE FOREST, JOHN W. *History of the Indians of Connecticut from the Earliest Known Period to 1850.* Hartford, Connecticut, 1853.

DENSMORE, FRANCES. *Chippewa Customs.* Bureau of American Ethnology Bulletin 86. Washington, 1929.

DENYS, NICHOLAS. *Description, Geographical and Historical, of the Coasts of North America,* edited by William F. Ganong. Toronto, 1916.

DONCK, ADRIAEN VAN DER. "Description of the New Netherlands," translated from the Dutch by Jeremiah Johnson. *New York Historical Collections,* 2d series, 1:125–242. New York, 1841.

DOYLE, JOHN A. *The Middle Colonies.* Vol. 4 of *English Colonies in America.* New York, 1907.

DRAKE, FRANCIS S., ed. *The Indian Tribes of the United States.* 2 vols. Philadelphia, 1884.

DU CREUX, FRANÇOIS. *Historiae Canadensis.* Paris, 1664.

DULUTH, DANIEL GREYSOLON. Letter dated April 12, 1864. *Wisconsin Historical Collections,* 16:115–119. Madison, 1902.

DUNTON, JOHN. *Letters from New England, 1686.* Boston, 1867.

DU PONCEAU, PETER S., and JOSHUA F. FISHER, eds. "A Memoir on the History of the Celebrated Treaty Made by William Penn with the Indians under the Elm Tree at Shackamaxon in the Year 1682." *Memoirs of the Pennsylvania Historical Society,* vol. 3, pt. 2, pp. 141–203. Philadelphia, 1834.

ESHLEMAN, HENRY F., ed. *Lancaster County Indians: Annals of the Susquehannocks and Other Indian Tribes of the Susquehannah Territory from about the Year 1500 to 1763, the Date of Their Extinction.* Lancaster, Pennsylvania, 1908.

EVANS, LEWIS. *An Analysi. of a General Map of the Middle British Colonies in America and of the Country of the Confederate Indians.* Philadelphia, 1755. Benjamin Franklin, printer.

FAILLON, ÉTIENNE MICHEL. *Histoire de la colonie française en Canada.* 3 vols. Paris, 1865–66.

FARRAND, LIVINGSTON. *Basis of American History, 1500–1900.* Vol. 2 of *The American Nation, a History,* edited by Albert B. Hart. New York, 1904.

FELCH, ALPHEUS. "The Indians of Michigan and the Cession of Their Lands to the United States by Treaty." *Michigan Pioneer and Historical Collections,* 26:274–297. Lansing, 1896.

FERLAND, JEAN B. A. *Cours d'histoire du Canada.* 2 vols. Quebec, 1861–65.

FISKE, JOHN. *The Discovery of America with Some Account of Ancient America and the Spanish Conquest.* 2 vols. Boston, 1892.

FISKE, JOHN. *The Dutch and Quaker Colonies in America.* 2 vols. Boston, 1899.
———— *New France and New England.* Boston, 1902.
FLICK, ALEXANDER C., ed. *History of the State of New York.* 10 vols. New York, 1933–37.
FRANKLIN, BENJAMIN. *A Narrative of the Late Massacres in Lancaster County.* Philadelphia, 1764. Pamphlet.
FRANKLIN, SIR JOHN. *Narrative of a Journey to the Shores of the Polar Sea, in the Years 1819, 20, 21, and 22.* London, 1823.
GALINÉE, RENE DE BRÉHANT. "Narrative of the Most Noteworthy Incidents in the Journey of Messieurs Dollier and Galinée, 1669–1670." Louise P. Kellogg, ed. *Early Narratives of the Northwest, 1634–1659,* 167–209. Also in *Papers and Records of the Ontario Historical Society,* 4:1–75. Toronto, 1903.
GALLATIN, ALBERT. "A Synopsis of the Indian Tribes of North America." *Transactions of the American Antiquarian Society,* 2:2–422. Cambridge, 1836.
GENDRON, LE SIEUR. *Quelques particularitez du pays des Hurons en la Nouvelle France.* Paris, 1660. Twenty-five copies reprinted at Albany, 1860; one hundred copies at Albany, 1868.
GIROUARD, DÉSIRÉ. *Lake St. Louis Old and New Illustrated, and Cavelier de la Salle,* translated from the French by Désiré Girouard. Montreal, 1893.
———— "Une Page sombre de notre histoire: L'expédition du Marquis de Denonville." *Proceedings and Transactions of the Royal Society of Canada,* 1899 (2d series, vol. 5), sec. 1, pp. 87–101.
GRIGNON, AUGUSTE. Letter in the *Wisconsin Historical Collections,* 3:136. Madison, 1857, 1904.
GROULX, ABBÉ. *Le Dossier de Dollard.* Montreal, 1932.
HABIG, MARION A. "The Site of the Great Illinois Village." *Mid-America,* new series, 5:3–13. July, 1933.
HAKLUYT, RICHARD, ed. *The Principal Navigations, Voyages, Traffiques and Discoveries of the English Nation.* 12 vols. Glasgow, 1903–05.
HALE, HORATIO E. *Indian Migrations as Evidenced by Language.* Chicago, 1883. Reprinted from the *American Antiquarian* for January and April, 1883.
HARRISON, WILLIAM H. "A Discourse on the Aborigines of the Ohio Valley." *Fergus Historical Series,* vol. 5, no. 26, pp. 1–52. Chicago, 1883.
HAWLEY, CHARLES. *Early Chapters of Cayuga History.* Auburn, New York, 1879.
HAZARD, SAMUEL, ed. *Annals of Pennsylvania from the Discovery of the Delaware, 1609–1682.* Philadelphia, 1850.
———— *Pennsylvania Archives, 1664–1790.* 12 vols. Philadelphia, 1852–56.
———— *Pennsylvania Colonial Records, Index.* Philadelphia, 1860.
———— *The Register of Pennsylvania.* 16 vols. Philadelphia, 1828–36.
HECKEWELDER, JOHN G. *History, Manners, and Customs of the Indian Nations Who Once Inhabited Pennsylvania and the Neighbouring States,* edited by William C. Reichel. Philadelphia, 1876. Also in *Transactions of the American Philosophical Society,* vol. 1.
HILL, ASA R. "The Historical Position of the Six Nations." *Papers and Records of the Ontario Historical Society,* vol. 19. Toronto, 1922.
HINSDALE, WILBERT B. *The First People of Michigan.* Ann Arbor, 1930.
HODGE, FREDERICK W., ed. *Handbook of American Indians North of Mexico.* Bureau of American Ethnology Bulletin no. 30. 2 vols. Washington, 1907, 1910.
HOLAND, HJALMAR R. *Old Peninsula Days: Tales and Sketches of the Door County Peninsula.* Ephraim, Wisconsin, 1925.
———— "Radisson's Two Western Journeys." *Minnesota History,* 15:157–180. 1934.
———— "St. Michael, the First Mission of the West." *Mid-America,* new series, 5:157–164. January, 1934.

HOLAND, HJALMAR R. "St. Michael, the Gateway of the West." *Peninsula Historical Review*, 2:41–62 (1928). Sturgeon Bay, Wisconsin, 1930.

HOWITT, ALFRED W. *The Native Tribes of South-East Australia.* New York, 1904.

HUBBARD, WILLIAM. *The History of the Indian Wars in New England.* 2 vols. Roxbury, Massachusetts, 1865.

HULBERT, ARCHER B. *Indian Thoroughfares.* Vol. 2 of *Historic Highways of America.* Cleveland, 1902.

HUMBOLDT, FRIEDRICH W. VON. *Personal Narrative of Travels to the Equinoctial Regions of America during the Years 1799–1804,* translated by Thomasina Ross. 3 vols. London, 1877.

HUNTER, ANDREW F. *A History of Simcoe County.* 2 vols. Barrie, Ontario, 1909.

———— *Notes of Sites of Huron Villages in the Township of Tiny (Simcoe County) and Adjacent Parts.* Toronto, 1899. Reprinted from the *Report of the Minister of Education.*

HYDE, GEORGE E. *Red Cloud's Folk.* Norman, Oklahoma, 1937.

INNIS, HAROLD A. "Interrelations between the Fur Trade of Canada and the United States." *Mississippi Valley Historical Review*, 20:321–332. December, 1933.

JAMES, BARTLETT B., and J. FRANKLIN JAMESON, eds. *Journal of Jasper Danckaerts, 1679–1680.* New York, 1913.

JAMES, CHARLES C. "The Downfall of the Huron Nation." *Proceedings and Transactions of the Royal Society of Canada*, 1906 (2d series, vol. 12), sec. 2, pp. 311–346. Ottawa, 1906.

JAMESON, J. FRANKLIN, ed. *Narratives of New Netherland, 1609–1664.* New York, 1909. A volume in the *Original Narratives of Early American History* series, edited by J. Franklin Jameson.

JENNESS, DIAMOND. *The Indians of Canada.* National Museum of Canada Bulletin 65. Ottawa, 1932.

JOHNSON, AMANDUS. *The Swedish Settlements on the Delaware: Their History and Relations to the Indians, Dutch, and English, 1638–1664.* 2 vols. Philadelphia, 1911.

JOHNSON, IDA A. *The Michigan Fur Trade.* Lansing, 1919.

JONES, ARTHUR E. "Identification of St. Ignace and Ekarenniondi." *Archaeological Report of the Ontario Provincial Museum*, 1902. Toronto, 1903.

———— *"8endake Ehen," or Old Huronia.* Report of the Bureau of Archives, 1908. Toronto, 1909.

JONES, PETER. *History of the Ojebway Indians, with Special Reference to Their Conversion to Christianity.* London, [1867].

JONES, URIAH. *History of the Juniata Valley.* Philadelphia, 1856; Harrisburg, 1889.

Jugements et deliberations du conseil souverain de la Nouvelle-France. 6 vols. Quebec, 1883.

KELLOGG, LOUISE P. *The French Régime in Wisconsin and the Northwest.* Madison, 1925.

KELLOGG, LOUISE P, ed. *Early Narratives of the Northwest, 1634–1699.* New York, 1917. A volume in the *Original Narratives of Early American History* series, edited by J. Franklin Jameson.

KENNEDY, JOHN H. "Thomas Dongan, Governor of New York (1682–1688)." Catholic University of America Studies in History, vol. 9. Washington, 1930.

LAET, JOHAN DE. "New World." J. Franklin Jameson, ed., *Narratives of New Netherland, 1609–1664,* pp. 36–60. New York, 1909.

LAFITAU, JOSEPH. *Moeurs des sauvages Ameriquains, 1724.* Paris, 1874.

LAHONTAN, LOUIS A., BARON DE. *New Voyages to North America,* edited by Reuben G. Thwaites. 2 vols. Chicago, 1905.

LAMBRECHTSEN, SIR NICOLAAS CORNELIS. *A Short Description of the Discovery and Subsequent History of the New Netherlands*, translated from the Dutch by Francis Adrian Van der Kemp. *New York Historical Collections*, 2d series, 1:75–122. New York, 1841.

LANCTÔT, GUSTAVE. "Was Dollard the Saviour of New France?" *Canadian Historical Review*, 13:138–146. June, 1932.

LA SALLE, ROBERT CAVELIER, SIEUR DE. *Relation of the Discoveries and Voyages of Cavelier de la Salle from 1679–1681: The Official Relation*, edited by Melville B. Anderson. Chicago, 1901. The text is a reprint of the "Recit de Nicolas de la Salle—1682," in Pierre Margry, *Découvertes et établissements des Français dans l'ouest et dans le sud de l'Amérique Septentrionale, 1614–1754*.

LA VÉRENDRYE, PIERRE GAULTIER DE VARENNES, SIEUR DE. *Journals and Letters of Pierre Gaultier de Varennes de la Vérendrye and His Sons, with Correspondence between the Governors of Canada and the French Court Touching the Search for the Western Sea*, edited by Lawrence J. Burpee. Toronto, 1927.

LAWSON, PUBLIUS V. "The Potawatomi." *Wisconsin Archaeologist*, 19:41–116. April, 1920.

LESCARBOT, MARC. *History of New France*, edited by William L. Grant and Henry P. Biggar. 3 vols. Toronto, 1914.

LIGHTHALL, WILLIAM D. "The False Plan of Hochelaga." *Proceedings and Transactions of the Royal Society of Canada*, 1932 (3d series, vol. 26) sec. 2, pp. 181–192. Ottawa, 1932.

——— "Hochelagans and Mohawks: A Link in Iroquois History." *Proceedings and Transactions of the Royal Society of Canada*, 1899 (2d series, vol. 5), sec. 2, pp. 199–211. Ottawa, 1911.

——— "Signposts of Prehistoric Times." *Proceedings and Transactions of the Royal Society of Canada*, 1916 (3d series, vol. 10), sec. 2, pp. 475–480. Ottawa, 1917.

LORIN, HENRI. *Comte de Frontenac*. Paris, 1912.

LOSKIEL, GEORGE H. *History of the Mission of the United Brethren among the Indians in North America*, translated from the German by Christian I. LaTrobe. London, 1794.

McGEE, W. J. "The Siouan Indians: A Preliminary Sketch." *Annual Report of the Bureau of American Ethnology*, 1893–94. Washington, 1897.

MACKENZIE, ALEXANDER. *Voyages from Montreal, on the River St. Lawrence, through the Continent of North America, to the Frozen and Pacific Oceans in the Years 1789 and 1793*. London, 1901.

MACLEAN, JOHN. *Canadian Savage Folk: The Native Tribes of Canada*. Toronto, 1896.

McLENNAN WILLIAM. A Gentleman of the Royal Guard: Daniel de Gresollon, Sieur du l'Hut." *Harpers' Magazine*, 87:609–626 (1893).

MACLEOD, WILLIAM C. *The American Indian Frontier*. New York, 1928.

McSHERRY, JAMES. *History of Maryland from Its First Settlement in 1634 to the Year 1848*. Baltimore, 1849.

MALLERY, GARRICK. "The Former and Present Numbers of Our Indians." *Proceedings of the American Association for the Advancement of Science*, 26:340–366 (1877). Salem, 1878.

——— "General Field Studies." *Tenth Annual Report of the American Bureau of Ethnology* (1888–89). Washington, 1893.

MARGRY, PIERRE. *Découvertes et établissements des Français dans l'ouest et dans le sud de l'Amérique Septentrionale, 1614–1754*. 6 vols. Paris, 1878–86.

MARIE DE L'INCARNATION. *Lettres de la révérende mère Marie de l'Incarnation (née Marie Guyard), première supérieure du monastère des Ursulines de Quebec*, edited by L'Abbe Richaudeau. 2 vols. Paris, 1876.

MARQUETTE, JACQUES. "Journal." Louise P. Kellogg, ed., *Early Narratives of the Northwest, 1634–1699*, pp. 261–280.

MARSHALL, ORSAMUS H. "Narrative of the Expedition of the Marquis de Nonville against the Senecas in 1687," translated from the French. *New York Historical Collections*, 2d series, 2:149–192. New York, 1849.

MARTIN, FELIX. *The Life of Father Isaac Jogues, Missionary Priest of the Society of Jesus*, translated from the French by John G. Shea. 3d edition. New York, 1885.

MARTIN, HENRI. *Histoire de France depuis les temps les plus reculés jusqu'en 1789.* 16 vols. Paris, 1855–60.

MASSICOTTE, EDOUARD Z. *Dollard et ses Companions.* Montreal, 1920.

MICHELSON, TRUMAN. "The Identification of the Mascoutens." *American Anthropologist*, 36: 226–233. June, 1934.

MINER, CHARLES. *History of Wyoming in a Series of Letters from Charles Miner to His Son, William Penn Miner, Esq.* Philadelphia, 1845.

MINER, WILLIAM H. *The Iowa: A Reprint from the Indian Record, As Originally Published and Edited by Thomas Foster.* Little Histories of North American Indians, no. 2. Cedar Rapids, Iowa, 1911.

MOONEY, JAMES M. "Siouan Tribes of the East." Bureau of American Ethnology Bulletin 22. Washington, 1894.

MOORE, CLARENCE B. *Additional Mounds of Duval and of Clay Counties, Florida; Mound Investigation on the East Coast of Florida; Certain Florida Coast Mounds North of the St. Johns River.* Museum of the American Indian, Heye Foundation, Indian Notes and Monographs, Miscellaneous Series, no. 26. New York, 1922.

MOLONEY, FRANCIS X. *The Fur Trade in New England.* Cambridge, 1931.

MORGAN, LEWIS H. *Ancient Society, or, Researches in the Lines of Human Progress from Savagery through Barbarism to Civilization.* New York, 1877.

———— *League of the Ho-dé-no-sau-nee or Iroquois.* Rochester, New York, 1851; New York, 1904.

MORGAN, WILLIAM T. "The Five Nations and Queen Anne." *Mississippi Valley Historical Review*, 13:169–189. 1926.

MOULTON, JOSEPH W., and JOHN V. N. YATES. *History of the State of New York, Including Its Aboriginal and Colonial Annals.* 1 vol. in 2. New York, 1824, 1826.

MYERS, ALBERT C., ed. *Narratives of Early Pennsylvania, West New Jersey, and Delaware.* New York, 1912. A volume in the *Original Narratives of Early American History* series, edited by J. Franklin Jameson.

NEILL, EDWARD D. "History of the Ojibways." *Minnesota Historical Collections*, 5:397–510. St. Paul, 1885.

New York Colonial MSS, in the office of the Secretary of State of New York. 3 vols. *Index* by Edmund B. O'Callaghan. Albany, 1870.

NOBLE, JOHN. "Notes on the Trial and Punishment of Crimes in the Court of Assistants in the Time of the Colony, and in the Superior Court of Judicature in the First Years of the Province [of Massachusetts]." *Transactions of the Colonial Society of Massachusetts*, 3:51–66. Boston, 1900.

O'CALLAGHAN, EDMUND B., ed. *Documents Relative to the Colonial History of the State of New York.* 15 vols. Albany, 1853–87. Herein cited as *New York Colonial Documents*.

———— *The Documentary History of the State of New York.* 4 vols. Albany, 1850–51.

———— *Index to the New York Colonial Manuscripts.* Albany, 1870.

———— *History of New Netherland, or, New York under the Dutch.* 2 vols. New York, 1855.

ORR, ROWLAND. "The Attiwandarons or Nation of the Neutrals." *Archaeological Report of the Ontario Provincial Museum*, 1913, pp. 7–20. Toronto, 1913.

[ORR, ROWLAND]. "The Ottawas." *Archaeological Report of the Ontario Provincial Museum*, 1916, pp. 9–25. Toronto, 1916.

OSGOOD, HERBERT L. *The American Colonies in the Seventeenth Century.* 3 vols. New York, 1907.

PARKER, ARTHUR C. *The Constitution of the Five Nations, or, the Iroquois Book of the Great Law.* New York State Museum Bulletin no. 184. Albany, 1916.

———— "The Origin of the Iroquois as Suggested by Their Archaeology." *American Anthropologist*, new series, 18:479–507. October-December, 1916.

———— "Iroquois Uses of Maize and Other Food Plants." New York State Museum Bulletin no. 144. Albany, 1910.

PARKER, R. J. The Iroquois and the Dutch Fur Trade, 1609–1698. Doctoral dissertation, University of California, 1932.

PARKMAN CLUB PUBLICATIONS, Milwaukee
Nicolas Perrot. Vol. 1, no. 1. 1895.
Radisson and Groseilliers. Vol. 1, no. 2. 1896.
Rene Ménard. Vol. 2, no. 11. 1897.
Tonty. Vol. 1, no. 3. 1896.
"Uses of Maize by Wisconsin Indians." Vol. 2, pp. 65–87. 1897.

PARKMAN, FRANCIS. *Count Frontenac and New France under Louis XIV. France and England in North America*, pt. 5. Boston, 1877.

———— *The Jesuits in North America in the Seventeenth Century.* 30th edition. Boston, 1867.

———— *La Salle and the Discovery of the Great West*, Boston, 1892.

———— *The Old Régime in Canada. France and England in North America*, pt. 4. Boston, 1874.

PEET, STEPHEN D. *The Location of the Indian Tribes in the Northwest Territory at the Date of Its Organization.* Cleveland, 1878. Reprinted from the *American Antiquarian*, 1:85–98.

PERROT, NICOLAS. *Memoir on the Manners, Customs, and Religion of the Savages of North America*, translated from the French. Emma H. Blair, ed., *Indian Tribes of the Upper Mississippi Valley and Region of the Great Lakes*, 1:42–293. Cleveland, 1911.

POWELL, JOHN W. *First Annual Report of the Bureau of Ethnology*, 1879–80. Washington, 1881.

PROUD, ROBERT. *The History of Pennsylvania, 1681–1742.* 2 vols. Philadelphia, 1797–98.

PRUDHOMME, LOUIS A. "La Baie d'Hudson." *Transactions of the Royal Society of Canada*, 1909 (3d series, vol. 3), sec. 1, pp. 3–36. Ottawa, 1910.

RADISSON, PIERRE ESPRIT. *Voyages of Pierre Esprit Radisson, Being an Account of His Travels and Experiences among the North American Indians from 1652 to 1684*, edited by Gideon D. Scull. Publications of the Prince Society, vol. 16. Boston, 1885.

RASIERES, ISAACK DE. "New Netherland in 1627." Letter in Jameson; *Narratives of New Netherland*, pp. 102–115.

ROCHEMONTEIX, LE P. CAMILLE DE. *Les Jésuites et la Nouvelle-France au XVII siècle.* 2 vols. Paris, 1906.

SAGARD-THÉODAT, GABRIEL. *Le Grand Voyage du pays des Hurons situé en l' Amérique vers la mer douce, ès dernier's confins de la Nouvelle France dite Canada avec un dictionnaire de la langue huronne.* Paris, 1865.

———— *Histoire du Canada et voyages que les Frères mineurs recollects y ont faicts pour la conversion des infidèles depuis l'an 1615.* 4 vols. Paris, 1866.

SCHOOLCRAFT, HENRY R. *Historical and Statistical Information Respecting the History, Condition, and Prospects of the Indian Tribes of the United States.* 6 vols. Philadelphia, 1851–57.

SCHOOLCRAFT, HENRY R. *Notes on the Iroquois; or, Contributions to the Statistics, Aboriginal History, Antiquities, and General Ethnology of Western New York.* New York, 1846.

SHEA, JOHN G. "An Historical Sketch of the Tionnontaties." *Historical Magazine,* 5:262–269. New York, 1861.

————— "The Identity of the Andastes, Minquas, Susquehannahs, and Conestogues." *Historical Magazine,* 2:294–297. October, 1858.

SHEA, JOHN G., ed. *The Discovery and Exploration of the Mississippi Valley.* New York, 1852.

————— *Early Voyages up and down the Mississippi.* Albany, 1861.

————— *Edict du rois pour l'etablissement de la Compagnie de la Nouvelle France.* New York, 1860. This was originally published in Paris, 1635.

————— *Vie de Chaumont.* New York, 1858.

SHETRONE, HENRY C. *The Moundbuilders.* New York, 1930.

SKINNER, ALANSON. "The Mascoutens or Prairie Potawatomi." Milwaukee Public Museum Bulletin, vol. 6, nos. 1–3. Milwaukee, 1924–27.

SMITH, BUCKINGHAM, ed. *Letter of Hernando de Soto and Memoir of Hernando de Escalante Fontaneda.* Washington, 1854.

SMITH, JOHN. *The General Historie of Virginia, New England, and the Summer Iles.* Richmond, 1819.

SMITH, SAMUEL. *History of the Colony of Nova-Caesaria, or New Jersey.* Burlington, New Jersey, 1765; reprinted at Trenton, New Jersey, 1890, with the same pagination.

Sommaire de l'instance pendante au conseil prime entre les Associez en la Compagnie de la Nouvelle France defendeurs, et la Sieur Guillaume de Caen defendeur. Photostatic copy in the Wisconsin State Historical Library.

SOWTER, T. W. E. "Indian Trade, Travel and Transportation." Ontario Provincial Museum, *Archaeological Report,* 1916. Toronto, 1916.

SPECK, FRANK G. "Algonkian Influence upon Iroquois Social Organization." *American Anthropologist,* new series, 25:219–226. 1923.

————— *Family Hunting Territories and Social Life of Various Algonkian Bands of the Ottawa Valley.* Publications of the Anthropological Section, Canadian Geological Survey, no. 8. Ottawa, 1915.

————— *The Functions of Wampum among the Eastern Algonkian.* Memoirs of the American Anthropological Association, vol. 6, no. 1. Lancaster, Pennsylvania, 1919.

STITES, SARA. *Economics of the Iroquois.* Lancaster, Pennsylvania, 1905.

STOCKWELL, QUINTIN. "A Story of Indian Captivity." *American History Told by Contemporaries,* edited by Albert B. Hart, 1:501–506. New York, 1897.

STRACHEY, WILLIAM, ed. *The Historie of Travaile into Virginia Britannia.* Works Issued by the Hakluyt Society, vol. 6. London, 1849.

STREETER, SEBASTIAN F. "The Fall of the Susquehannahs, a Chapter from the Indian History of Maryland." *Historical Magazine,* 1:55–73. March, 1857.

SULTE, BENJAMIN. "La Baie Verte et le Lac Superieur, 1665." *Proceedings and Transactions of the Royal Society of Canada,* 1912 (2d series, vol. 6), sec. 1, p. 3–34. Ottawa, 1913.

————— "Les Coureurs des bois au Lac Superieur, 1660." *Ibid,* 1911 (3d series, vol. 5), sec. 1, pp. 249–266. Ottawa, 1912.

————— "Découverte du Mississippi en 1659." *Ibid,* 1902 (2d series, vol. 9), sec. 1, pp. 3–44. Ottawa, 1903.

————— "Les Français dans l'ouest en 1671." *Ibid,* 1918 (3d series, vol. 12), sec. 1, pp. 1–31. Ottawa, 1919.

————— "Guerres des Iroquois." *Ibid,* 1920 (2d series, vol. 15), sec. 1, pp. 85–95. Ottawa, 1921.

————— *Histoire des Canadiens-Français, 1608–1880.* 8 vols. Montreal, 1882–84.

SULTE, BENJAMIN. "Notes on Jean Nicolet." *Wisconsin Historical Collections*, 8:188–194. Madison, 1879, 1908.

———— "Le Pays d'en Haut, 1670." *Proceedings and Transactions of the Royal Society of Canada*, 1913 (3d series, vol. 7), sec. 1, pp. 67–96. Ottawa, 1913.

———— "The Valley of the Grand River, 1600–1650." *Ibid*, 1898 (2d series, vol. 4), sec. 2, pp. 107–137. Ottawa, 1898.

———— "The Valley of the Ottawa in 1613." *Papers and Records of the Ontario Historical Society*, 13:31–35. Toronto, 1915.

THOMSON, CHARLES. *An Enquiry into the Causes for the Alienation of the Delawares and the Shawnees*. London, 1759.

THWAITES, REUBEN G., ed. *The Jesuit Relations and Allied Documents*. 73 volumes. Cleveland, 1896–1901.

TOOKER, WILLIAM W. *The Bocootawanaukes or the Fire Nation*. New York, 1901. Algonquian Series, vol. 6. New York, 1901.

TRUMBULL, JAMES HAMMOND. *Indian Names of Places in and on the Borders of Connecticut*. Hartford, 1881.

TONTY, HENRI DE. "Memoir." Louise P. Kellogg, ed. *Early Narratives of the Northwest, 1634–1699*, 281–322. New York, 1917. Also in *Louisiana Historical Collections*, edited by Benjamin F. French, 1:52–78. New York, 1846.

TYLER, LYON G., ed. *Narratives of Early Virginia, 1606–1625*. New York, 1907.

UPHAM, WARREN. "Groseilliers and Radisson." *Minnesota Historical Magazine*, 10:449–594. 1905.

VAN LAER, ARNOLD J. F., ed. *Correspondence of Jeremias van Rensselaer, 1651–74*. Albany, 1932.

———— *Minutes of the Court of Fort Orange and Beverwyck, 1652–1660*. 2 vols. Albany, 1920–23.

———— *Court Records of Rensselaerwyck*. Albany, 1922.

———— *Documents Relating to New Netherland, 1624–1626*. San Marino, 1924.

———— *Van Rensselaer Bowier MSS*. Albany, 1908.

WAKE, C. STANILAND. "Migrations of the Algonquins." *American Antiquarian*, 16:127–140. 1894.

WALKER, FRANCIS. "The Indian Question." *North American Review*, 116:328–388.

WARREN, WILLIAM W. "History of the Ojibways, Based upon Traditions and Oral Statements." *Minnesota Historical Collections*, 5:21–394. St. Paul, 1885.

WASSENAER, NICOLAES VAN. *Historisch Verhael*. J. Franklin Jameson, ed., *Narratives of New Netherland, 1609–1664*, pp. 67–96. New York, 1909.

WEBB, WALTER P. *The Great Plains*. New York, 1931.

WEST, GEORGE A. *Copper: Its Mining and Use by the Aborigines of the Lake Superior Region*. Milwaukee Public Museum Bulletin, vol. 10, no. 1. Milwaukee, 1929.

WILLIS, BAILEY. "The Northern Appalachians." *The Physiography of the United States*, 169–202. National Geographic Society, New York, 1895.

WILLSON, BECKLES. *The Great Company: Being a History of the Honourable Company of Merchants-Adventurers Trading into Hudson's Bay*. Toronto, 1899.

WILSON, DANIEL. "The Huron-Iroquois of Canada, a Typical Race of American Aborigines." *Proceedings and Transactions of the Royal Society of Canada*, 1884 (1st series, vol. 2), sec. 2, pp. 55–106. Montreal, 1885.

WINCHELL, NEWTON H. "Were the Outagami of Iroquoian Origin?" *Proceedings of the Mississippi Valley Historical Association*, 4:184 (1910–11). Cedar Rapids, Iowa, 1912.

WINSHIP, GEORGE P. "The Coronado Expedition, 1540–1542." *Annual Report of the Bureau of Ethnology*, 1892–93, pt. 1, pp. 339–615. Washington, 1896.

WINSOR, JUSTIN. *Cartier to Frontenac: Geographical Discovery in the Interior of North America in Its Historical Relations, 1534–1700*. New York, 1894.

WINSOR, JUSTIN. *The Mississippi Basin: The Struggle in America between England and France, 1697–1763.* New York, 1895.

WINSOR, JUSTIN, ed. *Narrative and Critical History of America.* 8 vols. New York, 1884–1889.

WINTEMBERG, WILLIAM J. "Indian Village Sites in Oxford and Waterloo Counties." *Archaeological Report of the Provincial Museum of Ontario,* 1900, pp. 37–40. Toronto, 1901.

WISSLER, CLARK. *The American Indian: An Introduction to the Anthropology of the New World.* New York, 1922.

———— "Societies and Ceremonial Associations in the Oglala Division of the Teton-Dakota Sioux." *Anthropological Papers of the American Museum of Natural History,* vol. 2. New York, 1912.

WOOD, JOHN W. "The Mascouten of the Fox River Valley." *Proceedings of the Wisconsin Historical Society,* 1906, pp. 167–182. Madison, 1907.

WOOD, WILLIAM. *Wood's New England's Prospect, 1634.* Boston, 1865. Publication of the Prince Society.

WRAXALL, PETER. *An Abridgment of the Indian Affairs . . . Transacted in the Colony of New York from the Year 1678 to the Year 1751,* edited by Charles H. McIlwain. Cambridge, 1915.

WRONG, GEORGE M. *The Rise and Fall of New France.* 2 vols. New York, 1928.

INDEX

Abenaki Indians, 45, 61
Adario, 49
Albany, 29–30, 31, 64, 141, 157
Albany Records, 26
Algic tribes, 120
Algonquin confederacy, *see* Algonquin
    Indians
Algonquin Indians, 6, 7, 13, 38, 46, 54,
    59, 61, 76, 84, 94, 95, 110, 123, 135, 137,
    145, 161; confederacy of, 7, 111; at
    peace with Hurons and Dakota, 20;
    role in peace of *1645*, 77 ff.; invasions
    of Iroquoia, 134; and Hurons united,
    160. *See also* Migrations; Population
Allouez, Father Claude, 104, 113, 114, 120,
    127, 147; among the Nipissings, 106–
    107; first priest at Chequamegon, 123,
    124; efforts to maintain peace, 136–
    137; among the Illinois, 148
Allumette Indians, 43–45, 54, 61, 63, 80;
    economy of, 44; relations with the
    Nipissing Indians, 46, 106. *See also* Pop-
    ulation
Allumette Island, 43, 44, 45, 60
Altona, 140
Amikoue Indians (Beaver People), 49
Andastoé (Andastogue), 88, 137
André, Father Louis, 107
Andros, Governor Edmund, 29, 139
Annenraes, Onondaga chief, 89, 99
Anthropology, Huron, 41–42
Antoine Creek, 45
Archeology, Iroquois-Algonquin, 14;
    evidence for Iroquois migrations, 16
Arkansas Indians, enemies of Illinois
    tribes, 148
Arquebuses, *see* Firearms
Artillery of the Susquehannah, 10, 36–
    37, 140
Assiniboin Indians, 125

Attikamegue Indians, 77, 107; trade
    route of, 53; trade with Hurons, 60–
    61; economy of, 60

Bacon's Rebellion, Susquehannah in, 143
Bancroft, George, 66
Beauchamp, William, 26, 32, 67
Beaver, 6, 33, 36, 51, 65, 74, 76, 96,
    125, 149, 152
Beaver People, *see* Amikoue Indians
Bell River, 60
Beverwyck, 10
Black Minquas (Mingo), *see* Erie In-
    dians
Black River, 104, 122, 124
Blockades: Iroquois, on the Ottawa
    River, 75–76, 104, 134, 139, 159; Sus-
    quehannah, of the Seneca, 139, 159
Blue Mountains, 42
Blue Ridge Mountains, 68
Bouillon Lake, 45
Bourdon, Sieur, 84
Bourier, Brother, 132
Bradford, William, 21, 32
Brébeuf, Father Jean de, 50, 55, 56, 72,
    92, 133, 142
Bressani, Father Francisco, 4, 55
British, *see* English
Brouet, Brother, 132
Bruce Peninsula, 42, 48
Brulé, Étienne, 138
Buffalo, 57, 65
Burpee, Lawrence S., 124
Bushnell, David, 16
Buteux, Father, 60
Butterfield, Consul W., 110–111

Canada, 18, 25, 87, 110, 142; tribes of,
    105–107
Cannibalism, among the Hurons, 94;